PETROGLYPHS
Garth C. Nielsen

Credits & Copyright

Garth C. Nielsen - Author

Description-
Petroglyphs is a collectionof short stories, thoughts, observations and impressions about traditional Native Americans I have known and the landscapes they inhabit.

Printed in the United States of America /First Edition
First Printing 2015

"Dying is much more difficult than one imagines..."
-- Gabriel Garcia Marquez

"Out of darkness, let light shine..."
-- 2nd Corinthians, 4:6

Dedication–

For Barb, Lars and Carrie, Pete and Val,
Nol, Kathy and Hunter, Joe and Maria, Tom and Kim
Aho Metakuye Oyasin

A number of people must be acknowledged for their help in the production of this book:

To my wife, Barb, loving thanks for her tireless hours of editing;

To my friend, Tom Watson for his many critically important suggestions and his unselfish efforts in helping me get this book published;

To Kim Victoria, many thanks for all of her helpful suggestions, the use of her beautiful petroglyph photos, and her help in creating the graphics used in this book and for the cover design;

To Don Criswell for the permission to use the photo on the back cover;

To Peter Genovese, for his critical read through and pertinent suggestions, for his continuing friendship and his willingness to spend hours on end discussing my efforts long distance. A ho, Kola.

Preface–

The stories in this book are compiled from not only my own thoughts and experiences, but from tales told to me over the years by many people from many walks of life. In some cases, I have reworked these stories to make them my own. The thoughts, anecdotes and impressions of my wanderings are part of my personal odyssey. As described in my first book, *Odyssey of a Spiritual Nomad,* many people and many places have contributed to enlightening me to hidden secrets that have broadened my perspective of what our time on earth is all about. I feel a responsibility to share with you, that which was shared with me. May your own odyssey begin.
Metakuye Oyasin

Table of Contents–

AMOS CHALK

Coyote trotted softly through the sagebrush, his head held low, sniffing the ground. The god of the day was announcing his arrival with heraldic banners of pink and trumpets of orange. The last of the night breeze snaked along the tops of the sagebrush and gently ruffled the fur on Coyote's back. The breeze carried also a small sound, a sound of far away -- beyond the still, black hills. Coyote stopped, motionless, and listened to the faint rumble. He raised his head and sniffed at the last rags of the almost gone night wind, glanced up at the waning pallor of the night god and trotted on.

Amos Chalk sat dozing in the back seat of the small plane, thinking over the last couple of days. The conversations in front between the doctor and the man from the Bureau faded into nothingness and Amos was alone in this capsule flying through the sky. He was not convinced that his sister and her husband were thinking of him when they suggested that he go to the Stewart Indian School. They told him he would meet new people from other reservations and that he would make good friends there. He would also be close to exciting things to see and do there in Carson City.

What was wrong with his friends here in Duck Valley, he had asked? He had told them he didn't want to leave his home. But his sister's husband had gone to the Bureau Office in Owyhee and made arrangements for him to go and see Stewart. Well, he had gone and it had been as he thought. No one seemed to care whether he was there or not.

The sudden sputtering of the motor brought him out of his reverie.

"Amos, snap your belt on," the doctor said, flipping switches. The Bureau man did likewise and glanced nervously at the Doctor.

"This is November 573, Romeo, Delta, calling Battle Mountain, over," the doctor yelled into the radio. The motor gave one gasp and died, putting the plane into a free glide.

"Everyone hold on. I'm going to try and clear that ridge ahead and put it down on the flats of the other side."

The screaming wind was now in complete control of the plane and seemed to be trying to tear it from the sky. The ridge rimmed with juniper and sage loomed near and the expanse of salt flat hemmed with far mountains tilted back and forth. When they were almost over the ridge, with the trees a few feet below, the momentum of the plane stopped and it was sucked down like a stone in a pool by the reaching, holding fingers of a down draft. The Bureau man covered his eyes with his arms and cried, "Jesus!" and it was over.

Amos awoke to find himself hanging, bent in half by his belt, his head and knees resting on the back of the Doctor's seat. Blood covered the remains of the inside of the plane. The door had burst open from the impact and faint wisps of steam and smoke rose from the rubble in front of him. Putting weight on his knees, Amos released his belt and slid out the opened door. Standing shakily, supporting himself on one of the bent struts, he rubbed his head. Gazing at the two men, it was obvious they were dead.

The silence on this mountain was made more overwhelming by the shrieking wind of a short while ago. But it was the silence of home, of the Owyhee River, a silence he knew well and was used to. Amos sat down, his head on his arms. A dull ache was pounding its way out of his head and he would sit there until it was gone enough for him to stand.

As he sat there, he thought of another time, another wreck, which moved slowly into his mind's eye. He had been just a small boy then, when the sheriff's men came with their tow truck and his father's pickup on the hook. They had come slowly and he could see the front end, a mass of crumpled chrome and glass, raised by the hood to expose its underside. He hadn't been sure what death was then, but he did know that he would never see his mother and father again. Sue, his sister, had become his mother from then on.

Tears slid down Amos' cheeks and sank into the sand. A small sound in the sagebrush interrupted his thoughts and he moved his head slightly in that direction to see the head of a coyote nervously moving, staring at him, his nose twitching. Amos watched the coyote move slowly around the wreckage, trying for a more advantageous spot to more readily acquaint himself with the situation that had intruded into his world. His nose soon told him all that he wanted to know and he started down the slope, stopping once to look back over his shoulder.

All that day, Amos sat near the plane, trying to decide what to do, while the sun burned down upon him. The heat caused the mountains across the valley to shimmer and float above the valley floor on a hazy mist. No sound reached this spot save the sounds he made or those of the buzzing insects.

The sun had crossed the entire sky and would soon be sliding behind the mountains behind him where he sat. His only protection against the night chill would be his jacket. The thought of again seeing the broken bodies studded now with clotted blood, nauseated him, but he steadied himself and walked to the plane. His jacket was lying on the back of the seat of the man from the Bureau. He reached over the collapsed body of the doctor with his seat pressing him into the instrument panel and pulled his jacket free.

Wondering about the coming night, Amos saw a juniper and decided he would climb into it for the night. At least any bobcat would wake him if it tried to climb up to him.

Once more, he turned to the plane, but could not bring himself to put his hand into the pocket of the doctor for the cigarette lighter he knew was there. As he stood there, he noticed a broken strut hanging loose and, with a little effort, he broke it off. Thus armed with a metal rod, he climbed into his tree to spend a wakeful, fitful night. Amos placed the rod in a small fork of the tree, zipped his coat to his neck and put his hands deep in his side pockets. Discovering the two chocolate bars he had purchased in Carson City, he proceeded to eat one, dropping the wrapper to the ground.

With the rising of the moon over the edge of the mountains, again, the night wind rustled the tops of the sagebrush. The coming of the wind was the herald for more subtle sounds. Crickets which murmured feebly from sunset to moonrise, now formed the background orchestration for another night – another night of searching for the essentials of existence -- food, water or a mate for the many animals on the mountain.

From off a low, black hill that formed a platform for all the mountains that rose and marched into the north, a wisp of haze moved. This haze, which had form in its formlessness, moved about the caves of the ancient ones. It paused and passed over marks on the cliffs, leaving small beads of moisture that were absorbed into the dry stone. It blew through the branches of the juniper tree, chilling the boy.

From out of a blanket of blackness, the small clusters of stars shone, blinking brightly. Amos gazed up at them through the softly moving branches. He thought of Mrs. Charlie sitting on the bench on the porch of the store in Owyhee. Her faced was lined with wrinkles with her hair in a bun, as she sat in her faded old dress, watching the day, remembering other days. No one ever seemed to see Mrs. Charlie take her place on the bench, and no one ever saw her return home. She would just be there in the morning and suddenly be gone at night. Amos turned his face into his shoulder, the tears starting again.

"Mrs. Charlie, pray for me," he whispered, drifting into a fitful sleep.

Coyote moved softly through the sagebrush. The smell of the ones who walk upright was all around this place. Lowering his head, his eyes straight ahead, he approached the shiny thing with its bad smell cautiously and stopped and looked up at the tree. A stir in the branches caused him to freeze in his tracks. He backed away, turned and went back down the mountain without looking back, pausing only to smell the discarded candy wrapper.

Amos stood and stretched slowly, his sore muscles stiff and aching from the night in the cramped tree. Reaching into his pocket, he ate the second candy bar and gazed at the expanse of mountains and valleys about him. Amos knew he should start walking, but in which direction he did not know. The doctor had planned on setting the plane down on the alkali flats. Maybe he should go in that direction. The summit of the ridge was just a few yards above him, and, in a matter of minutes, he was standing at the top. The wind blew his hair and clothes in little snapping sounds. Looking across the miles of white, he saw no sign of any living thing. No planes were overhead, though far in the distance, the sky was streaked with two fragmented con trails. They became small wispy clouds as he watched them. He started down the slope of crumbling rock. It broke apart at each step he took and he slid halfway down the mountain. Stopping to rest beside a large bolder covered with pale green and rust colored lichens, he covered his eyes again and looked across the expanse of the salt flats.

The only movements were small dust devils that whirled madly for a few feet and then evaporated into nothing. The floor of the valley shone with an intense brilliance that caused Amos to shield his eyes. The ground was split and cracked into rounded sections that looked like parts of a large puzzle. Amos turned and looked up at the mountain he had just descended and then he began walking out into the heart of nothing.

He thought of his friend, Jess, and wondered what he was doing -- probably chopping wood for his mom or down at the store, just sitting in the shade. He remembered the time he and Jess had been hunting jackrabbits in the hills and had discovered the girls bathing at the sulfur springs. They had watched the girls, lying flat on the ground behind some sagebrush. He smiled and kicked at the cement hard alkali pieces, his hands in his pockets. Turning and looking up into the sky for a plane, he saw only flat blue with no mark upon it.

Mirages danced against the low hills across the valley, shimmering with reflections of a steel tower and heavy machinery. Amos knew no things such as these were there – he would have seen them from the mountaintop. As he walked slowly forward, a figure came toward him through the shimmering mirage. Knowing the image would evaporate, he nevertheless watched it moving in his direction. The figure came closer and he recognized Mrs. Nichols, the good-looking wife of the Bureau man he had been with in the plane. She ran toward him as if in slow motion. The image dissolved slowly from the legs up, as if the devouring heat was consuming her. The image faded until only her head with her long hair and dark glasses remained. Then, that, too, was gone. Amos took his jacket off and placed it over his head and walked beyond the place where Mrs. Nichols had been.

The afternoon sun was slanting westward and Amos was nearly across the flats. He stumbled occasionally, cursing the heat and the dead doctor's airplane. The mirages were behind him now. Ahead were only the hills, the color of the sheriff's khaki pants, with darker outcroppings of stone and juniper at the summits. Amos stopped walking and stared down at an object before him. There, half buried amid the puzzle pieces, was the skeleton of an animal, with parchment skin and hair near the buried parts. It had been a coyote – Amos knew that. It was strange to see it here. Amos looked at the sky, but it was still flat and uncluttered. He sat on the white surface, crossed his legs, propped his chin in his hands and stared at the gaping mouth now partially filled with drifted dust.

A dust devil twirled around him and forced his attention away from the skeleton. Amos lay flat on his stomach, his head on the dust and gazed through the twigs of a half-buried piece of tumbleweed at the mountains across the valley. Shimmering air slowly rose around him. Amos closed his eyes and sighed deeply.

He dreamed again of the plane, of the doctor and of the man from the Bureau. He dreamed also of Sue and her parting words when he had left for Stewart. "Jesus!" the Bureau man had yelled, and again, the blackness.

Amos awoke with the sun only an hour from the mountain's rim. Starting up the sandy slope, he used the metal pole as a walking stick, slowly switch backing toward the summit. Amos used the last of his strength to climb into the sticky branches of a twisted piñon. His head was pounding and his stomach hurt.

"I ain't goin', Sue!" he said out loud. "Stewart can screw! The Bureau man is dead. The Doctor's dead. And if you don't want me, I'll move in with Jess."

Then, more to himself than to Sue, wherever she was, he murmured, "I might even go and live with Mrs. Charlie. I could cut wood for her, go for food. She ain't got nobody either. Nobody's got anybody. How do I know I'll ever get home anyway? I don't even know where I am or if I'm going the right way."

Amos sat up and yelled, "Mrs. Charlie, can you hear me? Hey, Mrs. Charlie. I'm goin' to be your boy now. I want to help you, Mrs. Charlie...."

Amos Chalk began to cry and Coyote trotted softly through the sagebrush, his head held low, sniffing the ground.

THE VOICES OF THE PEOPLE

When I hear the speech of The People, I understand not one word. But the passion in their hearts speaks to mine. It is the music of their speech, not one word of which I understand, that sings in my heart.

THE SKULL

My father was born and bred in a large eastern city. For years, all his thoughts were shaped by decisions from a crowded and consensual accordance until he moved to Nevada as a young adult. A change, subtle but unyielding in its grasp, began to occur within him and call into question all of these old thought patterns. He fell under the influence of the spirits of limitless horizons of sagebrush and piñon dotted hills, mirages that shimmered across the salt pan playas, and vistas where the vestiges of the early settlers and of those who had passed through, bound for the glories of California, could still be found.

When the turquoise gem of Pyramid Lake first met his astonished gaze, the die was cast. Every opportunity that presented itself was a reason to make the thirty-two mile drive from Reno, summer or winter. During the summer, nearly every weekend was spent under a lean-to of furniture blankets, while my brother and I swam or skimmed stones as flat as silver dollars across the placid surface of the lake. My father even bought a boat that he sailed straight across the lake so that he could look more closely at the namesake pyramid. We never went ashore on Anaho Island, a federally protected bird refuge.

One incident that stands out vividly in my memory is the day my father found the upper half of a human skull on the beach at Pyramid Lake. The gentle waves washed around it, making the long, green moss clinging around it appear as undulating hair. I remember thinking that it could have been the remains of a mermaid. Was it from a drowned swimmer or someone sucked down by quicksand patches found on the northwest end of the lake? We were told that the lake had been used as a bombing range during World War II. Perhaps it was the remains of a lost airman. Or was the skull much older? We never knew. I won't say that this beautiful, mysterious lake took what rightfully belonged there. Rather, I will say that some long forgotten soul returned to our Creator and became part of the mystique, one with the spirit of place.

One has to wonder about such a death. I long ago abandoned the concept that accidents happen. Things happen for a reason. But still, what was the reason for this death? Was this a man or a woman? I believe all life returns to our Creator, so all that we see is the residue of life on earth.

THE WORLD THAT WATCHES

The spiritual yet natural landscape is a world that watches my every footfall. It is a land of hidden beings who view my progress across the landscape. I am never alone. Those who have been considered dead by the dominant society are yet among us, transparent as the air, asking only for our memory of them.

THE SAFE

It's an old cliché that a desert holds many secrets, and Nevada's deserts hold as many as any desert on earth.

My father had discovered an area east of the city of Reno known as Squaw Flats. It is an area laced with alkali playas that become ephemeral lakes when the winter snows melt in the near hills and mountains. In summer, mirages tell lies of water and shrubs, while dust devils race across the sand and dry flats. The playas, as hard as concrete, appear to be composed of enormous puzzle pieces.

What drew my father to the area was the fact that Squaw Flats was where the covered wagons had traveled through in the nineteenth century on the way to California. The many metal wagon rims from broken wheels were still scattered beside the yet visible ruts left by the struggling wagons. Pieces of discarded furniture or other household items were also frequently uncovered by the wind driven sand dunes. Many history books have labeled the westward migrating pioneers as courageous. They were also desperate and often disappointed. Death was a constant companion.

There is a local legend that the area was a prehistoric battleground. The Paiutes have a story about red haired cannibals who were exterminated in what is now called Lovelock Cave. This cave is in the same general area as Squaw Flats.

What I recall is part of the mystery of the Nevada desert. I was about twelve years old and my interest in the native peoples of the state was earnestly taking hold of my thinking. I wanted to learn as much as I could about these people and I hoped to find at least an arrowhead on that day.

What I found, out on the sagebrush dunes of Squaw Flats is a mystery I doubt has ever been solved. If it has been, I know nothing of it. On that day, my father was looking for artifacts or maybe some trace of the red-haired cannibals. His friend, who had accompanied us, sought mineral specimens, since his interest was in the field of geology. I was there to explore and find whatever I could.

As I climbed up a dune that had a large sagebrush holding it in place, there, before me, at the base of the dune, was a very large safe. It was of the type once found in banks or mercantile stores from the last century. Beside the safe, with its hinges bent and curled by the explosion of a large quantity of dynamite, lay the door. The safe was black with gold piping and the lettering on the door was so abraded and faded that it was impossible to read. It had obviously been out there for a long, long time.

I called my father, who came and stood, staring in amazement. How could this huge safe, at least three feet tall, have been lifted and then brought out here with no one's knowledge? The interior of the safe was empty, its contents long gone, and it was now filled with windblown sand. When and where was it from? I have read that Jesse and Frank James stopped at Winnemucca on their way to California to avoid arrest in Missouri. But no mention has ever been made of a bank heist by these two in Nevada.

The safe that I found leaves questions, not just about where it came from, or when it was brought and left at this place, but also who it was who left it there. All indications show that it was a violent act. What desperation urged this act? Were these people ever apprehended?

The old safe is once again buried beneath the sand dunes of Squaw Flats, no doubt. It is but one more mystery. Only the desert knows it's secret.

A CONVERSATION WITH A DINÉ FRIEND

"My people have always been here, my family has always been here. I was born in that hogan you see there. I have always been here except when I was sent to a boarding school. This is our home place where we are at one with our Creator, with ourselves and with our earth. We want only to sing our songs, care for our sheep, weave our blankets and to work on our silver and turquoise."

'Those others who have come among us steal our land, the bones and blood of our earth. They dirty our air and want to move us from our place. Our old ones don't understand or know how to live in square houses. They don't know Social Security or VCRs. Look into our eyes. What is there – deceit? We want only to live and speak with the Holy People, to live between our four sacred mountains. We want only to honor the ways of White Shell Woman and Flint Boy. Big Mountain, Window Rock, Denebito and Ship Rock are sacred names on our land. The Holy People live there and so do we."

COLUMBUS DAY, PASCUA PUEBLO

The sky was barely hinting of the coming sun. Long, banner clouds stretched across the eastern horizon. The morning stars slowly dimmed. Orion and the Pleiades had been shining brightly.

Some people were waiting in their cars when I arrived. Tobacco and mesquite smoke floated in the air. Around a small fire, near the capilla, the Yoeme Coyote Warriors stood in a small group, talking in whispers.

The spiritual and political leader of all the Yoeme suddenly appeared and I walked to him and shook his hand.

"Good morning," he said, "welcome to this day here."

Three pow-wow drums arrived and were set up as more cars arrived. People walked slowly, talking softly, shaking hands with friends. English, Spanish, Yaqui and O'odham mingled melodically. It felt good to be here.

The spiritual leader called the people together and spoke to those assembled.

"My sisters and brothers, my friends, thank you for being here. My people have suffered much over the last five hundred years. Be thankful you are here. Welcome our white friends. The Creator has spoken to their hearts to be here. Perhaps they were here once before, long ago."

"Drums, follow my lead. We men face the east -- we are still at war. You women, face the west. Pray for the men.

We will drum up the sun."

Facing the clouds that had now massed into a solid line, the drummers indeed "called up the sun." The sun's rays poured into my head and filled my body with a sense of power. The pulse of the earth beneath my feet was in time with the drums. What a blessing!

DESERT SPRING

The desert in the warmth of the new spring is preparing itself for the coming summer heat. This day is only a hint of the coming blasts. No breeze stirs the bushes. Everything is still. Only filmy and torn clouds pass across the flat blue.

In a draw, a lone cottonwood stands naked now in the seam of two hills, waiting to be clothed with a soon to be green. I work my way up to the tree and stop beside an outcrop of gneiss, encrusted with green, rust and grey lichens. No one has ever seen lichens grow. Their colonies form slowly, taking eons to grow even a quarter of an inch.

The silence is absolute here. I have found that when the noise of disturbance has quit the air, the silence billows over me and engulfs me. I can feel the silence and the waiting – waiting for the ancient inland sea to return. Will the saguaros turn into kelp forests and the cholla into coral? Perhaps, it's the return of the ancient ones, with ceremonies and stories even older yet. What the desert waits for, no one knows. That is known only to the living spirits and to Coyote, the Trickster.

A TALE TOLD TO ME BY AN
OLD COYOTE WARRIOR

Once, in the eighteen hundreds, in the Bacatate Mountains of Sonora, near the Yoeme villages in the Rio Yaqui valley, there lived a Yoeme family. This family had some small children. The father kept some cattle, sheep and goats.

One day, while the father was out, tending his animals, a raiding party of Arizona Apaches attacked the small rancheria, kidnapping one of the small boys. The child was taken back to the Gila River area and his parents never heard from him again.

This child grew to manhood to become the most famous of the Apache freedom fighters. History knows him as Geronimo.

WHY DON'T YOU COME BACK

I read once of an old man of the Crow Nation who said, "It is not good to die among strangers."

For me, the mountains, the valleys, the sagebrush and piñons, the lichens on the stones, the streams and alkali playas – all are my relatives. They have helped to shape me into what I am. When I passed through this land not long ago on my way to somewhere far away, everything my eyes rested upon seemed to cry out:"Nephew, where are you going? Why don't you come back?"

EL ABUELO

The village of San Ignacio nestled in an elbow. The Rio Grande had formed that elbow after thousands of years of meandering through the Rocky Mountain foothills that are known locally as Las Sierras. The outer edge of a meandering river flows the fastest, and time, like water, flowed passed San Ignacio in a rushing tide. But the little village of adobe and stone homes stood largely unaffected by the rushing wave of days and years. Little had changed in the pueblo since the first European settlers marched into the beautiful valley two hundred years ago. What the eyes of those farmers saw, then, is the same as what the eyes of the bands of Southern Utes and the Pueblo People had seen for centuries, uncounted and uncountable.

An elbow can open to unprotected change, or it can guard from all that is unwanted or unnecessary. San Ignacio accepted changes cautiously and scrutinized each one. And yet, some changes were inevitable. Although horses yet stood in the pastures, belly deep in grass, they were seldom, if ever, ridden now. There had always been horses in the pastures, and there always would be. The bloodlines of most of the horses were from animals traded from the Utes almost two centuries ago. The horses would always be there.

The bloodlines of most of the families of San Ignacio

descended from the Utes, from the people of the Pueblos, and from the European settlers. This had been a change that had sunk family roots deep into the rich soil of their beautiful valley. It was not a few of the families that had stories which were told on occasion, of some ancestor who had chased the buffalo herds, or had occasion to raid the large, slumping mass of adobe which is Taos.

These farmers and horse breeders spoke an old world tongue; they spoke a Spanish not understood readily by some family members in Arizona or California. They could read Don Quixote in the original language of Cervantes. Thus, time swept through this elbow of the Rio Grande, bringing with it some changes. Pick-ups replaced horses. Men wore Levis now, with pointed cowboy boots. A weathered sign of an Anglo woman drinking a bottle of soda, pock-marked with bullet holes, stood sagging on its wooden frame near the road. But some things stayed the same. Time cannot change what is true.

Working the land was not economically profitable any longer, but all of the people in San Ignacio had small kitchen gardens. To even think of looking at a seed catalog was never a thought on anyone's mind. Tepary beans were what had always been grown. Yes, and squash and corn came from seeds which had been traded from San Juan Pueblo one hundred and fifty years ago. And so it was with the melons and chilies.

The river lowered or rose according to the season, and the white, puffy clouds always massed over the mountains. The horses stood in the fields munching grass and swishing their tails. Time cannot change what is true.

Isidro Arriola had become restless, intranquilo; nothing

ever happened in San Ignacio. The small adobe he lived in with his parents and abuelo looked as run down and shabby as the rest of the homes in the village. All the pick-ups were battered. Nothing was new. There was nothing exciting to do or see. He wanted to leave, but wasn't sure about where he wanted to go. He stood by the hulk of an old pick-up that had belonged to his father, the weeds of the field half hiding it from view. He looked out on the fields of his neighbors and up to the mountains. The far noise of the interstate faintly reached his ears. Glancing in that direction, he saw the black smoke of an eighteen-wheeler spurt from the twin stacks behind the cab, the driver shifting gears as he met the rising road up into the Raton Pass leading north out of the valley. Picking up a stone from the ground, Isidro slammed it at the already broken windows of the rusted wreck, and the last few shards of the broken glass sprayed the tall weeds.

"Cabron," he shouted at no one.

Fulgencio Arriola leaned on his cane, shaking his head from side to side.

"What is wrong with my grandson, my nieto?" he asked himself. "The rage that resides within him is not the stirring of the young colt becoming a stallion. It is more, much more. Perhaps I should speak with the boy."

The patriarch of the Arriolas, old Fulgencio, knew all there was to know about horses, the valley, the village of San Ignacio and the history of his family. He remembered well his father's parents. His abuela had been half Castiliano and half Taoseño. His abuelo had been half Ute and half Castiliano. He had learned much from them both. It was his grandfather who had taught him about horses.

His grandmother, on many a cold night, talked of the wanderings of her Taoseøño people, centuries in the past, and their search for a home place that the Creator would show them. His grandparents also knew the medicine ways of their peoples.

For years, Fulgencio had kept a small, personal altar in his tiny room with a Santo of the Cristo on the cross. Tied beneath the pierced feet, an eagle feather was suspended. Oh, he knew all of the stories from the Bible, his rosary and creed, but he also burned cedar and sage in a small clay pot. Old Fulgencio knew many things. Perhaps the time had come to now talk with his nieto and begin the process of passing along his knowledge. Someday the boy would be where he was now, the oldest Arriola, and he would pass on to a grandchild the same stories, the same knowledge. Time cannot change what is true.

Some deep thing afflicted the boy. What could it be? Fulgencio removed his shapeless old hat and scratched his head. His wispy, infant-fine white hair fell about his ears. Tonight, after the evening meal, that's when he would speak to the boy. The anger is strong within him now, he thought. His nieto would not listen, and perhaps, most disrespectfully, would simply walk away. Tonight, after his mother's good cooking had calmed the boy's soul, then he, Fulgencio, would speak with him.

Catarina Arriola was a good cook and prided herself on her art. The evening meal on that early autumn evening was no exception to her abilities. She had cooked the rack of pork ribs her husband, Santiago, had earned working on a neighbor's pick-up truck. Along with the ribs, she had prepared a red chili, cilantro and tomatillo salsa, a stack of warm corn tortillas, and chilies rellenos. All of the family at the table, except the baby, Nubia, crossed themselves devotionally and plunged into the fragrant meal. Caterina kissed the topmost tortilla and passed the plate to her father-in-law.

"Gracias. How went your day?"

And so the meal passed pleasantly, with the idle conversations of a family content, a family who knew what would change and what should be left alone, and who knew that time cannot change what is true – all but Isidro.

For as long as he could remember, although he could not remember when it began, old Fulgencio had gone out into the night before retiring to say good night to Grandmother Moon, if she was out and about, or to the stars, whom he called The Eyes of God. For him, it was the way a person should end the day. Contemplation on the creation allowed a person to know his place in the scheme of things. This night was no different. He stood outside in the dark, allowing his eyes to adjust to the lack of light. A sharp breeze blew down out of the mountains and across the fields and pastures of the valley.

The leaves were changing colors rapidly. Soon it would grow bitter and ice and snow would press down upon the land. Toward the middle of the valley, the distant headlights of vehicles on the interstate appeared as beads being strung on an invisible thread. Fulgencio stood in the night, thinking, saying his evening prayers, and The Eyes of God slowly revolved above his head.

"Grandson, I would speak with you."

Isidro had walked to the outhouse and was returning,

when his grandfather spoke to him.

"What is it, grandpa?" Isidro asked in English.

He knew the old man understood him. Isidro spoke English most of the time, trying to throw off the perceived provincialism of his native tongue.

"Grandson, why do you not speak in the language you were born to?" Fulgencio asked in his formal, archaic Spanish.

"Grandpa, this is the United States, now. Not New Spain! Geeeez!" he said, angrily, and turned and looked at nothing but the night.

"This 'geeeez' you say, is it not a form of the name of our Lord, Cristo? Grandson, you should show respect for the Son of God."

"Yeah, yeah, grandpa. Okay, what did you want me for?"

"The anger within you. What is it? You turn from those who care for you. You draw inside yourself like a turtle and shut out all. This is not good."

Isidro turned to walk away from the old man, when, like a snake striking, Fulgencio's hand reached out and grasped the boy's arm in a grip that Isidro had never before felt. Suddenly he was scared of the old man.

"You will listen to my words. Then, how you choose to act upon them will be up to you. But, you will listen."

"Si, Grandpa," the boy said, almost silently, in Spanish. The old man released his grip and Isidro's arm fell to his side.

It had been agreed upon that the following afternoon, the two would talk privately, man to man.

"To make the boy feel like he is a part of something, not a child being scolded," Fulgencio had said to his son and daughter-in-law.

But, in truth, Isidro now felt more restless than ever. A part of him felt he was to be chastened for something he had not done, and a part of him was a little scared, yet, of his grandfather. Lying in his small bed that night he rubbed the sore muscle in his arm.

The afternoon sun shone warmly as Fulgencio addressed Isidro.

"We will talk of serious matters, as men. There is much you know little or nothing of, and for you to take your place someday as head of this family, I must now confide in you," so began old Fulgencio.

Isidro's interest was caught on his grandfather's words, and the choice of the one word, 'confide', did what Fulgencio hoped it would do. Isidro leaned forward on the stump he was sitting on, his hands clasped firmly together, staring at the ground between them so as not to let any distraction interfere with what would be coming.

"Nieto, let us begin by addressing what appears to your family as an anger. Who or what angers you?"

"Abuelo, it is hard for me to put such feelings into words."

"Try, grandson. Right now, it seems this problem, whatever it may be, looms large in your life. But you have only fourteen seasons of experience to try and find the answer. Your family cares deeply for you. You carry the blood of many noble and brave people in your veins. Face this squarely, and your old abuelo will assist you."

It seemed that the school in Caborca, to which Isidro rode in the yellow school bus each morning, had been using a television for a teaching aid. Many new thoughts and ideas buzzed in Isidro's head, like the flies that swarmed around the carne asada his mother, Catarina, made.

"What ideas disturb you most?" his grandfather asked.

"It seems the people speaking on the programs all assume we will attend the university in Albuquerque. That, and no class is taught in the Spanish we use here in San Ignacio. They only speak English."

"And these things are what cause the anger?"

"It is all very confusing, Grandpa."

"Si, this I realize, grandson."

The old man placed his cane on the ground, removed his hat, and mopped his head with his handkerchief. Replacing his hat and wiping his thick glasses, he continued,

"Many years ago, our Ute ancestors would take a young boy your age out to a hill, to speak with the Creator of All Things and our departed, in order to find answers to questions of how the young one would find his life's path."

"Is that what you did, Grandpa?"

"By the time I was a young boy, most of our relatives had been killed off by the army. Those who remained were herded like animals onto parcels of land far away, and they were told to stay there. I believe these pieces of land are called reservas. We, who had started farms here in this valley, were allowed to stay. So now, we have only stories of the deeds of the Old Ones in our families. We had a priest, once, who stayed down at the small capilla."

Isidro knew that no priest had said mass at this small chapel for many years, but that the women of the village still continued to repair the walls with fresh adobe plaster after the summer rains. Any heavier work was done by the men.

"The priest would come to each home in the village for a meal and talk with the families. He taught us the ways of our people who had immigrated from Mexico and Spain. On Saturdays, he instructed the children in the catechism, the stories of our Lord, Cristo, and the saints. Slowly, the ways of our native ancestors were forgotten. Only a few remembered, and these ways were taught in secret. My father's people always burn the sacred yerbas to cleanse their homes of all that is unwanted. The smoke puts your soul and mind at ease and allows the Creator and the saints to show you the answers."

For as long as he could remember, the smells of smoldering sage and cedar had filled Isidro's home with their pungent perfumes. The burning yerbas had always been referred to as incencio. His mother had once told him that the elders down in Taos continually burned the herbs in their daily rounds of prayers. Isidro thought that perhaps this is what he would do each night as he prayed to the sorrowing Cristo painted on the retablo over his bed.

Fulgencio sat silently for a while. A meadowlark trilled somewhere off in the tall grasses, and a red-tailed hawk glided silently, while its shadow trailed on the ground.

"La lengua," Fulgencio began again, "what is language but words? True language is your thoughts, and your actions are your thoughts made visible. How many tongues have crossed this valley in a thousand years? A thousand years is as a moment in the eyes of God. What you see about you, the fields of grasses, our small village... this is the language of The People. Yes, and even the hard road that runs through the middle of our valley is a language, a teaching to us. It was built by those who have forgotten to listen to the will of God. They cut the skin of our Mother, the earth, to build their road, yet our small village stays as it has always been."

"That's it, abuelo. Nothing changes here. Everything is old. I would like to see new things. Some of the children at the school speak of things I know nothing of."

"Grandson, you have lived for fourteen years in our valley. You have gone as far as the school in Caborca. But, have you really seen all that is in our valley, our beautiful valley, the place of our ancestors, our family – la sagrada tierra?"

"Grandpa," the boy replied, reverting to English, "how can dirt be holy? Forgive me, but you seem to talk in circles. I don't understand."

Fulgencio replied in his native Spanish. "This day will live in your memory for as long as you walk this earth. You will recall when you are old, like me, the slant of the sun and the rustle of the cottonwood leaves in the trees. Something will trigger the memory of this day. The exact words may, in time, be forgotten, but the content will remain. Time cannot change what is true, mijo. I will take you somewhere new. Somewhere you have never before been."

Within the elbow of the Rio Grande stood a hill, and the river flowed between it and the larger cerros. The hill was steep and rocky, with outcroppings of large, sunburned boulders at its summit. The old man and the boy walked along a path beside the river, which flowed on their right. Cattails lined the banks, and red-winged black birds held precariously to the bending stalks. The path was bound on the left by lush fields of grasses. Two horses lifted their heads, tufts of grasses sticking out from their mouths, to watch passively as the two walked near them. The path became faint as they neared the hill. A water snake raced to the river. Fulgencio patted his face and neck with his kerchief.

"Nieto, can you see where the stones there seem to be stacked in a pile?" he said, pointing with his cane. "That is where we will go."

After a short climb, they stood before the pile of stones. A cross of small branches leaned to one side, the cross arm bound to the upright with wire. A few, faded plastic flowers lay beneath the cross, and a rosary was wound around the wood. Isidro instinctively crossed himself.

"Who lays here, abuelo?" he asked, respectfully.

"Mi padre," the old man replied, removing his hat. "I will explain, now, why this earth is sacred."

So saying, he walked a few feet up the hill and bent down and picked up a large stone. Returning slowly, he placed it on the grave.

"Let us go down to the shade and cool of the river. I have two burritos your mother made for this day. We will eat as we talk."

"When I was a boy about your age, we owned sheep."

Isidro saw, in his mind's eye, the old weathered ram's skull that hung over the door of his father's shed behind their home. But no sheep had been raised in the valley for many years.

"One night, in early spring," the old man continued, "a fierce and mighty storm raged out of the mountains. Its fury left much destruction in the valley. All of the acequias were choked with mud and branches. Many fences were broken and stock had fled at will before the storm.

So it was with us. Most of our sheep escaped into the night to be devoured by coyotes. The day after the storm, mi padre and I went out to try and retrieve all that we could. It was near mid-morning when we came to this spot. The river was swollen above its banks and all of the ground was mud. Many rocks had tumbled down from yonder hill from which we just descended. As we paused about where we stand now, my father heard a lamb bleating from the hill and went to investigate. As he climbed to where he thought the sound came from, with a roar, more stones crashed down upon him, killing him. My father, Efren Arriola, was dead! My grief knew no bounds, and I threw myself upon his battered body. When I could weep no longer, the sun was at the high point of the sky. But, what could I do? My father was a large man, and I was but a boy. I could not carry his body home, and if I left him and went to get help, coyotes would devour him. I prayed that God would help me in this."

Fulgencio paused in his story and unwrapped a cloth holding two burritos. He passed one to Isidro. Isidro had said nothing since they had sat down in the shade by the river. He took the burro from his grandfather's hand and looked at the old man's face. How changed he now seemed. Isidro had never thought of his grandfather as a boy. He had always thought of him as the old man he had always known. The link in the chain of family events was suddenly welded in place for Isidro.

"Grandpa, please continue. Why is my bisabuelo buried on the hill and not in the campo santo near the capilla?"

Fulgencio continued, "I prayed to God to help me to know what to do. It came to me then, that the stones from the hill had killed him. The stones would now protect his resting place forever. I climbed to the top of the hill where my father lay. The stones that had fallen on him had loosened others. With some effort, I loosened them more and half of the hill gave way. The slash has grown over with sage and grass, but it is still discernable," Fulgencio said, again pointing with his cane. Isidro could barely make out the slide's face.

"The slide carried me down, but I was unhurt. I went to where my father's body had been. One of his arms protruded from the earth. His hand reached up, as if to grasp me. I placed a stone in his hand and placed more around it until there was no trace of him."

Fulgencio crossed himself, saying, "When I returned home, my dear mother, rest her soul in peace, swooned to the floor of our home. My uncle was there, and he carried her to her bed, where she remained for three days. My younger brother, also named Efren, who would die in a tractor accident many years later, was sent to fetch Father Ochoa at the capilla."

"When he arrived, I was made to go over the whole incident in detail to him. I told him why I had buried my father, and that I had knelt and said the rosary after I had put a cross of sticks on the spot. Father Ochoa arose from his chair, placed his hand on my head, and made the sign of the cross. He said I had done correctly. I have since that fateful morning come on this exact day to place a stone on the pile."

The two sat in silence, with only the sound of the river in the background. The clouds massed over the far mountains. A light breeze bent the grasses.

They returned to their home, down the faint path, the only sound being Fulgencio's cane tapping the ground as he walked.

"Grandson, look closely at what the outsiders bring to our valley, those things that we think of as bright and new."

That night, the old man and the young boy stood before the door of their home beneath the star filled sky.

"What they bring," Fulgencio continued, "does it last? To be sure, there are some things that help us, like the pick-up of your father. But the other children in your school, what are they like? Are they not quarrelsome, disrespectful? Do they not taunt you and other children of The People?"

Isidro could see the image of a boy named Pete from his school. His hair was straw yellow and he had large freckles on his face and arms. He always seemed to have a look on his face that said, "I know something you don't." And this boy liked to fight, goading the other students unmercifully. Isidro recalled what could happen if anyone crossed him. Last year, this boy had whipped a boy named Juan, breaking his arm and nearly gouging out his eye.

"These outsiders," Fulgencio continued, "they seem to have forgotten what is true. They seek to only make themselves mighty. They live not as we do. Have you never noticed your mother, in the spring, after the last frost? She plants a garden in the earth your father and I have tilled for her."

Isidro nodded his head. Yes, he had noticed. For three years now, he had helped till that same garden.

"Your padre could, I am sure, move his family to Santa Fe or Albuquerque, and make a living. But we belong here, with our hands in the soil, planting, as your mother does each year. The soil is our life, our past and our future. You saw the past today where your bisabuelo lies beneath the pile of stones. And I will tell you this, mijo. You, Isidro Arriola, are our future. What will you make of those days to come?"

Easing himself down onto an overturned five gallon bucket, Fulgencio continued:

"To be sure, you may go to some large town or city. Yes, go, with my blessing. But, go to see, to compare, to observe the truth of what I say. There will be much that appears new, but look closely. There is a constant repair of things, roads, buildings. The earth seeks to regain those places. Our little pueblo is built on the top of the soil. We have no paved roads. We don't try to cover our Mother Earth with black tar. We use only what she provides and take nothing else. New? Look above you and see the stars. See, there, the three bright stars in a row, The Three Marias? To the left, there is a star and another. Look tomorrow night and you will see another you didn't see tonight. That will be new. Grandson, the newness is within you."

Isidro could say nothing against his grandfather's words. Much of what he said made sense, and yet, Isidro wasn't quite sure that his grandfather could feel what he felt, or that he had seen what he wished to see.

That night, as he lay in his bed, with the sorrowing Cristo above his head, he said to himself:

"My abuelo has lived many years and seen much. Still, I would like to see what some of the others have seen."

He turned and faced the wall and fell asleep.

Out on the interstate, the beads of light were being

strung once again on invisible threads, and the Rio Grande also swept passed the village of San Ignacio, nestled in its elbow.

WOUNDED KNEE

I saw the moon's crescent brightness and its shadowy circular whole, and standing off clearly was the morning star, Venus. I climbed a hill of dead grass and stood by a chain link fence hung with hawk and eagle feathers and strips of red cloth and tobacco offerings. Spirits stood invisibly but they touched me and spoke on the wind. A white man stood and spit between his boots. This is Wounded Knee.

THE LAVA BEDS

A mist hung on the morning air. It caught and shredded on a juniper tree. It clung to the lava boulders and sagebrush and scented the air. A marker says that this is a self-guided trail, but I seem to know the way by heart.

They are all still here. Their shadows still lay on the

ground and their voices are still caught on the stones. A small sign reads, "Keep America beautiful."

THE BEAD

I had not been in Arizona for long when I met a man who had been in Tucson for years. Our conversation focused on hiking in the surrounding mountains. He told me that when he was a boy, now many years in the past, he had hiked on a trail on the western side of the Santa Catalina Mountains in Romero Canyon. This trail led into the farthest most reaches of the range. Up beyond Pusch Ridge there was an area where one could rest and look down upon the surrounding country, the Altar Valley and on into Mexico.

What made the area he was describing of such interest to him was that in the early decades of his life, in the dry washes that flowed out of the canyon, small pottery vessels were once found. Now, though, he told me that this was no more. I would find, perhaps, a shard or two, but nothing else.

The Saturday in May that my wife and I decided to explore the canyon was bright and clear. The weather was warm. Brittlebush and mallow were in bloom, adding to the stark beauty of the rust colored boulders that we climbed passed. It was exhilarating to be there, we both agreed.

We had been following the trail, which meandered,

switch backing, occasionally through the dry wash, when we stopped for breath near an area shadowed by a large rock outcropping. We were both in agreement that our decision to come to Arizona was a good one.

As we sat resting and talking, I picked up a small twig and stirred the fine sand. To my utter amazement, there before me was a small bead, almost unnoticeable at first glance. It had been tumbled through the years by occasional water, which had coursed down from higher up.

Finding it felt, for me, like a token of welcome. I put down a pinch of tobacco and said a prayer of thanks.

TABLE ROCK

Stillness rests on the land here like a blanket. The land looks burned. Lava stones and a few scattered pines are all that is here. Below me, the boulders are still stained red.

Voices from unseen mouths still cry out --

"The Blue coats have us trapped, surrounded.

Let us go now to our Creator. Grandfather, release our spirits. Let us go."

A snow shrouded peak in the east watched then and watches now.

Over my head, an eagle and a vulture are flying. Life and death still cling to this place.

THE LAKE

He drove his car up the graded road that reached up and over the summit of the hill, separating the dry lakebed behind him from the lake before him.

He drove off onto the rutted track, half hidden by the drifting sand. The car bogged and wallowed, struggled for a grip, and inched forward on buried rocks. Floundering once again, the car stopped, unable to maintain its momentum. Shutting off the ignition, the man waited for the silence to envelope him. But the silence he hoped for was replaced by a buzzing in his head. Opening the door, the man got out and stood and gazed about him. Walking, his shoes instantly filled with sand and he aimlessly picked his way, slowly, almost mindlessly.

Before him, at some distance, the sheet of water was blinding, reflecting and intensifying the sun. Around him, scattered in the sand, pieces of lava cluttered the ground. They seemed dull and without luster. But when he held one in his hand, he noticed that its surface was smooth and it gleamed almost iridescently. Turning it in his hand, what appeared to be a blackish, chocolate brown became a reddish umber, with a metallic oil slick rainbow sheen. He dropped the rock back into its impression in the sand. Although he had replaced it exactly where he had found it, he was taking a part of the stone, perhaps its essence, its spirit, with him, however inadvertently. He liked stones. He had collected some. He remembered many. Their memories sat on the shelves of his mind.

Continuing to walk, he stopped beside a large boulder and sat down. He gazed at the ancient sagebrush that grew sparsely around him in the sand. It had been at least five hundred years since the water had been up that high and it would be another thousand before the sagebrush would be as thick there as it was on the low sand hills behind him.

"What are you doing? We've been watching you. You don't belong here. We got your car out for you and we could use a little something for that."

The man on the stone turned and looked at the Indians walking toward him, but he said nothing. His hands rested on his knees and he looked as if he were expecting someone or something.

One of the Indians, his white t-shirt barely covering his stomach, seemed unsure of what to do next. The others moved into a half circle around the man on the rock, but no one stood in front of him, and the man continued to stare out at the lake.

"What's he doing? What's he want?"

With the late afternoon sun, an old man with a faded print neckerchief tied around his head, walked up to the men. His grey hair hung about his ears. He looked at the man on the rock and then at the others, who shook their heads and shrugged their shoulders.

The old man looked back at the man on the rock and walked slowly, stopping nearly in front of him. The man on the rock glanced at the old man and then back to that point, far away, that only he could see.

"You can't die here," the old man said. "You'll take what you're seeing with you." The men in the half circle looked at the old man questioningly.

"He is dying. He wants to take this memory with him. He wants to remember this place, for some reason."

Turning to the man on the rock, he continued, "You are taking minute parts of our place into your death. You used to take our spirits away with your photographs. And we all know of the other taking. But this is different – to take a place away by dying in it. Why couldn't you die somewhere else? Why here? Why is this place special to you?"

The man in the white t-shirt moved to look out in the direction in which the man on the rock was gazing.

"Ain't nothing but the lake and the mountains. What's he looking ...... My God! The lake's gone... it's vanished!"

The man on the stone fell backwards. The old man began to chant softly.

ZODIAC RIDGE

Ancient eyes looked to the heavens, then hands placed the stones. The People lived according to the movements of the sun, the rhythm of their lives. Now only the stones remain. The People have gone.

I have held in my hand broken shards and touched the symbols carved at the shrines of stone.

The whispers of The People linger in the mesquite and palo verde trees. A hawk's shadow ripples over my head when I stand at the center stone and Coyote sits and watches.

THE PLACE OF THE ANCIENTS

I have stood in the caves of the most ancient ones, the walls blackened by cooking fires. I have held their conception of the spirits of the land in my hand. I saw the bones of one crushed by falling stone.

Visions came to my mind's eye: I saw the preparations for boys becoming men, women carrying water in skin bags, lookouts scanning the heavens. All was now silent.

"Boys like you once lived here," my father said to me.

I remember. In my heart, I know.

VAIL

It is early morning, and not a sound can be heard across this eastern corner of Pimeria Alta. The sun has just brightened the top of the tallest mountain, painting it a soft orange. The day comes softly at this time of year, gently awakening the earth, as a loving mother would stir sleep from her young child's dream journeys.

What as yet unrealized memories lie in its unfolding?

A far saguaro now bristles with a golden halo as a ray of the sun cuts through a rock formation on the ridge at my back. A cactus wren bounces on the air, from bush to tree, as if pulled by unseen strings.

The desert comes alive. The mountain before me is now streaked with orange light and blue grey shadows. The full moon is fading in the western sky as the sun inches slowly through a bosque of mesquite. The tortolilla doves stretch and ruffle their feathers and the saguaros march up the slopes.

The sky is a pale turquoise. There is not a stirring of the air – all is stillness around me. Down in the mesquite bosque, where an arm of the creek percolates when flowing, a congress of cactus wrens appear to be in filibuster over a perceived issue. The quiet is disturbed further by a suddenly swooping, low flying, black, shiny raven, screaming out the only sound he knows.

TO LIVE IN THE DESERT

For me, to live in the desert and the mountains is not an escape from reality. The desert absorbs my grief, fires my joy and it keeps hopes alive when nothing else can. I often wonder if I would have any life at all if it were not for deserts and mountains.

THE COWBOYS

The silence of the desert was broken occasionally by wind in the mesquite trees or the call of a cactus wren and the mutterings of a flock of quail. From the ridge bordering the dry wash to the south where I sat, faintly at first, then steadily louder, came the lowing of cattle and whistles and shouts.

I walked down the fence to where it turned sharply to the south. There, a cattle guard crossed the road and then, suddenly, out of the brush, topping the rise, came a herd of cattle. Black Angus with a few Herefords began plodding across the road, bawling their discontent. The drovers, swinging the lariats, whistled and shouted to keep the herd together. The cowboys passed in front of me, driving the herd into the wash toward the holding corrals. The entire sight lasted little more than a half hour. In my mind, I was suddenly transported to the Chisholm Trail, or the King Ranch, or the XIT. Images from books or movies of my childhood were suddenly before me. All of the old feelings welled up within me. How I had wanted to be a cowboy and do what these drovers were doing. The Old West lived again for me, if for only a few minutes.

When they had passed, once again, there were the sounds of quail and cactus wrens and soft winds blowing.

THE SUMMONS

The tracks led upward into the foothills and it appeared that they would follow the obvious course, straight into the wide and angular canyon that was now half in shadowy blues and half in brilliant sunlight. Loud cracks of thunder shook the earth and the wind began to pick up. The mesquite and palo verde trees jerked and bent in its furious force.

The man pushed on, planning to make camp in the shelter of some small cave or overhang before the full force of the storm overtook him. The ground became more littered with stones. The soft, padded tracks became more difficult to follow and the sun began to slant more rapidly. It would soon disappear entirely. With a rending roar, the thunder echoed across the eastern sky, now a dark, blue-grey color. The wind eased some. As yet, no rain pelted the ground to wash the tracks away. Perhaps the storm would stay to the east and behind him to the south. The far, pointed mountains there were totally obscured by the storm.

No rains came and the winds departed. Once more, the calm and the sun held the desert. The shadows in the canyon deepened to a night black and inched slowly up the mountains.

The man sat by his small, smoldering fire, thinking of the footprints he had followed for several days. The desert had been hot, the sun like the burning eye of the Creator. Tomorrow he would walk into the canyon before him, perhaps climbing up into the cooler reaches.

The vision of the now hidden split in the mountain appeared once more in his mind. Two days in the past, it had been but a blue slash across the buff and dun colored mountains. Yesterday, after the sun had passed its zenith, he could look far into the interior of the mountain. Today, the immensity of the gash and the solemn stillness waited in awesome wonder. The faint smell of water blew down out of the blackness before him where he sat, mixed with the aroma of pine and oak trees. Coyote wailed and cried somewhere unseen.

The man watched the sun disappear behind the far grey mountains. Clouds of the same color hung overhead. As darkness approached, a dull sunset touched the landscape. Little spots of sun shone momentarily on a hill or mountainside and then faded out. When the sun was completely gone, the clouds and the mountains retained an afterglow that caused everything to be rimmed with light. A golden mist floated in the far canyons on the other side of the wide valley.

Stars began to twinkle, one by one, piercing the sky like gems dropped on a blue cloth. The man sat against the stone, his legs drawn up, his arms wrapped around them, with his chin on his knees. He wondered if he was the last person on earth and if this would be the last night the world would ever know.

The moon rose slowly, large and yellow through the torn clouds. To him, this was an ensign of hope, telling him he was not alone. This would not be the last night on earth.

The moon's radiance flooded the hills and valleys. The cries of the night were all about him.

****

The sun's light seeped into the night sky, faintly at first, but it deepened in intensity to a blood red crimson. The dawn dusk brightened slowly to expose huge, mountainous, cotton clouds forming and growing over the pointed southern mountains. Perhaps the rain would come today.

The man covered the ashes of the night's fire with sand. With a broken branch, he smoothed the area he had rested in. The first winds would eliminate any trace of his passing.

He turned his eyes to the waiting silence of the gaping canyon. The trees began half way up and were printed blue black against the tan rocks and earth. He began to walk into the waiting stillness, not knowing what he would find. The footprints had now disappeared in the stones, broken twigs and bent grass. All telltale marks had been erased by the wind of the day before. He would walk and climb, guided by his senses.

Seven nights in the past, he had been awakened by the sounds of faint bells and the weeping of a woman from far out on the desert. He lay on his narrow bed and listened, unable to tell from which direction the sounds came. They grew neither fainter nor stronger. The silence of the night had muffled the sounds somewhat. At first, he had thought they were sounds from within his dream wanderings.

Standing to clear the sleep from his mind, he walked to the door of his low clinging home and listened, staring out into the blackness of the night. The stars shown so brightly that the mesquite cast shadows of a deeper black into the black desert. Again, from out of the night came the soft, barely perceptible sounds of far away bells and a woman in deep distress, wailing from her soul. Coyote had heard as well, for he made no sounds in the night.

The man stood and listened until the dawning of the day, when the sounds ceased. To the north, over the far mountains, a column of clouds stood, rising from the massed thunderheads. As he watched, it slowly curled and twisted, growing larger, nearly filling that part of the sky.

All morning he walked, looking for signs of who or what had stirred him from his sleep. When the sun was half way to its highest point, he found the tracks, unrecognizable in their form. They seemed as disturbed animal tracks, partially weathered by the wind, but, of what animal?

Now on this eighth day, he stood in the entrance into the earth. The saguaros climbed around him up the sides of the canyon. No shadows curled in this place. All about him was exposed to the intense light of the day; all was laid bare and folded back. The trickle of water springing from far up the mountains sank into the sand at a small, moist mound and disappeared. The man placed his fingers to the damp earth and then to his tongue. The water tasted sweet.

With audible prayers for guidance, he placed a carved stick, tied with hawk feathers, deep into the earth. The feathers fluttered in the light breeze. Rising to gaze once more into the split in the earth, between the small stones of the spewed talus, he saw the tracks begin once more.

He stopped half way into the canyon, not so much for rest, but to view the land behind him. Far away, near the base of the far mountains, a faint haze hung and disappeared in the heated air. His small home was there. His old mother would be sitting in the shade, moving as the sun moved, going about her daily chores. Her face came to him. She would be gazing in this direction, no doubt.

A stir in the brush brought his attention back to this place. Far above, against the blue sky, Grandfather Eagle looked down and screamed his long, trailing cry. A cactus wren clung to a low growing limb, cleaned its beak and cocked his head, looking at him. He had now climbed to where the oak trees were giving way to pines and Manzanita.

The unrecognizable tracks somewhere in the rocks became recognizable, the naked prints of a human foot. How had he mistaken them, he wondered? Who was this person? The prints were obviously those of a woman.

As the sun began to set, he sat upon a rock at the head of the canyon and the pines unburdened upon the air their load of fragrance. He thought about this journey. Somehow, this time mirrored his life and origins. His thought took him late into the night. He listened attentively to his thoughts, recalling his childhood, his efforts to be accepted as a member with standing among his people. He had sought answers from the wise ones for the whole of his life, this life given to him by the Creator. He was totally absorbed in these thoughts and the calm of the canyon.

Sitting thus, he mused, "The Wise Ones have taught me

to listen and to open myself up to the knowledge of all there is to know of life in this desert. They have taught me how to live within the Creator's will. As much as I have learned, I will always learn more. I will listen with a still heart and an open soul. When the heat of summer comes and our people depart for the cooler elevations in the foothills and the desert shrivels one's words to a whisper, the voices of everything born and everything that ever was, is or will be, can be heard in the voice of the desert."

And so the man sat and listened silently to mountain and to the desert far below him. The desert and the mountain spoke with the voice of life, of continually becoming.

****

With the dawn, he began to walk again and the tracks, now easy to follow, took on the unrecognizable form they had had on the desert floor. When the sun had reached its highest point, he followed the tracks across the ridge and once more rested. He lay upon his back, gazing up into the sky and watched

the clouds that moved across the vast expanse of blue. The breeze blew softly and stirred the branches of the tall pines. Little birds darted occasionally from bush to tree. The insects buzzed and the ants crawled. All was still about him. So also was everything in movement; an unfathomable mystery. What he saw and was a part of was the Great Mystery.

He walked once more through the manzanita. The tracks began to fade upon the white sand resting upon living rock. He now questioned whether they were human prints after all. What woman would wander alone in these mountains? He now questioned his judgment. There had been tracks – of that he was sure. For days now, he had followed them – across the desert, into the canyon, up into the mountains. But what made them? Tracks are made by the passing of some creature – human or animal – something from here, from within the creation of the Great Mystery.

He turned and looked behind him. His own marks upon the soil were fresh and clear. With the first wind or rain, they would be gone. No trace of his passing would be marked after one phasing of the moon. He stopped and looked about him, his thoughts racing like the wind. This place of mountains and wind, heat and cold – it has a feeling of peace. It conceals and reveals meanings and is haunted by the Great Mystery.

He glanced up through the swaying pines.

He said to himself, "I have become obsessed with following what may simply be the tracks of Coyote. I have been seeking and my seeking shows in my confusion and fatigue."

The man had walked for many days and had entered the Earth Mother. The rhythm of her body became one with his own.

"Coyote made the tracks I have been following," he whispered. "He it was who disguised them as human and animal. He and the Earth Mother worked together in this mystery. She it was who called me from my bed in the still of the night. And it was Coyote who led me to this lesson."

Shielding his eyes to the sun, the man turned and began retracing his path. He felt an almost imperceptible shudder from the Earth Mother and the throbbing of her heart in the mountain. Stopping, he glanced over his shoulder to look once more at the ridge where he had sat and gazed at the expanse of the heavens and the undulating ripples of the desert floor.

The Great Mystery had reminded him of his purpose as a two-legged creature, something the four-leggeds and the wingeds never forgot – the fine line of balance between spirit and body. This was the lesson of the cloud nation, the placement of the trees on the mountains, the movements of the ant nation and the sounds of the insects. All that he could see was as it should be. All was in place.

The man came to realize that the desert was like his life, a mirror in which, once he had been young and now was older. Where the desert had once been fresh and green, now it held brittle, sharp edged stones and poisonous plants that could both kill and heal. He knew that the desert held many secrets hidden from the eyes of those who didn't care. He knew that for those who seek to understand, the desert will shed its mystery and stand unashamed.

Grandfather Eagle screamed once more his long, whistling cry.

BEGGING

I pray that I am not a beggar who steals scraps of power from native cultures to decorate my own life that is bare of enchantment.

PASSAGES

The four men rode their horses at a leisurely walk and crested a knoll. From there, they had an unobstructed view across the undulating ocean of buffalo grass. The knoll that the men rested upon, a ground swell in this sea of grass, hid a small, slow flowing brook lined with stunted willows where small birds flitted and chattered. Nothing was to be seen in all directions but toward the east, where low, wind-blown sand hills lay naked to the sun and where the buffalo would, when near, wallow and where the bulls would duel for supremacy.

None of the men spoke – what was the need for wasted words? A buzzard swept the sky, its shadow rippling across the grass. The riders paused and the horses began munching the grass around them. First one horse, then the other three raised their heads, their ears alert and pointed forward.

One of the younger men, who had been on scouting forays, shielded his eyes and pointed toward the sand hills. The blue sky was uncluttered but for wispy clouds far to the southwest, announcing the coming arrival of the Thunder Beings. The buzzard glided toward the sand hills.

A small plume of dust rose from the direction of the hills. As the men watched, riders appeared, paused and continued into the plain before them, their pace never faltering. The men on the knoll reached for their weapons.

They were as yet uncertain as to who the riders were that were approaching them.

"They may be enemies," said the man who led the other three. He was a man of middle years who had seen and experienced much. He had led many scouting parties.

"One of their party holds something above his head," one of the younger men said.

When the advancing riders were about as far as a horse can run in five breaths, the older man spoke.

"Put your weapons away. He holds a sacred pipe. Whoever these men may be, they come in peace. There is to be no blood spilled before the sacred pipe."

Descending the knoll, the four men dismounted and stood silently as the strangers approached. When the man who held the pipe above his head had come close to the others, he lowered the pipe and dismounted. Those with him dismounted as well. Letting go of the reigns of their horses, they sat in a half circle. No word had yet been spoken by either party.

When all had settled themselves upon the grass, they sat in a circle. The pipe that had been carried aloft was placed upon a small red stone the pipe carrier took from a colorfully quilled bag. Using hand signs, the pipe carrier began to tell his story.

"We come from the land far to the east. We have travelled long. Our village, to the south and east of this place, was destroyed by our enemies. Our people all were killed. Those who weren't killed were taken captive. Nothing was left but ashes and the bodies of our loved ones. We had returned to our village from a trading journey and found that all had been destroyed. Thus, we six are the last of our village. We counseled among ourselves after we had placed our dead upon burial scaffolds. What were we to do? Where were we to go?"

The man signing paused, and then continued, "We have relatives who live far to the south, the Quapaw, and also relatives far to the north, the Ponca. They, like ourselves, have been at war with our enemies. When we discovered our destroyed village, it was decided among us that we would seek to know those with whom we may come in contact. The pipe of the red stone has allowed us safe passage through the nations we have crossed. We asked only to be left in peace, that the Creator of All Things might continue to show us the path we have been following. We will pass through and out of your country, taking only what will sustain us on our journey. We wish to keep the memory of those we meet as being brothers. So that you may know who it is that sits before you, we are The People of the Village near the Hill Rising from the Center of the Plain. We are of the Omaha. I am called The Panther."

So saying, The Panther motioned to one of the men, who handed him a tortoise shell that issued wisps of smoke. Placing a coal within the bowl of the red stone pipe, he began to smoke and then passed the pipe to the one on his left side. And so the pipe passed to all of the men in the circle. When only ash remained, there was a brief silence. Then, using signs, the conversation continued.

"Visitors from the east, we of the prairies find your words hard on our ears. I am called Spotted Crow. We are of the Osage. My men and I seek the herd. We need meat in our village. Take what you need to live on, but do as you have done. The sacred pipe held aloft is your safe passage. Be warned, though. To the west are our enemies. They may think of you as spies if that is the direction you intend to follow."

Again, The Panther signed, "May we rest here awhile and refresh both ourselves and our horses near that small stream? We will depart this place with the rising of the sun after a night's rest."

Spotted Crow signed, "Rest peacefully and may you be guided by the Great Spirit on your journey."

Spotted Crow and his men rose, mounted their horses and headed east where they rode, four abreast. One of the men, Prairie Chicken, asked,

"How is it that a whole village may be taken out? What type of a man would kill children, women and old ones? This I can hardly understand. As the one who called himself The Panther signed, I saw, in my mind, our village. The image of it made my heart sore."

Spotted Crow responded, "Do you recall but three moons back, men from beyond The Butte Where the Bear Lived came to our village? They spoke of ones who seek the beaver, how they take the hides and leave the ground bloody and then move on. Always they take more than is needed. Our holy man, Mole, asked the visitors to our village if perhaps they might be mistaken. But no, they said, they were speaking true. I asked myself then how the ones spoken of could do this. Perhaps the ones who seek the beaver act in the same manner as the ones who took out the village of The Panther and his people."

One of the other men, Hairy Moccasin, said, "I think these destroyers to be spirits of evil who have clothed themselves with flesh. Their bodies should be destroyed. Then perhaps they would return to where they came from."

Spotted Crow and his men travelled two days more when the herd was found. The men rode slowly outside of the herd, so as not to frighten the animals and then turned their horses.

"We are four days from home. We must hurry and report all that we have witnessed. We have much to tell."

When the men returned to their village, the hunters were informed of the location of the buffalo. The camp crier passed among the tipis with the news. Soon, the women were striking the camp with the dogs barking in excitement. Small children were gathered up. Only the council tipi was left. Spotted Crow and the men who had been with him sat with the elders of the band. The sacred pipe was lit, prayer was said, prayer that the words that would be spoken would be true, with nothing left out or forgotten.

Spotted Crow began, "The herd was found two days beyond the small brook with the stunted willows. This you all know already. What we have to relate is something most unusual. Those who were with me will verify what I am about to tell. We have smoked the sacred pipe so that no words can rise above it or below it, but will fly straight to your ears."

When the words of all that had occurred with the strangers had been spoken, the holy man, Mole, addressed the men.

"We must speak more on this mystery, but now we must prepare for gathering meat. Aho."

Spotted Crow's people did not need to travel four days to reach the buffalo. The herd had wandered but a day and half from where the people had been camped. Twenty animals were taken. Immediately, the women began to cut the meat into thin strips to dry in the sun.

Large pieces were roasted over open fires. Hides were staked to the ground to be scraped clean. Hungry dogs prowled near and were chased away with sticks by little boys.

The tipis were once more in a circle. All of the doors faced the east to greet the morning sun. Words of thanks were offered by all of the people in Spotted Crow's village. All of the people were happy and at peace. Everyone had had enough to eat, even the dogs that sprawled in the shade of the tipis.

Spotted Crow and the men who had been with him scouting the herd, were summoned by the camp crier.

"Mole requests your presence," was all he said.

Mole sat facing the door as Spotted Crow and the other men entered and took their seats. Again, Mole held the sacred pipe in his hands, the stem pointing away from him. His head dropped to his chest, his long, gray hair hanging about his shoulders. His lips moved in silent prayer. All within were still and silent.

"I have gone into the purification lodge and spent a day and a night out on the prairie. I have taken the words you men spoke within my mind. I can but wonder about the men you met. Had they anything about themselves that might tell us that they were who they said they were? You said they came from the southeast. That is a big country. You, Spotted Crow, would have been able to tell if they were enemies of ours. But, no, they came in peace with the pipe. My mind is sure of this."

A silence rested within the tipi. Spotted Crow then spoke.

"Mole, these men and myself have told all that occurred. We spoke on the pipe, as you know. We saw no indication that these men were our enemies. They were dressed in clothes similar to ours. The one who called himself The Panther had many blue marks on his arms and chest. From his ears, long strings of small shells hung. That is all. Had I not known differently, they could have been some of our own people."

And so the words went back and forth across the fire, each man holding the sacred pipe before he spoke.

The meat had been taken and all was as it should be; bellies full, children playing, each person with his or her own duties. The keeper of the winter count came to Spotted Crow to record the encounter with the six men from the southeast.

****

The Panther and his men heeded Spotted Crow's words and took a more southwesterly direction, never hurrying, resting their horses when the need arose. They met no people. One afternoon, they found what had been a camp circle of tipis. The Panther dismounted and knelt beside a fire ring, touching the ashes.

"The people left this place at least six to eight days ago. See how the grass has begun to grow green once more around the stones?"

The people who had been there had left nothing to indicate who they might have been.

Since leaving their camp by the little brook with the stunted willows, they found little water seeps or hidden trickles in the buffalo grass, enough for themselves and their horses. Soon, the land became flatter and the grass shorter. They were passing into new country. Buffalo herds had left huge swathes of torn earth through the short grass. Here and there were the marks of horses, small herds of them roaming free.

It was discussed that perhaps they could try and capture new mounts from one of these herds and release the mounts they had been riding. This was agreed upon.

The Panther and the men with him had no definite destination in mind as they rode. It was a journey to try and open their minds to a new life, to rid the anguish from their hearts, but never to forget the memory of their destroyed village and their loved ones. Perhaps, they would someday, somehow, be accepted by a people and their lives would begin once again. Their own people adopted those of other nations and this is what the men hoped for themselves.

The land became more broken and plants they had not seen before began to appear, plants with clusters of sharp spears. Water became more infrequent. One day, the men observed a deep cut in the side of a large hill that soared abruptly and rose to a high crest. Pausing at the entrance of the split in the hill, the men had to hold tight to the reigns. The horses smelled water within. Slowly they entered the split in the hill, which widened and became a valley, lush with green grass, willows, chokecherries and stunted oak trees. Swallows swooped and dived around the cliff faces. As the men proceeded slowly, they touched their weapons. They halted beside a sheer face of smooth stone upon which were carved symbols strange to them.

"Do you think we are being watched?" one of the men asked The Panther.

"I feel no fear," he responded.

Dismounting near a small stream that flowed down from somewhere further up, suddenly a horse hidden from view, let itself be known. Instantly, each man had his sinew-backed bow in his hand, an arrow notched. No one appeared. Their own horses responded to the one hidden, who now came into view, leading a small herd behind him.

"I feel no one is about," The Panther said. "If we had been seen, it is doubtful their horses would have let us know. These must be free roaming animals. We may have new mounts."

Walking six abreast, the men slowly forced the wild herd back into the far end of the little valley. When they could go no further, they forced the horses into a large pond that was formed from a spring at the side of the cliff. The horses swam, milling in the water where it then became an easy matter to mount a tired animal and so acquire it.

Each man spoke to the horse he had ridden for so long, thanking it for its friendship. Then, these horses were turned loose, but they did not wander far. The new horses the men now had were hobbled near their camp. These horses were stroked and spoken to, establishing a bonding.

The Panther said that he felt that the Creator of All Things had guided them to this spot and that they needed to pause and rest here and to counsel among themselves about how to proceed.

For five days, they worked with their new mounts, riding up and back through the little valley. The horses soon became as willing to allow a rider as if they had always done so.

One day, a man whose name was Water Snake said that he would ride out of the valley to see if he could kill some meat, for, strangely, no large animals other than the horses, seems to live in the valley.

When he returned, late in the afternoon, Water Snake had a number of the rabbits with the long ears tied to his saddle. Approaching The Panther with his catch, he said,

"I feel that it has been discovered that we are here. Not far from the mouth of this valley, I found many horse prints. There were riders and one of them dropped this."

He handed The Panther a quilled eagle feather.

"Someone will suffer for this oversight, this carelessness. We must be on our guard. We will keep watch."

The next morning, a lone rider slowly approached. The Panther held aloft the sacred pipe once more. The stranger rode directly to The Panther and spoke words none of the men understood. The Panther lowered the sacred pipe and placed it on the red stone. Then, signing, he addressed the stranger.

"We are strangers in your land. We come in peace. We are The People of the Village by the Hill Rising from the Plain. We are Omaha."

Before he could sign more, the stranger signed,

"Why are you here?"

The Panther related all that had occurred.

"Come with me," the stranger signed. "Gather all that

you have with you. I will take you to my village."

As they proceeded to leave the little valley, The Panther held the sacred pipe once more.

When they approached the village, many riders rode out and surrounded The Panther and his men. They pointed at The Panther, who yet held the sacred pipe. The village was large. Many children ran and stood staring at the strangers. Camp dogs growled around the horses' hooves. Women stopped what they were doing and stood watching.

The Panther and his men were taken to a large tipi where a man of great size sat waiting. When he saw The Panther, who still held the sacred pipe, he moved from his place opposite the door and motioned for The Panther to take that place. After they seated themselves, The Panther began to sign, telling all that he and his friends had experienced. When he finished signing, the large man pointed to the fire. The Panther took a pouch from his waist, filled the pipe and lit it from a twig in the fire. He passed it to his left to the large man. All within smoked until only ash remained in the pipe. The large man spoke, his words not understood. There was a silence. The large man wiped his hand across his forehead, as if to clear his mind. Then, signing, he said,

"I am called The Bear's Shoulder. We are the Yamparika. You say you wish to pass out of our country. Why is that? Have you been harmed while you have been here?"

"No harm has come to us. Since we have wandered, we have agreed among ourselves that since we believe we are being guided by The Creator of All Things, we would end our travels only when we felt guided to do so.

We mean no insult to you or to your people," The Panther responded.

Continuing, he said, "With your permission, we request of you the right to sleep one night in your village and we will leave you when the sun appears."

The Bear's Shoulder rose, as did the others. The Panther took from a pouch he wore across his shoulder the quilled eagle feather.

"This," he said, "was found not long before your man led us to your village. It lay upon the ground."

The Bear's Shoulder stood and gazed speechless at the plume and then took it from The Panther. Then, more to himself than to those about him, he said, "This carelessness will be paid for."

Stopping at the entrance to the tipi, The Bear's Shoulder turned to The Panther and said, "So that it can never be said that The Bear's Shoulder refused hospitality to strangers, I offer you a place to stay. The cold season will soon be upon us."

The Panther and his men accepted this invitation gratefully.

"While we are with you and your people, we will do as you and your people do. If you need for us to accompany your hunters, we will do so. We will do as you bid us to do. We do not wish to be a burden on your kindness and generosity."

The Panther and his men lived and hunted with the Yamparika all through the cold moons.

One night, when the season was warming, The Panther and his men lay in their robes. The night's stars shined brightly above their heads. In the center of the Yamparika village, a large fire burned, throwing a halo of light in which men danced. They carried long staffs, from which fluttered freshly taken scalps. The Panther and his friends watched silently.

As they watched, a young girl, totally nude, was brought to the fire circle. Her hands were tied and she was led by a tether around her neck. The Panther and the others rose from their robes and walked to the edge of the lighted area. The Panther signed to the one who held the tether,

"Who is this white girl? What has she done?"

"Like you, she is a stranger in our lands. But, unlike you, she and her people did not come in peace. They killed with their thunder sticks a number of our people. So now, I offer her for adoption to one of our poorer people to replace a murdered son."

The young girl was led away by an old woman.

At dawn the next day, The Panther and his friends departed the village of the Yamparika. As they left, they saw the young white girl, hands still tied, tethered to a tipi peg. They had smoked the sacred pipe with The Bear's Shoulder and pledged a peace between themselves.

The new horses that The Panther and his friends rode, as well as the six spare mounts, served them well. These new horses were spirited mounts and a pleasure to ride. The men again rode six abreast, each with his spare horse tethered behind him.

"The Bear's Shoulder answered my query about the people and the land beyond where we are now," The Panther began. "He said that in three or four days of easy riding, we will come to people who live in large, square blocks made of mud and stone. They live near a large river. Many tongues are spoken there. He said he and his people trade hides and meat for corn. It is the same as what our people grew. The Bear's Shoulder said also that these people spoke of making wraps from looms similar to the feather cloaks our chiefs once wore, long ago. But he also said that these people are wary of strangers and that we should proceed slowly with caution.

****

It was in The Moon of Popping Trees when Mole, the holy man, walked from the prairies and into the spirit world to gather with his ancestors. There was little to debate as to who would now take his place. Few men had the experience or wisdom needed to protect and guide The People, such as was possessed by Spotted Crow.

Spotted Crow and his people had camped within a deep and narrow cut in the earth. This place received little snow and wind. The winter storms would blow across the top of the ravine, leaving only a sifting of snow below. A vein of water, now coated in a glaze of ice, flowed down the middle of the defile where small boys gathered water in bladder bags by first breaking a hole with stones.

On such a morning, a boy of about ten winters had wandered up the frozen trickle. The camp was slowly awakening for the day. There seemed no need for haste. Smoke issued from a few of the already dark tops of the tipis. A loud scream from up the frozen creek brought all the people out into the frosty morning, staring, wondering, fearful.

Two men, lances in their hands, ran but a short way when the young boy ran toward them. Blood covered the boy's chest and his left hand was missing. Spotted Crow's camp had had no way of knowing that the trappers had been in the ravine at an earlier time and had forgotten one of their traps. A flaming stick from one of the fires was placed to the bloody wrist of the young boy where the hand had been. The boy was known as Hand Cut Off from then on. The beaver trap was brought to the camp and memories and words from visitors, now many moons in the past, were recalled. Again, counsel was taken about the ones who took and left only bloody earth.

Questions were in everyone's mind. How would it be if we were to meet these strange ones? Would there be blood spilled among our people? Fear and apprehension now walked beside the people in Spotted Crow's camp.

Spotted Crow had taken a second wife. She was the sister of his closest friend, White Horse. Her name was Willow and she and her sister-wife were resting from the work of quilling new moccasins. After sipping choke cherry juice from her horn cup, Willow asked her companion,

"Why must we, the two-leggeds, be always on guard from others of our own kind? It is only during the time of mating that the buffalo bulls fight among themselves. That seems to be nothing more than jealous challenging. They don't seek to kill each other. The great grizzly lives alone and takes only what he needs to survive. Yet the two-leggeds kill one another for what is called glory and honor. This I find most strange. What do you say, my sister?"

Willow sat looking at her sister-wife expectantly.

Butterfly, Spotted Crow's first wife, sat long before answering.

"It is said that long ago, it was not then as it is now. Peace and harmony ruled the hearts of all of the two-leggeds. I'm sure that you have heard from our elders that, at that time, the people and the animals spoke the same language. Why this is not so now, I'm not sure anyone can tell. Many reasons are given for answers, but I don't feel that anyone knows the certainty of it."

Again, Willow spoke to her sister-wife, taking the hand of Butterfly as she spoke, "You are most kind to me, sister, and your wisdom is a blessing to me. I am happy in my heart to be your sister-wife, for, you see, I am with child."

Butterfly gently patted Willow's hand and replied, "It will be good to have a little one in our home. My hope is that those strange ones who come for the beaver will leave us in peace.

Spotted Crow's camp was not confronted by the trappers. But, the young boy, Hand Cut Off, as he grew to young adulthood, vowed, someday, to take the life of the one responsible for the loss of his hand.

The cold winds and snows departed and the sun warmed the earth. Tiny flowers began to appear here and there in the open places. Long trailing vees of geese sounded their returning as they wended their ways north on paths in the sky that only they knew. The camp crier in Spotted Crow's village walked to each tipi to announce a gathering of all the people in the camp. When all were assembled before Spotted Crow's home, a hush fell over the people.

"My relatives," Spotted Crow began, "we have fared well during this time of cold. Only one incident of note occurred – to the young boy now known as Hand Cut Off. This tragedy has been duly recorded on the deer skin winter count."

A toddler who had gotten free from her mother waddled toward Spotted Crow. Stopping and glancing down at the little one, he smiled and stooped down, picking the child up. Then he continued his speech to the people, holding the young girl in his arms.

"Although it is yet early in the season, we must begin to get ourselves prepared to move to The Home of the Bear, the great rock pillar to the north. If we move without haste, but with purpose, we will have more than enough time to set up our camp before the great ceremony of renewal begins. There will be many camps gathering there and we will all proceed to our place within the sacred hoop of the people. So, my relatives, let us gather our belongings. When the sun appears after a good night's sleep, we depart this ravine that has sheltered and protected us from the snow and the wind. Aho."

The same word of confirmation was spoken in response. The people felt that it would indeed be good to once more be a part of the great expanse of the prairie and leave the overhanging walls of the ravine.

The people walked for many days without seeing anyone. The tipi poles, now used as travois, carried the people's belongings, as well as infants and the very elderly. One day, as they neared a large stream, far in the distant southwest, a long column, such as theirs, was seen by the scouts.

Spotted Crow said, "They are headed in the same direction that we follow. They must be friends."

As Spotted Crow's people neared their destination, they saw more columns of people. All would meet at The

Home of the Bear, the place of the sacred Sun Dance. The place selected for this, the most sacred ceremony of all the people of the plains, had been shown to the people far back in time – no one knew how far. But all of the people, whether Kiowa, Lakota, Comanche or any of the many other people of the plains, knew the story of The Place of the Bear.

One of the elders in Spotted Crow's band gathered all of the young children about him. This is the story he told them.

Long in the past, seven sisters were picking berries. These sisters had a brother whom some say was unkind to his sisters. One day, as the girls were attending to their duties, the brother suddenly began to change into a grizzly bear. He attacked his sisters, who fled in terror. Some say that it was a bird who told the girls to stand upon a certain rock, which they did. Suddenly, the rock began to rise up into the air. Their bear-brother, growling fiercely, reached for the girls, but could not touch them. His claws scarred the sides of the rock as it rose into the air. When the rock reached its present height, the girls rose into the sky and became the seven stars.

Spotted Crow, as well as all of the other band chiefs, was summoned to the counsel tipi in order to discuss ceremonial procedures for the pending ceremony.

The large cottonwood tree had been taken in the traditional way and placed in the hole prepared for it. Streamers of colored strips of leather hung from the fluttering branches. The tethers, which would eventually be used in the piercing of the pledgers, were also tied around the trunk of the tree. A heightened sense of excitement and expectation was everywhere felt by all of the people.

A huge encampment was now home to many people, many of whom, at one time or another, had been known to be at enmity with one another. Here, at this sacred ground, all was, if not always forgiven, at least forgotten for this time. Cheyenne were camped near Hidatsa, Lakota near Arikara, Assiniboine near the Blackfeet. The Way of the Pipe held all The People in a feeling of camaraderie, of oneness, and of being together. All of the camps knew and felt deep within themselves that The Great Mystery dwelt within this camp of The People.

It was during this time of celebration and thanksgiving that Willow, Spotted Crow's second wife, gave birth to a little girl. Willow and Butterfly had long anticipated the birth and had prepared many gifts to be given to the family friends and leading elders of the Sun Dance. Butterfly, who had never given birth, had welcomed the young girl, Willow, into her home. When the little one made her appearance, it was Butterfly who attended Willow. It was Butterfly who shed tears of joy as she held the infant, wrapped in soft fur.

****

The Panther and his friends had camped by a small stream that widened and branched. Returning to their horses, the men sat in a circle and The Panther took the sacred pipe from it's quilled bag, filled it, lit it and passed it to his left. When the pipe was empty, it was taken apart and returned to the quilled bag.

"I have some hesitation about these people described by The Bear's Shoulder," one of the men said after the pipe had been put away. "They sound like people far more strange to us than any we have met so far."

"This may be so," said The Panther, "but we have been led this far – to retrace our steps at this time, to my mind, would be wrong. Do you not wish to continue? Speak your heart."

"You have led us with the pipe. We have met and been welcomed by all with whom we have come in contact. I find no fault with anything. I am but weary of travel. I long for a warm fire and a sweet companion to lay beside me in my robes."

"My friend," The Panther replied, "that is the wish of each of us."

The Panther and his friends descended the slope toward the slumping mass of adobe. They noticed a small rivulet that separated the dwellings with a bridge leading across it. No one was about, but from the rooftops, they noticed lines of men looking in their direction – men who stood watching, waiting to see who these six strangers might be.

The Panther carried the sacred pipe above his head as he had done before. The men lined on the rooftops gave no indication of either their friendship or aggression – they stood like carved wood.

"My thoughts are that these people have enemies. It may be best that we do not linger here," one of The Panther's men remarked.

"You may be correct. Let us turn to the south."

The Panther continued to hold the pipe as the men turned their horses, but he lowered it to his chest. When they had crossed the small stream, from behind one of the out structures, a very old and wrinkled man stepped toward them, supported by a long staff which he gripped in his gnarled hands. Raising his left arm, he slowly hobbled toward the men on horseback, who then reigned in their mounts.

The old grandfather walked directly up to The Panther's horse and took hold of the loose hanging reigns. With the staff still in his hand, he shielded his eyes with his arm. He spoke words unfamiliar to the men, but looked at each one in turn questioningly. The Panther signed and the old man chuckled a toothless grin. Then, he waved his hand as if to dismiss the signed words of The Panther.

"You men have traveled far," the old man spoke, slowly enunciating and pausing between each word.

The six men on horseback looked at one another, then at the trembling figure before them.

"You know our tongue. How is this so?" asked The Panther.

"I am not of these people," the grandfather replied, turning slightly and waving a hand toward the mass of adobe and stone. "I have been held here for a long time. I was traded to these people from horse people such as yourselves. I have passed through many hands. You should return to your own country or else go in another direction. Do not linger here. These people trade only with the Yamparika and fend off all others."

"We will heed your words, grandfather." So saying, the men on horseback slowly moved toward more open ground.

"The Great Mystery has put the correct thoughts within all of us. I wonder about the old one – what a story he must have."

When the men from The Village Near the Hill Rising

from the Plain had left the homes of mud and stone, they dismounted and stood to stretch aching muscles.

"We must listen more closely now to the guidance of The Creator. Each of you, speak your hearts – what do you feel we are being shown?"

One man, a stern and taciturn warrior who had been in the forefront of conflicts for his people before he had been asked by The Panther to join the trading venture, now spoke.

"We have seen our village destroyed, our people dead and left lying where they fell, like offal. We have journeyed far and long. We have seen those we have met who, had it not been for the sacred pipe, would have not welcomed us into their lands. This I feel sure of. My old wounds pain me daily. I, like the others, seek the pleasantries of peace and the comfort of a loving companion. Though, in truth, I find it difficult to imagine another who could ever compare to the one I buried when we returned to our ruined village. Perhaps someone of those whom we have met would, if we returned and were welcomed, allow us to spend whatever days we have remaining with them."

He continued, "Each of us has something of value that would benefit a welcoming people. Should we be welcomed somewhere, we are still able to bear arms. The one who spoke for the four we met before we met the Yamparika – his name escapes me – although a warrior for his people, carried himself with the dignity befitting a chief. My inclination is to seek this man and his people. That is all I will say on this. Whatever is decided by all of us, I will abide by. Aho."

The positive response, unsolicited, was unanimous.

"So be it," replied The Panther.

The men began to transfer their tack to the spare horses.

"Let us ride past the mud and stone dwellings and out of this country. We don't want to be taken like the old grandfather," said The Panther. "I feel we should go north of the Yamparika. They showed no inclination for bloodshed toward us, but I recall the young white girl tied like a dog. I would not want to fight with The Bear's Shoulder. It would be more than uneven."

The men smiled in agreement and chuckled. They all knew The Panther was no coward, only careful.

The Panther and his five friends traveled slowly for many days, seeking to avoid further contract with any of the people from the area, always moving to the north and to the east. Tall pointed mountains lined the western horizon, the open prairie spread before them in all other directions in slight, undulating rolls. Nothing was to be seen except the grasses that began again to reach high on the horse's legs.

One day, the buffalo, masters of the prairies, threw a great cloud of dust into the air as they stampeded north. The men reigned in their horses, unsure if the herd was being culled by hunters who, if they wanted no strangers in their country, would report their presence to their elders upon return. The men on horseback watched long, but no riders appeared.

"We should seek a stray," one of the horsemen suggested. "Fresh meat would be most welcome."

When finally the herd had passed beyond the northern horizon, the men slowly rode to where the huge beasts had passed. The grassland was torn and trampled in a great swath. It was there that they saw a yearling who hobbled on three legs. One of its back legs hung loosely as the animal tried to walk. An arrow ended the animal's suffering.

Dismounting, the men dismembered the yearling cow, each man taking a large piece and wrapping it in a portion of the hide. Mounting their horses, The Panther said,

"Let us look for a sheltering area and spend the rest of the day resting."

Late afternoon found the six men in a sheltered dale with a small pool that was fed by a seep of water where delicate ferns and watercress were growing. They had made a fire from the dried buffalo dung and the meat from the young buffalo was pierced with sticks and placed over the smoldering coals. The horses were hobbled and grazed nearby. The men did not sleep, but lay in the shade. One man took from the pouch on his horse a clay pipe which he filled and then passed to one of his friends nearby.

The sun was a hand's width wide where the sky and the earth lay as one, when one of the men rose to gather more fuel for their slow burning fire.

"Brothers, come look," he said in an even voice. "There, to the north and west of us are riders. From here, I cannot make out who they might be. It appears that they have not realized that we are here."

The other men stood and looked to where he pointed.

"The four riders we met so long ago before we met with the Yamparika said that their enemies, the Padouca, lived to the west of them. Now, I recall! His name was Spotted Crow, was it not?"

All agreed that the remembered name was correct and

that it was possible that the distant riders could be the ones Spotted Crow had spoken of.

"If it is meant for us to speak with these people, and we are able to determine that they are enemies of people further east, we will not mention Spotted Crow's name."

Each day, the direction they traveled became more to the east.

****

Spotted Crow was born during the season when the rivers ran full. His people had been camped near the Niobrara River and they had been trading with other bands. The People all were at peace. New and unusual items had come from the trading: shiny copper kettles, bolts of red cloth and even sharp edged hatchets. No longer would buffalo bladders be used to carry water by the wealthier among the people. There were a few side-ways jealous glances.

Among the family who lived in the home near the holy man, Mole, little trading had taken place. Everyone knew and joyfully anticipated the coming of the new member. Would it be a boy who might grow to be a great hunter or an important headman? Or would it be a girl who would be taught the home maintaining arts so important to the life of The People? Only the Great Mystery knew.

Spotted Crow's arrival was announced by a "Give Away." Spotted Crow's father gave Mole a horse. After he was placed in a cradleboard made especially for him, no name had yet been given to him. His mother said it would come when the time showed itself.

Then, one day, many days after his arrival, a most unusual bird dropped from the sky and strutted around the village, cocking its head as if listening for something.

It appeared as though it was kangi, the crow, or, kangi tanka, the elder brother, raven. This strange bird, although black, with the sun shining and reflecting from his wings, had white spots on his breast. No bird such as this had ever been seen before. The mother of the new arrival stood with a small group of her friends watching the bird picking at a bone that a dog had forgotten.

"My new son will henceforth carry the name of this bird. I feel he is destined to be a lasting memory of our people."

The name, Spotted Crow, was carried by him for the rest of his life. Even as a child, he never acquired a nickname.

As Spotted Crow grew to manhood, he received praise from his elders – always he was one of the first to volunteer on scouting forays. It was Spotted Crow who gave large pieces of fresh buffalo meat to the elders who had no one to hunt for them. He gave the whole hide of the first buffalo he killed to an aged grandmother who had only a daughter in her home. Spotted Crow's mother recalled her words when the strange bird strutted around the camp. And so it was Spotted Crow who was asked to lead a scouting party on the day that he met The Panther and his friends out on the prairie.

More and more, the people of Spotted Crow's band looked with anticipation to the traders who brought with them items that were strange, yet helpful. Wool blankets began to be used in all of the homes. Copper buckets, iron ladles, glass beads and German silver conchos were appraised and found to be useful. Soon the usefulness became a need. No longer did the arrows carry stone points, but iron tips hammered from nails. But the question in all of the men's minds was this -- what could be traded for the thunder sticks, and would the traders show them how to use them?

Drastic changes were everywhere. The people from the east and from the north were crowding in upon the Osage, Spotted Crow's people. Why were their neighbors, both near and from a distance, moving from their long, established homes? The People wondered. Goods, which the people could not produce, were being traded for their lands. All that was needed was to place one's thumb on some black paint and then print it on a white leaf that the white man held in their hands. The thumbprint was placed near the cross of the four winds and the men would also make a mark from a bird's feather dipped in the black paint. The people understood this to be a sacred trust. They would some day come to realize that this trust had been misplaced.

European traders moved north as well as south, bringing not only foreign goods, but also smallpox. Many of Spotted Crow's people succumbed to this disease. It was at this precarious time that war was continuing between the Lakota and the Pawnee, which caught many of the nations in a pincher. Again, many of Spotted Crow's people were killed.

The trade in buffalo robes was beginning to take its toll on the herds, which was why Spotted Crow and the men with him were seeking the herd, when they encountered The Panther and his friends.

The Osage had been forced to seek the herd in the hunting grounds of their enemies, the Lakota. Osage hunters stayed near the southern most borders of this area, avoiding, as much as possible, the possibility of contact with Lakota war parties. The Osage had once traveled north to parley a peace with the Oglala Lakota and this had been successful. But, on the way home, they were waylaid by a large band of Teton Lakota and the party had been nearly wiped out. Spotted Crow and the other elders of his band spent long hours in council, debating their predicament.

It was on a day of blustery wind, the sky massed with gray clouds, that a rider approached and dismounted before Spotted Crow's home. Butterfly entered and said that a man wished to speak with him. Being made welcome, Spotted Crow bid the man to speak.

"A number of wagons approach our village. It is the hairy faced ones. They come slowly, looking all around our country. They do not appear to be people of war. They have women and children."

When the small caravan stood beyond the village, a man clad in greasy buckskin pants and shirt approached, carrying no thunder stick. Instead he carried a red stone pipe. The man's hair hung loose on his shoulders and he wore a floppy hat with an eagle feather on it. Spotted Crow approached him with his left hand held up, palm forward.

Speaking in a dialect barely understood by Spotted Crow, the man said, "I be called Jeb Thorn. I am guide to these here preachin' folk. They be comin' to yer lands to parley with ye. They be peaceable, meanin' no harm to ye or to yer kinfolks."

As he spoke to Spotted Crow, a man leaped down from one of the wagons and walked to the two men. He wore a black frock coat and a black tall crowned hat. No hair grew on his face, which Spotted Crow saw was a bright pink color. Addressing the guide, Jeb Thorn, he said,

"Tell him that we bring him good news for him and all of his people."

Spotted Crow and the elders of the village sat in a circle upon the ground with the men from the wagons. The sacred pipe was lit and passed among the men. The man in the floppy hat took four puffs and passed it the man in the frock coat. As he held it, he took from his coat pocket a white cloth. He wiped the stem of the pipe with the cloth before he placed it in his mouth.

Spotted Crow, as well as the men of his village, had never been so insulted. They said not a word.

"Perhaps these white men are ignorant of our ways," Spotted Crow said to himself. After the pipe had been passed to each person in the circle, the man in the frock coat, speaking through the guide, Jeb Thorn, said,

"I'm bringing you good news about your Great Spirit. The son of the Great Spirit was sent to live and die with us and to cover our sins with his blood. His name is Jesus."

There was a loud exclamation from some of the men who sat with Spotted Crow. How could this be?

"The Great Spirit has a son? Who, then, was his wife? Why have we not heard of this before now? And why does this message come from the white man? We have, all of us, sought visions for our lives. Not once were we told of this. To die and yet be alive once more? This is most strange. We will hear no more until we have discussed this in council."

So saying, Spotted Crow and his men rose and walked away. They still smarted over the insult to the sacred pipe.

Turning to the guide, Jeb Thorn, the man in the frock coat said,

"Appears I have some work here amongst these heathens."

Jeb Thorn spit a long stream of brown tobacco juice.

"Reckon so, parson."

The men who had met the white men sat with Spotted Crow. They all agreed that this rude white man spoke words most strange and he left many questions that needed answers.

"What was this thing – sin – that he spoke of being covered with blood? And that name he spoke of – what was it? Jee-gus? We should find out what all of this means for us. Who asked these white people to come here?"

The families of the white men set up their belongings all around the wagons and turned their animals out to graze. A mule wandered into Spotted Crow's village, braying loudly as the dogs snapped at its hooves. Bucking to defend itself, the mule upset a cradleboard that had been placed in the shade of a tree. The child was not injured, but cried loudly, bringing many of the women to investigate and sooth the child.

One morning, a young boy ran to his home, much alarmed. Talking rapidly, he pointed to where the white men's wagons were. When the boy's parents walked to where the wagons were placed in a circle, what met their eyes was as strange as anything the people had ever seen. The white families were all kneeling on the ground with their hands together, their eyes closed, and they were mumbling. When they stood, they began singing in a most unusual way. These white people were, indeed, most strange.

A few days later, more wagons of white people arrived. The circle of wagons got bigger and more animals grazed around Spotted Crow's village.

Jeb Thorn was summoned to Spotted Crow's home. After smoking the pipe, Spotted Crow began.

"How many more white people wagons will be coming and why do they come? We must move our village. Their animals have fouled the area all around our village. We did not ask them to come and we wish them to leave."

Jeb Thorn had no answers to Spotted Crow's questions. The white people did not move.

One day, the guide, Jeb Thorn, and the man with the pink face entered the village. With them came another white man. This man had much hair upon his face and he had two shiny clear pieces before his eyes. The three walked directly to Spotted Crow's home. The hairy-faced one began to enter the door when Jeb Thorn took his arm.

"Reckon I better learn ye. Scratch near the doorway. Don't jest enter. It's the same as knockin'."

"We are here to teach these .... these Indians about Jesus," the hairy-faced one responded.

Spotted Crow sat, his face set like a piece of carved rock. His eyes glinted like flint. He did not offer the sacred pipe. There was an uncomfortable silence and then the hairy-faced one said to his guide,

"Does this man understand why I am here?"

"Parson Gross let him hear some words prior to yer gettin' here."

"Very well, let us begin." Turning, he said to Jeb, "Spotted Crow, that is his name, right?"

"Yep," Jeb answered.

"Brother Spotted Crow," the hairy-faced one began again. "I'm here to tell you something of great importance. I want to tell you that I feel a kinship to you. We are both people, brothers in creation. I want to share with you the life that Jesus lived. When you hear of his life, it will place a power within your heart that you have never felt before."

Hairy-face paused while Jeb Thorn translated his words.

Continuing, he said, "When you feel this power in your heart, you will know that your life has been wasted and that you will now live for a purpose."

Jeb Thorn again translated these words.

Again, there was a silence.

Then, Spotted Crow began to speak.

"You call me brother. You say that I will feel a power in my heart. If I learn of the one you call Jee-gus, can his power be more that the power I have felt at our most sacred Sun Dance? Is it for you, a white man, a stranger in my village, to tell me that my life has been wasted?"

Spotted Crow paused, then said,

"I will hear no more of this talk. I have defended my people with my life. My life has been one of honoring my people. This is the life that has been given to me. There is nothing more to speak on this. I have never told anyone to leave my home. Visitors have always been welcome. You and those with you overstay your welcome. I would ask you and your people to take your wagons and your Jee-gus back to your own homes, wherever they may be. I have spoken. Aho."

Once outside, Jeb Thorn turned to the two men with

him.

"Gentlemen, my advice to ye both is to heed his words and skedaddle. He could be trouble for ye."

"Do you think he would bring his men to our wagons and murder us?" Pink Face asked in a voice full of trepidation.

"I wouldn't bet agin' it," the guide responded.

It took a day and a half for the caravan of wagons to regroup and depart.

****

The Panther and his men had turned more to the east, with the intention of meeting their distant relatives, the Ponca.

"It seems we are to return," said The Panther.

Little conversation had taken place among the six men since the decision to return east was decided upon. They were not sullen, but resigned to what they felt they were being led to do.

Continuing, The Panther said, "It is hard for a man to leave all that he knows and that he has been a part of. We have, by our journey, lifted our hearts from the ground. The memory of our village, now no more, and those whose faces live within our minds and hearts, will be forever with us. We can now – we must – as men, continue the life that has been given to us. The Great Spirit is guiding us to regain our standing as men of integrity. The grief pains have made us resolved to seek peace among the people, or, if this is not possible, to annihilate those who hate and wish to destroy us."

****

The bark covered long houses of The Panther's small village had stood on the banks of the swiftly flowing river for many generations. His people had large gardens of corn, beans and squash, pumpkins, persimmons and sunflowers. They also had peach trees that had been obtained from French traders. With the coming of the hot season, watermelons grew as sweet as honey. The well maintained gardens were the efforts of the women of the village, and great pride was felt when this bounty was harvested.

The Panther's people, the Omaha, the People of the Village Near the Hill Rising from the Plain, were in constant conflict with their neighbors, the Tunica and the Koroa. It was the Tunica who had raided The Panther's village when he and his companions had been on the trading venture.

It was toward the kindred villages of the Ponca that the six men now rode.

"Do you feel we will be welcomed?" one of the men asked.

"When all is explained, I feel that we will be accepted and welcomed," The Panther replied.

As the men rode east and they began to turn their faces more to the north. The Panther's people had knowledge of many of the people on the plains, but little contact had been made in trade or war.

It was agreed that their travels would now necessitate a stricter caution. The Panther carried the sacred pipe in the quilled bag in a large pouch over his shoulder. Feelings that had not ridden with the men now filled their minds: a gloom tied their tongues to sullenness.

"What is this oppressiveness that lays its hands upon us? My heart seems as heavy, once again, as it did when we came upon our village. My mind plays tricks before my eyes. I see danger behind each clump of buffalo grass. I feel as if I ride with a stone upon my shoulders. Does death ride upon the breeze?" the man on The Panther's left asked.

"I, as well as yourself, feel that we are being watched by unseen eyes. We must keep our medicine strong."

The men traveled for many days and saw no one. They found, as they once had, an abandoned camp circle, this one many days old. They were near the lands of the Pawnee. The camp circle showed a clear picture of what had taken place.

"Those who camped here were attacked," observed The Panther.

Scattered human bones showed that a violent confrontation had taken place. The men stood silent, looking at what had been a village, with thoughts of their own, now but a memory.

"Who were these people?" a man known as Snapping Turtle asked. "And why, I wonder, were they attacked?"

No answer was given, for who knew?

The six men saw the herds of buffalo frequently as they passed through the land. Many times, the torn and trampled earth was crossed, showing the path the herd followed in their stampedes. Yet no hunters were encountered. The men passed through the lands of the Pawnee without incident.

But one day, as they topped a rise, far below and away from them, was a strange sight – a number of what appeared to be a large circle of small hills. Proceeding slowly, they rode forward to investigate, their hands upon their weapons. It soon became apparent that they had entered an abandoned village of earth lodges similar to those their own people lived in on occasion. But why had the people left?

They knew the Pawnee lived in earth lodges. Dismounting, they stopped and looked at one another.

"I smell death in this place," Snapping Turtle said.

One of the other men returned, running, "I looked into one of the homes. All within were lying dead and rotting. My thoughts are that the white man's spotted sickness visited this village. Let us depart. They lie unburied. Their spirits linger."

The men riding with The Panther now rode through the last of the lands of the Pawnee. The land became increasingly dry, the grass only as long as the tops of the horses' hooves. Water became more infrequent. The men traveled more slowly, always following the path of the morning sun, which burst upon the sky from its home beyond the horizon. A number of dry creek beds added to the parched land they rode through.

"We must find water soon or we will be carrying our belongings on our backs. Our ponies suffer."

Later that same day, a muddied water tank of moderate size was discovered by the circling of birds. Many animals had been watering at this place, and a small herd of pronghorns fled at their approach. The horses were watered with care and it was decided that they would camp.

A fire was begun from dried dung and the few dried sticks they could find. As the men rested, they slowly ate the last of what dry meat they had.

"Do we risk a hunt after our horses are well rested?"

one of the men asked.

"We will find game along the way," The Panther replied.

Three days from their resting place, the men stopped beside a well-traveled and rutted road. Wagon wheels had cut deeply into the prairie sod. Scattered at places beside the road, broken wheels, metal tires and other pieces of refuse lay rusting or rotting in the sun.

"We may follow this white man's path to our friends. What say you?" a man known as Muskrat asked The Panther.

"Friends, perhaps. Enemies, perhaps. Let us proceed. The Great Mystery has led us this far."

The men followed the road for a day and a half. The country began to give indications of water near by. Small, wind-warped trees and shrubs grew, along with the ever-present cottonwoods. Clearing a rise, there, before them was a river of swiftly flowing water. Riding down the slope, they entered the water. As the horses drank, suddenly, shouts and whistles reached their ears. Looking at each other, it was apparent that these were noises made by white men. Turning toward the road and clearing the rise before them, they saw a wagon and then one more. Soon a caravan wended its way in the direction that the six men had ridden from. The men in the wagons looked at the six riders but kept their wagons moving. All the white men carried thunder sticks.

When the sun began to make its descent, the men with The Panther sat on their horses near the corrals of Bent's Post on the Canadian River. Smoke rose above the sod and adobe building from its chimney. The smells of food drifted on the air. Both white men and Indians of the surrounding nations milled near the wagons being unloaded. Oxen and mules stood waiting to be turned into the corrals and fed. Dismounting, the men tied their horses to a corral rail and walked toward a small group of eight or ten men, both white men and Kiowa, who stood watching the animals being led into the corrals.

Signing, The Panther asked if it would be possible to trade for new mounts. A white man, with a clay pipe in his mouth, walked up and signing, asked who it was he was talking with.

The Panther identified himself and his men.

"Holy Jumpin' Moses," the man shouted. "This be a long time we had Omaha in these parts."

Then, signing, he asked how they came to be so far from home.

All was related and the white man stuck his hand out to The Panther, who, at first, was unsure – then he tentatively took it within his own. The twelve horses of The Panther and his friends were traded for six new mounts. Again, they traveled toward the east, traveling always toward the sun.

They crossed the buffalo grass and many times were stopped by herds of buffalo. Now, though, the herds were many times smaller than those they had seen before. They forded streams and once, swam their horses across a swiftly flowing river. The feelings of gloom and foreboding had long since been left behind in the lands of the Pawnee and the abandoned village with the rotting bodies of the dead.

Before them, at the confluence of three large streams, they came to a cluster of villages. People were going about their daily chores as they entered the great Ponca villages.

The Ponca, at this time, were middlemen for a lucrative trade in slaves with the Spanish to the south. Wars with the Pawnee kept scouts continually riding out into the plains. When The Panther and the five riders with him were noticed, they were quickly surrounded by warriors carrying thunder sticks.

The Panther held the sacred pipe aloft and no shots were fired. The men were escorted to the village. As they approached the village of bark-covered homes, they passed through a gate in the stockade that protected the people. Still under guard, they approached a large structure with a door at each end, the home of the headman. Still holding the pipe, The Panther and his men sat upon their horses, waiting while one of the guards entered the structure before them.

A man of middle years emerged with the guard. His face was painted and his shoulders and chest were tattooed. His hair was cut close to the scalp, leaving a roach. Two eagle feathers stood straight above his head, with hawk feathers beneath them. A string of shells hung from his ears and he had a metal armband on each arm.

Looking long at The Panther, who yet held the sacred pipe, he signed, "Who are you and where are you from?"

Replying, The Panther explained.

When the chief understood the men to be Omaha, he greeted them and said, "Come."

The six men dismounted.

"My name is Elk Horns, and I make you welcome in my village, men of The Hill Rising from the Center of the Plain."

The pipe had been smoked and the account of all that had occurred had been told. Elk Horns listened intently.

"So, you have no intent to return to the land of your village?" Elk Horns asked.

The Panther answered slowly that the sight of their destroyed village and loved ones made the thought of returning like a knife in the guts.

"No, we will not return. Brother, the Ponca and the Omaha were, as you know, at one time long ago, one people. We ask for sanctuary in your village. If you agree, we will abide by your directions and live as the Ponca live. We will defend with our lives you and all you find and hold as sacred."

"Then let it be so," said Elk Horns with gladness in his voice.

****

The Panther and Spotted Crow never again met. Their peoples followed what the Great Mystery showed them. Many changes were taking place. The peoples of The Panther, Spotted Crow and Elk Horns, as well as the Yamparika and all of the peoples of the plains and prairies would succumb to the world of the white man. Diseases and wars would take the strength of the nations. Old alliances would become stronger and old grievances would be set aside. A common decision now faced all of the peoples – how to live in the new way being forced upon them. The names of Spotted Crow and The Panther would someday be forgotten, no longer even a memory.

PETROGLYPHS

In the southwest, one many times can see the petroglyphs of big horned sheep carved on the stones by the ancient ones. Not long ago, I saw a photo of petroglyphs that had been found in Pakistan. The caption under the photo identified these petroglyphs as ibex. To me, they resembled the big horned sheep of the American southwest. I wonder if there was a similar meaning being related.

THE COMING

Little light sat upon the land and the dark clouds covered the entire sky. The wind blew in gusts and carried with it the wetness of winter. Snow was upon the breath of the day and soon the whiteness from above would be covering the cluster of dwellings by the river. The cottonwood trees reached upward and moved in the wind like arms of long forgotten skeletons, their naked limbs clicking upon themselves as they moved.

The village appeared disserted, but for the webs of smoke that issued from the round brush shelters. The smoke reached upward, and then was carried sharply out and dispersed on the air across the silent desert.

The large lake was the color of flint and moved silently on its own. The black clouds dissolved into the water's far distant line and no reflections showed on the expanse of moving water.

The village of the Kuyuidikada was waiting for winter. All was in readiness. Flesh of the great Cui-ui fish was smoked and stored for the winter's use. So, too, the jerked meat of the rabbits with the long ears. Nuts from the twisted sticky trees were stored in baskets. All was in readiness.

The hunting was over. So, too, the gathering. Now was the time of the stories of the long walks, the times of mists and dreams. Now was the time, also, to talk of the awakening of the earth when the sun would shine brightly, when the sagebrush would blossom, and when the fish would run. Now was the time to listen, to be still.

A man, wrapped in a robe of rabbit fur, walked from a karnee to the grove of trees that surrounded the village. Stepping from the trees, another man, similarly robed, but not of the Fish Eaters Band, approached.

"Aho, Fish Person, I am from the village of the Ground Squirrel Eaters. I bring you words of magic and wonder. The words I would speak to you were brought to our village by a person of the Mountain Sheep Eaters Village. Something new and strange is upon our lands – something all The People should be aware of. New beings have come among us out of the east. They appear as men, but not as our men. Hair grows about their faces and is the color of the sand we walk upon. They sit upon beasts unlike any in our land. These beasts are large and wonderful. These new beings and their beasts are most frightening to gaze upon. So says the person from the Sheep Eaters Village."

The person from the Kuyuidikada answered, "Your speech is as rapid as the wind. We must speak more upon this. Come, my dwelling is there. What do these new beings seek? Know you that?"

"Yes, they kill the animals with the large teeth which cut the trees on the waterways. They kill them and take their skins."

The words about the new beings were taken to all of The People in a similar manner or they discovered the new beings themselves.

The new shaman of the Kuyuidikada of the village

beneath the cottonwoods would be pressed by his people for answers concerning the new beings. He sought for answers from The Spirit Which Moves Through All Things. Many times, as the moon moved through its phases, he went alone to the hill above his village and sat seeking wisdom and understanding. The Spirit Which Moves Through All Things was silent on this. The man was fearful for the first time in his life.

For half of a day, The People crouched behind rocks or lay flat upon the sandy soil, watching through the foliage of the sagebrush, at the steadily approaching cloud of dust. The shaman recalled the man from the Ground Squirrel Eaters Camp who had visited him many winters in the past. He recalled the words spoken then about new beings that looked like men – but not our men. Beings who owned strange and wondrous beasts. Now, on this day, the strange beings were coming – coming out of the desert – coming into their lands. The People would stay hidden until they were sure of the intent of these strange ones.

The large lake shimmered like the sea – a sheet of blue-green water surrounded by pale pink and buff colored hills. The men marched on wearily, their horses plodding forward, wallowing in the soft sand, urged on by their riders. The grove of cottonwoods along the river cut a pale green margin at the base of the tan hills. It was to these trees that the men rode. The trees would offer protection from the wind and a place to rest. Into the beautiful grove of close growing trees watered by the river that nearly surrounded it in a large bend, rode the men. No sound save the wind which rustled the branches of the trees, could be heard. As the men on horseback entered the grove, suddenly The People emerged from behind the sagebrush, the trees and the stones. Intense invocations to The Spirit Which Moves Through All Things were in the minds of The People, as they stood, staring at the strange beings.

The shaman stepped out from among the trees, his stance and dignity masking his apprehension.

"Welcome, men from beyond the desert. I have known of your coming for many winters. Sit and be welcome. If you hunger, we will feed you."

So saying, the fish with the blood red sides was presented to them.

The People, realizing that no harm would come to them, and following the words and gestures of their leader, walked to see the wonders which had come among them.

"We would show you courtesy, friends. Eat your fill. If you seek a way out of our country, we can show this to you. While you are here, your are welcome. Rest and be refreshed."

The strange beings stayed with the people but a handful of days. They departed as they had arrived, sitting on their wondrous animals. The hairy men and their animals strung out through the trees and slowly departed the land of the Kuyuidikada. They rode to the snow covered mountains, through the rugged hills and valleys. They straggled past the sharp boulders and The People wondered and stared long at the direction in which they left. The shaman wondered if The Spirit Which Moves Through All Things, moved also within these visitors.

Many Years Later–

The Old Man walked alternately between the cool shade of the cottonwood trees and the blasts of sunlight that bounced into his face from the bone-dry earth. He walked upon the stony ground, his soul on fire, with his shadow moving silently.

The People had moved in great numbers to the White Man's Town – people from all of the encampments – Fish Eaters, Ground Squirrel Eaters, Sheep Eaters. They built their dwellings under the trees as they had always done, but they were separated from the white man's dwellings. They were separated by a piece of ground on which the Old Man walked.

A wildness burned in his eyes and an anger belied his age. He walked in a fury. Within his soul, there lived a frailty and a meekness. These feelings were hidden and staked to the ground. They were feelings that lived half starved. No more did answers come to him from any sources or to any of The People. Perhaps the ones who had come among them had stolen the sources of all answers. They have answers and a strong magic. The People now found they had little of anything.

The earth beneath the Old Man began to tremble as he walked and he heard the far away scream of the magic box of smoke and steam that moved upon the long shiny lines. The Old Man was afraid of the noisy box that moved across the country. Others of The People had said that it was another of the magic beasts owned by the strange beings. Why did The Spirit Which Moves Through All

Things not give to his people also strange beasts?

The train began to slow as it neared the settlement. It would take on water and firewood -- the wood of the little trees in the hills that dropped their seeds each year when the cool weather approached. Water, which came up from holes cut in the earth, like blood from a wound.

A blinding sun caused the Old Man to shield his eyes as he watched the firebox move along the shiny hard lines. Clouds of mist issued from its undersides, and an ear splitting sound filled the air. Many of The People now traveled on this firebox of the white men. They sat huddled together along the back of this magic thing. They even opened its sides and sat inside it. On this day, many of the men of The People stood on its back and the Old Man felt alone. He had been shaman of his people for many winters. That now seemed like a dream from a long winter's night in the past. The women of The People, who rode in the boxes that followed the firebox, stared blankly out at him. He wondered if their souls had been devoured by this great beast.

Night overtook the day and the Old Man walked aimlessly the wide paths the white men made in their settlement. His anger and his meekness battled within his soul. The Old Man cried out in his anguish. In the homes of the white men, the fearful voice, now laden with sorrow, could be heard. They heard the cries and paused. They shivered and turned away. They drew their drapes and snuffed their lights, less the Old Man seek and try to enter.

****

The Old Man lay in his dwelling under the cottonwood

trees. The smells and the sounds of his people comforted and covered him like a rabbit skin robe. Soon, though, he would be taken by The Spirit Which Moves Through All Things and he would be with his ancestors. The stars blinked down at him and he fastened his gaze through the willow framework and gazed at them. Before the sun rose, he would be walking on the dusty road.

There were many new feelings in the hearts of The People since the strange ones had come among them. There was much fear now and sorrow. Many of The People were drowning in the rapid stream of new ideas that the strangers brought with them. The Old Man had despaired of this. He had realized for some time that he could no longer help his people.

Perhaps the Prophet, the Trout Eater from the village by the southern lake, had spoken to The Spirit Which Moves Through All Things, and ways for help for The People had been shown to him. The Old Man, weakened now from many seasons, had wondered if his people's dancing would return him to this place once he left on the dusty path.

"This Trout Eater from the Southern Lake appears kind and true," he had murmured to himself. "We shall see – we shall all see, soon."

****

Addendum –
Part of the Field Notes and Diary of a University Student Who Sought Out the Last Remaining People Who Had Been Taught the Old Ways

"I've always longed to know about the Indians who live in the state of Nevada. I would like to know their ways of living on the land, their relationships with each other, their ideas about the Creator, what they ate, how they dressed – all of it. On this day, I am driving to Nixon, the settlement at Pyramid Lake. A kind old woman I have been introduced to, who lives there, has agreed to talk with me. Hopefully, I will learn much from her.

MOAB, UTAH, 1961

Moab was a full-fledged boomtown in 1961! The quiet little Mormon town was holding precariously to its image, trying to live in harmony with the flood of non-believers. The cut, red stone homes of the pioneer settlers stood in stark contrast to the hurriedly built homes of the newcomers. The mobile homes that had been dragged in by construction workers seemed almost like a blight in the community.

Suddenly, Moab appeared to be trying to compete with Salt Lake City for having the biggest of everything. A uranium deposit had been discovered, which was so huge that a reduction plant had been built nearby to process the ore extracted daily. Then, down river only a few miles, a potash deposit was found which was being touted at that time as being the largest in the world. It was so extensive that if this had been the only deposit, it could have furnished the entire world with enough commercial fertilizer to last for twenty years. On top of that, there were oilrigs pumping black gold only a few miles from town.

With all of these riches suddenly available, sleepy little Moab exploded. There were simply not enough places for all of the men and their families to live. It was first come, first served. I knew a man who lived in a rented tool shed. There was an urgent need for homes. Carpenters were being paid premium wages.

There was no easy way to transport the potash for refining, so the Denver and Rio Grande Railroad had subcontracted to blast a tunnel through a mountain and lay tracks to get the ore out.

Moab was inundated with gandy dancers, hard rock miners, engineers, scientists, geologists, roughnecks and many others. Major companies were arriving daily to build branch locations. Moab was no longer a backwater town. The atmosphere everywhere was in a state of chaotic excitement.

I struck up an acquaintance with a man who was a scientist at the potash plant. We found we had a lot of interests in common. We both had fallen in love with the rugged beauty of the Colorado Plateau and the red rock canyons around Dead Horse Point and the Arches National Monument. The land, for both of us, had a siren's call.

No road had as yet been built for access to the potash plant. My friend had a small boat with an out-board motor which he used to go to and from work everyday. All of the employees had to travel that same stretch of the Colorado River by boat. One day, as we sat talking, we decided that we would go down river as far as we could before we hit any white water rapids.

We had left the boat dock only a mile or so behind

us. When we entered the canyon, the cliff walls towered above our heads for seven or eight hundred feet. The sun, reflected from the water, confined by the precipitous walls of brick red stone, held the temperature at well over 110 degrees.

Shutting the motor off, we drifted with the current. After a few miles, we came to where someone had painted a warning on the rocks: "No hard boats beyond this point, only inflatables. White water ahead."

Starting the motor, we turned back the way we had come. On the way down the river, we had passed a few side canyons. We decided to explore one of them. The water was much less turbulent in the narrow channel we now followed. Ahead, we saw where, in some ancient time, a part of the cliff wall had fallen. It had formed a small beach. When we reached it, we jumped from the boat and placed a large rock on the bowline to hold the boat from drifting. This spit of land was a treasure trove of fossils – crinoids, ferns and mollusks – all embedded in stone. My friend found an intact fossil snail that sat upon a rock with nothing holding it in place.

Further up the channel was the epitome of the day for me. When we had come to the place where we could go no further and needed to turn around, high above us, about fifty feet or so above the surface of the water, were petroglyphs. Carved into the surface of the stone were men and animals. The beauty took my breath.

The question of how they were carved carries two possible answers. First, the artists who carved these may have stood on rafts using scaffolding. This theory has been suggested by "experts." Others claim that these petroglyphs are so old that it is almost impossible to date their age. They suggest that these glyphs were carved when the water level was higher so that the artists stood on rafts without the aid of any type of scaffolding.

In one sense, does this matter? They are, for the most part, out of danger of vandalization except for someone with a rifle. Sadly, this destruction has been done frequently.

I wondered, what were these ancients artists saying? Why or for what reason had they carved these glyphs? What made this particular place so important for them?

These ancient ones, now known as the Fremont Culture, had lived near where Moab now stands. While I was there, I worked for an electrician, placing small power poles for a mobile home park that was under construction. One day, while grading the earth, I found a small piece of pottery on which was painted a Fremont Culture design.

Standing in the midst of this chaotic business, holding this shard in my hand, remembering the petroglyphs I had seen so recently, I could not help but wonder what it was like when the Fremont Culture people were here. What was life like for them? They grew corn and other staples in abundance. The soil along the river, because of centuries of annual flooding, is extremely rich and fertile. Where did they go? Why did they leave?

The spirits of these ancient ones still lives in this place, away from the confusion of modern society. The canyons still echo their presence. Thinking back over the years, remembering those petroglyphs and that small shard, and placing these memories against the memory of the frenetic confusion of Moab of the 1960s, I can again experience the incredible gift of this desert, its peace and its timelessness.

REALITY

It has been my years in the desert that have allowed me to see through printed words and what they try to say to me. It has been my own experiences that have disclosed reality. I find that it is only someone else's experiences and memories that words on a page convey.

IN THE TRACKS OF THE HORNED TOAD

"Dayton! Get your butt out of my truck! Dayton! You drunk!"

Dayton Bose was drunk again. Drunk as a skunk and twice as smelly. Lying in the bed of his friend's pickup was the Colony's worst drunk. One or two beers and he'd be on his way again.

"Come on, man, out! I got to go to work."

The numbness in his cheek, more than the yelling, was sinking into the slowly awakening mind of Dayton Bose.

"I'll get you out of there, dammit."

The man with the blue slacks and tie jumped into the cab and started the motor. He raced it a couple of times and looked back through the window. The silver surface of his dark glasses reflected the figure sprawled in the truck bed. Twice around the vacant lot over rocks and bumps with dust and small stones flying would do it. Dayton Bose was sitting up. He held the edge of the truck bed. Blood had clotted on his left cheek where he had lain on the tire jack all night. It held part of his hair stuck to his face.

The truck slid to a stop in front of a small house with a refrigerator on the porch near the front door. An old Bendix washer stood unplugged with the lid gone in the silt fine dust out in the front yard.

"You gonna get out or do I have to drag you out?"

"I'm going, I'm going. Thanks for the bed and the free ride," Dayton said sarcastically, climbing out of the truck bed.

Waving a hand at him, his friend roared out and down the road toward the Tribal Council Building. The dust snaked after him, sinking slowly back onto the dirt road.

"Hi, Ma." Dayton shuffled slowly into the house. The screen door slammed and hung loosely after him. His mother did not acknowledge his presence but continued her work at the decrepit old stove. Dayton walked to the catchall shelf that ran along one wall, took a cup and poured black coffee into it. He sat down at the table with chrome legs and a plastic top. He watched his mother move mechanically about the small room, to the table, to the sink and back to the stove. The lack of emotion on her face was what he had always known. Her blind eye seemed to bore into all with whom she came into contact.

His throbbing head, painful as it was, was not enough to keep out the memory of the story his mother had told him when he was a child, of how she had lost her eye. He thought, between sips of coffee, of this story.

When she was a child attending a boarding school, the teacher, in between geography and social studies, had heard her and another girl talking in the Paiute tongue. Without warning, the teacher picked up the black board pointer and hit the two girls across the face.

"This is America! We speak English here, not some foreign, pagan tongue. You understand?"

When the large welts formed, it became apparent that Dayton's mother would be partially blind for the rest of her life. The teacher was eventually transferred to another position back east.

"I'd like to beat her head in. I hope she rots in hell, wherever she is," he thought as he slammed the mug down on the table. His mother glanced at him and then went back to her work.

"Ma, I've been thinking. I'm going to try and go to the university."

His mother had heard him voice wishes and dreams before.

"Emerson Billy thinks he can get me a scholarship through the Tribal Council. Maybe I can do something for the people and myself at the same time. What do you think, Ma?"

His mother stopped and bit her lower lip.

"Dayton, don't ever forget who you are. What you do, you do. Emerson Billy is a brown skinned white man."

"Emerson Billy is no Uncle Tommy Hawk, Ma. He works for the people."

"Dayton, you hear what I tell you and you mind my words." She stared at him and then said softly, " Remember who you are."

"Ma, I'm going away for a few days – back in the hills. I don't know when I'll be back. I just need to get away and think. Would you get some things together for me?"

"You be careful now. You know where you're going?"

"I might go out around Pyramid Lake if I can keep out of the fishermen's way. Or maybe up in the high country up above Verdi. I'm not sure where exactly."

Driving west out Fourth Street, with the sun on his left shoulder, Dayton gazed at the wall of blue-black mountains that had been a part of his life for as long as he could remember. When he'd been a child, the mountains were somewhere in his vision at all times. He would stop and stare up at the mountains and play would cease until the spell was broken.

One day, he asked his mother, "Ma, does that high wall keep us in or does it keep something bad from us?"

His mother smiled and said, "No, the something bad is all around us. That high wall is where the Washoe People once lived and higher up is where God once lived."

Dayton stopped for a traffic light and watched two men walking toward the university. For some reason, his mother's words about Emerson Billy being a brown skinned white man came back to him.

"I wonder," he thought, "if it's possible to be an Indian with white skin?"

The houses soon gave way to open land with homes going up the hillsides into the trees. Fenced fields in which Herefords grazed lined the banks of the Truckee River. Even this far out into the country, the ranches were being absorbed by the subdivisions.

"They steal from themselves as readily as they steal from others," he said to himself grimly. An hour later, he pulled the car off the highway into the Floristan Exit. A number of years ago, Floristan had been a railroad and lumber town, with a paper mill and a fine old hotel. Now, all of that was gone. All that remained were a few old houses that had been renovated into weekend and summer homes. Some insane man had tried to burn the mountain down a while back and he had started with the hotel. Even the foundations of the old mill were now rubble. Dayton parked his car and walked into the trees.

Moving silently through the tall trees on a brown carpet of dead pine needles, he watched motes of dust and pollen float aimlessly in and out the long shafts of light which bore down through the high branches and into the dogwood and manzanita. Turning his head to the source of these filmy golden beams, he squinted into the bright sun, which burned like an all-seeing eye. The sun shown into his eyes and into his brain, filling his head with molten golden light, a light which caused his mind to reel in its weight.

Moving at random through the forest with the light and the shadows playing upon him, he was oblivious to direction or course. He wandered aimlessly and would have continued to do so, but for the natural barrier of the river. The sound and feeling of the rushing water, though a part of the mountainous terrain through which he walked, had, for him, a mind and feeling of its own, independent and yet one with its surroundings.

Below the small bluff on which he stood, willows now wove with the bear brush and dogwood into a pattern of green, creating a new design. Far above him and across the river somewhere, the roar of the interstate grated harshly with the sounds of jays and wrens, tumbling waters and breathing pines. Down the river and across it, a flume and railroad trestle tied the two halves of the earth together.

The willows below him nodded and swayed in the breeze like a pale green screen, permitting spangles of gold and silver from the river's surface, to shine through. It allowed him to glimpse something else moving slowly among the leaves. He had not been seen or heard, so he withdrew into the shadows, watching intently the half hidden figure. The sunlight shown upon the tawny hide of a large buck, that waded slowly into the water with its burnished surface. The deer did not splash or walk hesitantly, but moved smoothly and gracefully, as all deer walk when dusk calls them to the river to drink.

Moving almost imperceptibly, Dayton studied its every movement. The deer walked slowly through the water, bending to let its nose trail in the current. Raising its head, the liquid silver flowed down its chin and chest. The deer waded to shore and then turned once more to the river, standing in the slight waves at the edge, it's legs buried in the fine mud, the stones and the fool's gold. Holding its antlers to the sun, it gazed at the mountain above. Water raced down its legs to fan out and blend with the surface of the river.

Coming to a break in the foliage, still unseen, Dayton leaped to a large rock outcropping nearly level with the top of the willows. He then jumped onto the sand in the willows. Walking around a large, stagnant pool filled with tadpoles and protected by large, four winged dragonflies, he moved silently over an old fallen tree to a spot directly behind the wading deer. His feet sank into the moist sand as he came out onto the small beach. Standing motionless, his shadow now nearly filled the small opening and it fell across the deer's grey-tan back and into the water in front of it. Without turning around, its head, now held high, the deer leaped forward with its legs deep in the water. He trotted up river, looking for a place to enter the forest.

"I won't kill you," Dayton said, as he watched the deer flee into the trees.

A chill slid down off the mountain, pushed along by the light breeze, now that the sun was moving behind the sharp pointed rocks high above. The songs of the birds had stopped and only the wind in the tall pines was to be heard as the branches swayed.

Something within Dayton seemed to be dead or gone. A hollow ache numbed his limbs. This place of green no longer welcomed him. His feet cracked the dead branches with resounding snaps as he moved back to where his car was parked somewhere down stream.

He thought about his decision to attend the university and about how things had always been with him.

"Remember who I am," he said to himself. "Yeah, Ma, I'll do that. But who the hell am I? A Paiute? A would-be white? A no-good drunk?"

It seemed his life had always exposed him to the ridicule and derision of those around him. He felt he had always been simply playing parts: one for his mother, another for the people at the Colony, and still another for the whites. He wondered if in trying to make his bitter life more palatable, he had perhaps sold himself. He began to think that his hopes and goals were now somehow now worthless and of no value. This imposed bondage with the white world had torn out his inner self and replaced it with something that would fit or be acceptable to the routine and actions of the society around him.

Dayton thought of the deer and its vulnerability in the water. It had exposed itself, and had been pleading for its life as it fled, asking to be spared a greater pain. It had shown him its physical self in exchange for the intangible.

Turning, Dayton ran back through the trees to the small

bluff above the willows. The deer was gone.

"I'm sorry," he whispered. "Can you hear me? I'm sorry."

Only the sighing of the wind came back to him, the wind and the ever-present tumbling water.

He turned and retraced his steps. Leaning against the car, he lit a cigarette and then, after one drag, ground it out with his toe. From beneath the car, a horned toad ran. The horned toad stopped to glance up at him and then ran to the cover of a pile of railroad ties, leaving a trail of small tracks in the sand.

Night had come with its feelings of aloneness and Dayton stopped for gasoline in Verdi on the way home. He noticed across the poorly lit street of the sooty little railroad town, the neon sign: The Old Corner Bar and Restaurant. Pulling open the heavy stained door with its round window, the smell of stale cigarette smoke and liquor filled his nostrils. It was a smell with which Dayton had felt at home for some time.

The only lights in the room came from somewhere behind the bar and from the jukebox that was playing Tex Ritter's old recording of "High Noon." Three men sat at the far end of the bar, one of whom was playing gin rummy with the bar tender. The bar tender glanced toward the doorway as Dayton moved slowly toward a table and sat down, trying to grasp the feeling of the place. Except for the glance from the bar tender, no notice was made of his presence. After about fifteen minutes, the man behind the bar yelled "Gin," and slapped the cards down. Moving down the bar, with his short, fat fingers caressing the wood, he stopped at the droughts, poured a glass and, looking at Dayton, said, "What'll it be, chief?"

"Not again," Dayton thought. "No more fights."

"Hey, chief, you want something?"

The three at the bar were looking over their shoulders at him.

"Anything you got, I don't need, white eyes."

Dayton stood and turned toward the door. He hadn't anymore than touched the door handle when a shot glass hit the wall about two feet from his head, sending a shower of slivers to the floor.

The fight was over before it began. When Dayton turned to face his attackers, the three men at the bar were on him. He was knocked to the floor and the last thing he remembered until he awoke at the Washoe Medical Center, was a foot crashing into his mouth, sending waves of pain through his body.

Dayton was unconscious for a day and a half -- unconscious to all around him but for the dreams and memories of other times.

"Dad," he called out to no one. "Dad, where are you?"

The image of his father filled his mind – the image of an old/young man, whose face was lined and whose eyes saw nothing – only a child without, a wife without, a people without – eyes which seemed to see no way out, eyes which had once been friendly, eyes which pleaded and grew dim with hatred and now saw only a bottle.

Dan Bose had been dead drunk when the prowl car found him lying face down in the gutter. Water had washed cigarette butts into a dirty clump and they spun slowly around his head. A paddy wagon had come and hauled him away to the drunk tank, but Dan Bose never woke up.

"Dad, come home. Where are you?"

"Hey, man, what're you doing?" Emerson Billy grinned down at him. "That old boy sure took care of your face for you. You want to hear some good news? That bastard that kicked your teeth in was an off-duty cop. The attorney for the Tribal Council is going to tack his ass to the wall."

Dayton tried to speak, but the sparks of pain started in his head and he didn't try again. He closed his eyes and let Emerson talk.

"When the ambulance came, one of the attendants was a Washoe from down at Dresslerville, and his old man's on the Tribal Council. Anyway, this guy took notes. Seems he's run into this dude before, a real Injun fighter. When they got you here, he filed a complaint with the Council, and we got the law on him. He'll be lucky if he has a pair of shoes left when our lawyers get through with him. Oh yeah, that hunk of scrap metal you drive around in is down at your mother's."

Emerson laid a hand on Dayton's arm. "Our time's coming now, pal. Get well and take care."

"Yeah," thought Dayton. "I'll do that."

Months went by and that fall, Dayton Bose, with a scholarship from the Tribal Council, enrolled at the University along with a new set of teeth and a couple of scars.

After class one afternoon, he walked west on Commercial Row, looking up at the blue-black mountains now veined with the white of the first year's snow. Leaves from the maple trees turned to old parchment by the cold weather drifted into piles or clung to the fences and walls. They seemed to be trying vainly to hold the memories of the summer and its life.

Crossing Sierra Street, Dayton felt the rumble of the earth beneath his feet as a westbound freight began to pick up speed for the climb up Donner Summit. Directly in front of him, about a yard away, a car pulled into a parking space and a blond woman with a little girl got out. As the child was waiting for her mother to find change for the meter, she ran after some falling, wind tossed leaves. The woman never turned around, but struggled with her purse, her cigarette smoke blowing into her eyes, with the hem of her dress and coat rising in the wind.

Dayton was along side of her when the child walked near the tracks.

"Mommy, lookee, a choo-choo."

Dayton ran and caught the child, turned and threw her to safety as the diesel roared by. What happened next, no one knows for sure. The woman turned, screamed and fainted as Dayton was dragged along the cross ties. Blood stained the ground and splattered small patches of snow.

A large vee of geese flew high above, their cries unheard on the ground. No one saw them pass that way. They flew toward the great blue-black wall and then flew over.

THE EARTH

We are, or should be, interested in our relationship to the earth. As such, I feel that the dominant society has a great deal to learn from traditional native peoples, if they would but listen. Christianity need not be abandoned. Spirituality gives meaning and value to a person's life. The main points are not to confuse the outward with the inner way of life. I have found this to be true from my wanderings in the desert and the mountains – something from the core of my being perceives things that outwardly I may not realize. It is my soul and spirit that are responding. Even though I work at trying to observe all that is around me, I see very little and remember less.

FOCUS

It is when I am in the desert that I am provided with the barest of environments that may allow my deepest thoughts to begin to focus. It is when I walk this spare landscape with little to distract me that I am aware of spirits around me. I can see plainly where God has walked. The landscape has become spiritually transformed – all is Holy Ground, but I have yet to witness a burning bush.

THE PUEBLO REVOLT

The sky was a flat blue. It would be hot again. Already the sun had eaten the shadows out of the silent plaza and splashed the walls with golden light. The sun's warmth chased the cold out of the man's body in shivers, which rippled across his skin. He opened his eyes and tried to focus them on his surroundings. He didn't see the two hawks that glided slowly above the far mountains and the trembling leaves of the tall trees, quivering in the sun below and away from him at the streambed. Two days of hanging from the cross beam which had been set up in the white light of the sun was burning the sight from his eyes.

Don Rodrigo Torrel y Ibarra knew he would soon die, perhaps on this day. He thought of how quickly Fray Andreas had given up his spirit. But he, Rodrigo, hung yet from the cross beam, beginning his third day, while Fray Andreas had died before the sun had set on the first. He moved his head slightly to his right and tried to make out clearly the form of the dead man. He let his head droop again on his chest, the effort being much too painful.

Don Rodrigo tried not to think of his thirst. His mind wandered again through the fragments of his disturbed and painful night and the images that tormented his mind through the dark hours.

The face of the magician continued to appear and fade in his mind. The magician who came and danced and chanted in a loud whisper in front of him after they had tied him to this pole. The eyes of the magician were like the eyes of some mountain animal and they never ceased to look at him the whole time the ritual was being performed. The Old Man shook his rattle at him, and chanted in almost inaudible sounds, while his eyes pierced his flesh. For two days, again and again, the magician came to Don Rodrigo.

The chanting, the dancing and the sun, hour after hour, had caused Don Rodrigo's dizziness, a dizziness which caused a drowsiness, a drowsiness which in turn caused his body to jerk awake from the pain of the ropes cutting into the flesh of his wrists. The magician would be coming again soon.

"Blessed Mother in Heaven, Protector of the Faithful..." as he prayed, the words in his head began to follow the rhythm pattern of the magician's chant. He stopped his prayers.

Fray Andreas had prayed also, his words silent, but his lips moving, his eyes looking at the skies. So intently had Fray Andreas stared at the sky that Don Rodrigo had looked there as well. Perhaps the Blessed Virgin was descending to save them. But the sky had been a flat blue then as it was now.

"I hang as did Our Savior," thought Don Rodrigo. "I must try to have his strength, but this is a mockery! I am not their Christ. They are not Romans or Jews. But yet, I am a martyr. Perhaps this is the time for which I was born. Then maybe I shall yet escape or be rescued."

The magician stood to one side of him, watching him.

Don Rodrigo had not seen or heard his approach. Through half closed eyes, Rodrigo now stared at the strange man directly before him, who threw a white powder in the air toward him. Again the magician danced and chanted.

"Perhaps these barbarous beings are indeed the sons of the devil," Rodrigo thought. "Many of the friars say this is so. How dare they refuse the grace of the One True God and the protection of the Blessed Virgin? How dare they? They insult all that is sacred. They insult the monarch. Those who come after will again gain this place and will do what we have been unable to do. These plains and deserts will bloom with orchards and vineyards. This is New Spain and it will be as grand as the old. The banner of Christ will fly over this land with the banner of Imperial Spain."

The first arrow stuck in the ground near his feet. For a brief moment, the air was alive with the sound of arrows. Don Rodrigo Torrel y Ibarra was dead, his life sinking into the hard packed plaza floor.

****

"Word has come from all of the villages that the hairy-faced ones are all dead. Not one remains. Many of their kind have fled to the south. Their dwellings are destroyed and many of their children and women are captive. We have succeeded, Running Ground Squirrel! We walk as free men upon our land once more!"

On this day, when the last of the invaders was put to death, Running Ground Squirrel, primary shaman of his pueblo, glanced at the now limp form hanging from the pole and then he turned and gazed into the ever blue sky. For three days he had come and matched his faith against that of the invaders. He had won. Perhaps his companion was right. Perhaps they had succeeded. But, perhaps, also, they were doomed.

****

For forty years, the villages of the mesas and the villages of the river valley would be free. Children would grow to middle age before the hairy-faced ones would come among them once more. The names of Don Rodrigo Torrel y Ibarra and the first settlers, Fray Andreas and the first friars, would burn on the lips and in the memories of those who came after.

ANCIENT SPIRITS

Within the stillness of the desert where the mountains reach to grasp the sun, where at night with only the low hanging stars for light, ancient spirits can be felt. Faintly on the wind, the strains of ancient chants drift on the air and float about me.

LANDSCAPES

I have incorporated the landscapes of the deserts I have traveled through into the core of my being. What makes the desert spiritually important to me is what is not there.

THE INTERNATIONAL BORDER IN SUMMER

The heat has come: like a devouring animal, it stalks the land. With unsated jaguar breath, it seeks out the weak. The sacred mountains heave and sigh with the heat. The silence is impermeable and rides above the ubiquitous and callous noise of the city. The silence is as fierce as the heat. It is a silence that can steal one's soul, one's mind, and one's identity. Screams of agonizing death search for respite in any hidden shade. An empty plastic water jug marks the end of hope.

GRAVES IN A POTTER'S FIELD

I walked on the path of death, one that is torturous and cruel. It is a death where the life giving sun now becomes an instrument of inhuman suffering and desperation.

My eyes begin to dry and crust forms around their edges. Sweat, which trickled down my back and from under my arms, is dried against my skin. I can no longer sweat – I am dry. Here among the creosote and mesquite, my feet take voice and scream their agony. Pain, like burning comets, sears my legs. I must go on. I must.

Rest, I must rest now. I will wait until night. Black spots

dance before my eyes. Are they vultures who wait – are they demons who live in this hell? My thoughts are now my words – I can no longer talk. My tongue swells out of my mouth. God of my ancestors, pity me. I cannot go on. The blood of the people is from the earth and now it returns. Gringos will weep at my unmarked grave in a potter's field.

In a village in a far valley, an old woman crosses herself. Her dim eyes can no longer weep. No word. No word will ever come. Dios, por favor, no mas muertes: basta!

ON THE HUMBOLDT TRAIL

It was toward the middle of the century when one more of a long stream of wagon trains made the harrowing journey from the east and slowly plodded down the Humboldt Trail. The now rutted road crossed endless miles of sagebrush plains and around and through rugged mountains. Further east along the main road across the Great Plains, the travelers had had to contend with herds of buffalo and winds strong enough to take a wagon cover flying. But now, it was alkali dust that swirled up from the wagon's wheels and burned everyone's eyes red.

Will Hardy, the wagon master of the long train of Conestoga wagons, reigned in his buckskin horse and took a map from the leather bag he had slung across his chest. Will had obtained the map in the town of St. Joseph, Missouri, from a friend of long standing, who, a few days before, had returned from California.

"How ya been, Jed," Will said with a broad grin, as he held out his hand.

The other man grasped his hand warmly and said, "Well, I'll be. It's been a while, ain't it?"

"I'm fit as a fiddle. It's good to look on you. You plannin' to take another train back down through New Mexico territory?"

"Not this time," Will responded. "I'm hankerin' to see

this Willamette Valley everyone is talkin' about. You been up there, ain't ya?"

Stepping into the street to the horses tethered at the rail, the two men talked of their adventures and trials leading the settlers' wagons.

Now, many weeks later, Will Hardy sat on his horse, studying the map his friend, Jed, had given him.

One of the wagon owners yelled down from the seat on his wagon, "S'cuse me, Mr. Hardy, when you s'pose we'll be gettin' to this here cutoff you told us all about?"

"We should be comin' to the Applegate Road before we circle for the night," Will replied.

The wagon train was bound for Oregon and the legendary Willamette Valley where, it was rumored, a farmer could grow nearly anything – the area was said to be that fertile.

All through the remainder of the day, the oxen plodded and dust from the wagon wheels hid the trail like a mist.

Will Hardy rode back beside the slowly rolling wagons.

"Catch up," he yelled at a man on a wagon, "keep the pace."

The man tipped his hat and cracked his whip. "Git movin'," he yelled at his team, and cracked his whip once more.

All along the train, horses and mules were sweating in streams and wagon axles groaned. All one hundred and sixty wheels were turning toward Oregon and the Willamette. True to his prediction, as the sun began it's descent behind the western mountains, Will's voice called a halt for the day.

"Circle up," was heard and echoed from wagon to wagon.

All forty wagons had reached the Applegate Cutoff.

Cooking fires lit the area within the circle of wagons and children were chastened to stay near while the women began to prepare the evening meal.

A group of men walked to where Will Hardy sat on an overturned bucket eating near his fire.

"You reckon we'll fight off more of them pesky red skins?" one of the men asked as he filled his briar pipe.

"That's hard to say," Will responded. "But it's prudent to be wary. Is your piece loaded?"

The other man nodded.

"I've never sought out trouble with no body," an old man with a limp stated, patting his left leg. "Yet I never once, in all my years expected to catch an injun arrow."

The man across from him replied, "The army's puttin' up forts everywhere, we'll be rid of 'em soon enough. I know I took down at least three, maybe four, where we joined 'em after we got into them salt flats east of here."

A man with wire spectacles said, "I've been thinkin on that ruckus. I ain't no parson, but seems to me thems people, same as us. Why are they so all fired up to try and kill us? I don't git it."

One the men in the group who had been listening, now spoke up, after first letting go a stream of brown tobacco juice into Will's fire, sending up a small spiral of sparks.

"Families!" he said in a disgusted voice. "Why, them bucks 'll sleep with any squaw that's willin!"

There were chuckles from the others.

"I've not mentioned this till now," Will began, "but I've been watchin, and we've been followed ever since we threw down back there. All of you, keep your eyes on the teams you're drivin, keep the pace and also keep a glance now and then in the hills we'll be passin'. There's been men on horseback as well as a-foot watching us."

There was silence as the men stared at the wagon master.

Several weeks before, the well-equipped wagon train had been attacked and a number of natives had been killed. The men around Will's fire talked about the possibility of more Indians as well as the day's progress.

The following morning, when the sun was beginning to rise behind the eastern mountains, the camp was astir with preparations for the day. Will had given the yell to "catch up." Through the early dawn, horses were harnessed, oxen balled, chains clanked. The children clambered into the wagons, followed by the women.

Suddenly, a cry came, seemingly coming from all directions at once. It brought the well-armed men together. One man climbed up onto the wagon seat and was immediately hit with a stone tipped arrow. With a scream, his wife leaped from the wagon to his writhing body on the ground.

A cry rang out but it was not Will Hardy who gave the order for the men to ride out and give battle.

"Come back, you dad burned fools," he yelled, to no avail.

For nearly an hour, the air was pungent with black powder smoke. It appeared that the Indians were retreating.

As the men rode back to the wagons, thinking they had won the morning, Will Hardy stood ready to challenge the man who had given the order to attack. But just then, the Indians attacked the unprotected south side of the encampment. Before Will could utter a word, the mounted men again gave chase. The natives had the advantage of the familiar land around them. One by one, arrows dispatched the riders easily. The men still within the wagon circle unleashed a withering barrage. Women and young children loaded rifles as fast as they were fired. A number of the men's horses, now riderless, were captured by the departing Indians who were finally driven off, carrying their dead across their horses.

When the struggle was over, Will Hardy was barely able to restrain his rage, as he helped bring in the bodies of the slain men.

"I want all you people to think about what has just happened. I did not give that order to ride out and fight. We might still be talkin' to these men here if we had thought rather than acted so damn hastily. I'm the wagon master. This had been agreed upon by all. I give the orders. Look at this, all of you! Forty good men dead. And we still have more than a ways to go before we hit the Willamette."

"I'm sorry for these here children, now fatherless, or the ladies with no husbands. If any of you want to have someone else lead this train, say so now."

The only sounds were the weeping of the women and the wailing from the fatherless children.

"What are we goin' to do about buryin' our dead?" a woman asked. "My husband was a Christian man."

Placing his hand on the woman's arm, Will said, "If you or anyone else knows the words to say, after we bury them, they'll be said over them proper."

Shovels were unloaded from the wagons and all who were able started to dig a long trench. No one spoke. There was nothing to say. All the rest of the day, the trench got deeper. Will walked to each wagon. To those in mourning, all he could say was a heartfelt, "I'm sorry."

There were no accusations or verbal retaliations. All the people realized the horrible mistake that had taken their loved ones. Those wagons that no longer had a man to drive the teams were now driven by some of the women. Families in other wagons took many of the children who had lost their fathers.

So that no trace of the grave would be found by their attackers, should they want to take revenge on the departed, the oxen and horses were driven over the grave until it became totally obliterated.

Natives were again occasionally seen in the surrounding hills, but no attacks came and the wagons rolled. For those who had lost a husband, brother, or father, the hopes and expectations for a new life were now only a memory. The only thought in the minds of the people was to end this journey of sorrow. There were more than a few who remembered their lives as they once had been, and now, how it had been changed, tragically changed forever.

All that the people had endured made each one mindful of what lay ahead of them. Would they be able to cope? What lay in store?

In a loud, bellowing yell, Will called out, "Fall in," and the wagons began to roll to the promise of Oregon.

PATTERNS

I have found that the earth has lines, patterns to be followed. Over the centuries, people have travelled and migrated over the land, pulled by invisible chords stronger than steel.

SECRETS

The mountains have begun to relinquish secrets to me. In the past, I've been unsure of their whisperings. Their speech has been mummified echoes that hang on cliff walls in forgotten canyons. They are whistled by wraiths in a half remembered chant.

The sky is a canopy of white jade, splotched with virga, curdled clots of rain that hang but do not reach the earth. A pregnant stillness is moved by spirit dusts that shower the stones with tiger eye oak leaves. Doves and sparrows cling breathlessly.

Obsidian and turquoise merge on tendrils of wind sweep. Raven plays and dives on the air while a hawk holds garnet prayers and wishes in dripping talons. Sun sweat.

REFLECTIONS

I have come to a place in my life where I feel it is advantageous to review my past experiences. Who I am, is in great measure, the result of knowing many people who have been a major influence in my life. My early years were a blur. It wasn't until my father and mother moved to Nevada from Southern California that the influences from outside began to coalesce and give me a new perspective.

We arrived in Reno in 1946. For all intents and purposes, we were penniless. We were reduced to living in a one room converted chicken coop heated by a small wood stove that we also used for cooking. My mother referred to Rosco and Mattie, the owners of this hut, as "Okies." Whether or not they were from Oklahoma was immaterial. The Dust Bowl years had cast its pall over anyone who was perceived to be living in a state of near poverty, with no education to speak of, and with no understanding or inclination for the finer things of life. My mother thus stigmatized the owners of this property. She could not see in the reflection of her own life that we were no better, and actually, were worse off. Rosco and Mattie had a large, extended family, most of whom were cattle ranchers. A son-in-law came from a family who had been long in northern Nevada with ranch holdings across the state.

Across the backside of their house ran an uncovered porch on which, in summer evenings, they would sit, rocking in their chairs, listening to a radio turned up loud. Rosco would rock, either smoking or chewing on a cigar stub, while Bob Wills and the Texas Playboys, Spade Cooley or Hank Williams sang songs of drinking, cheating or rambling. Much to the chagrin of my mother, I loved the music, and especially the petal steel guitar that was then, as now, the integral instrument in county music.

Country music became ingrained into my being. Many years later, as a teenager, it became an enigma. Should I continue to listen to country music and love it or should I sophisticate myself with jazz or classical music?

It is only through hindsight that I am now able to see our desperate state at that time. Imagination in a young child can blind him to what is actually taking place around him. I always likened our humble house to the bunk houses in western movies, with me as a working cowhand. Having since been to Indian reservations, to the jungle village of La Garucha in Chiapas, and to barrio homes in the Southwest, I feel I can relate to the life ways imposed upon these people with genuine empathy.

What is the measure of a person? Is it the old argument of genetics or the culture one is raised in or the impact of the soul of the land upon a person? Why does a person live with the anguish of loneliness when people swarm around like bees in a hive?

The mountains are lonely. Their existence wears on them with a devastating weariness. They slumber, they breathe, they beckon. Leaving the chaotic poverty of my home, I clung to the mountains. I merged with their melancholy loneliness. I became a spirit that was freed by the acceptance of the mountains. I wandered aimlessly. I would stop to pick up a stone, attracted by its glitter, and then wander on. I once found an abandoned mine and I stopped beside the sagging entrance. Stepping but a few feet within, I could see the collapsed tunnel ahead of me. A soft, cool breeze lightly played on me from some fissure in the crumbling rocks. A trickle of arsenic laden water oozed beneath the rubble and sank into the soil at my feet. I returned to the opening and sat on a stone, resting my back against the portal timber.

Gazing down into the valley at the town far below, my heart burst with an overflow of pent-up tears. I was yet too young to accept that over which I had no control. I saw no images, I heard no voices. My soul was numb to everything about my life. Only the mountains and the vast sagebrush plains had a meaning for me. I knew this desert. It spoke to me, not in words, not even in a feeling. Just what it was I could not tell. I only knew that it made me feel welcome.

The desert can be threatening, but I had long ago made peace with that threat. It was the only thing in my life with which I had made peace. I had found skeletons in the desert, oftentimes, steers or rabbits, once even the remains of a mountain lion. I wondered how they had died. How would I die? I thought the desert was a good place in which to die.

I was invisible to my peers. They could see that my family was destitute. My attempts to hide were a continual failure. I discerned within myself a gradual weakening of the spiritual receptiveness that had initiated my earliest search to know God. This was followed by a gradual disillusion of all spiritual values. I was seeking for a discovery of new thought for a renewed hope for living that could breathe new life within me. God had almost become a non-entity for me. Like a snail sprinkled with salt, I withdrew into a shell, into darkness, hoping to die.

Near our home lived a woman whom the neighborhood children called "the crazy lady." On warm, summer evenings, she could be heard singing arias from *Aida*, *Madama Butterfly* or *Don Giovanni*. In the evening, she would stand in her slip, hose in hand, watering her yard, treating the surrounding homes with opera. She was no longer young and her voice was not what it had been once. When not regaling the night with Verde or Bizet, her huge Steinway grand piano thundered with Rachmaninoff, Tchaikovsky or Beethoven. Her piano playing was magnificent. I would open my bedroom window and listen to music that I would come to not merely appreciate but to hold most dear. This "crazy lady" was not crazy at all, just alone and very lonely. She lived in her glorious past, a past that included the opera company in San Francisco.

She befriended me and I would sit in her small home, with an offered soda, mesmerized by the concert grand piano that took up nearly the entire room. Paintings by Hans Meyer-Kassel, Venetian glass, Wedgewood, and crystal and gold candelabrum decorated the interior of her home. This place also became my escape and my refuge.

My refuge also became a catalyst for paradox: Hank Williams or Vaughan Williams? Self-doubt became my obsession. I succumbed to my inability to choose where I felt my choices lay. Choices were supposed to be yes or no, black or white. There could be no gray areas. My family and peer pressure had convinced me of this. My life was a morass of clinging vines of self-doubt, self-hate, indecision and the quicksand of lack of motivation. I was stuck fast and slowly sinking into the oblivion with thoughts of suicide.

When I began to reassess my need to re-establish some spiritual direction for my life is unclear to me, even now. The constant emotional exuberance of my mother's Pentecostal, born again weekly worship services had done nothing but to drive me further within my ironclad shell. I could not believe that the Divine would require anyone to become so agitated that rational behavior gave in to uncontrolled hysteria. Thus, confusion was another burden which, when added to my existing load of negative self-image, did little to become "a light unto my path."

Within the hardening shell of isolation, I devoted most of my energies to the literature of the time – Hemingway, Steinbeck and the like, as well as reading biographies of artists like Van Gogh, Renoir or Picasso. The creative urge to paint surged up within me, swirling around in my head, spurred by memories of my father's paintings.

In this time, in my late teen years, I began to spend more time with those whom I called my friends. Yet within me were feelings of melancholy and disassociation. Under my calm exterior, there were growing strong passions and an extant, powerful imagination. Behind this exterior facade if someone had only looked deeper, was a Daniel in the Lion's Den or a Job.

I remembered my father telling me about my paternal great grandfather, Hans Nielsen Cronberg, who had been a very staunch Lutheran. He had been knighted by the

King of Denmark, an honor bestowed on him as a reward for years of faithful service to the crown as organist in the King's church, and as a tutor to the royal children.

I knew little of Martin Luther or the revolution he had created within Christendom. Because of my father's heritage, I was drawn to Saint Luke's Lutheran Church in Reno. The building was influenced by the Gothic architecture of Europe. When I walked through the carved doors, I was immediately struck by the faint smell of candle wax and a deep sense of calm, enhanced by the colored light rays streaming through the windows.

The pastor was a middle-aged man of keen perception. I was instantly welcomed and he offered his assistance. With some acute sense, he recognized a troubled spirit. I began participating in weekly confirmation classes with the caveat that if, at the conclusion, I felt no calling to join his church, he would assist me in searching for a congregation that would perhaps fill my spiritual needs. A man of greater insight I have rarely met.

Painting was becoming a consuming passion. The categories of simplicity and color became absolutely fundamental to my artistic endeavors. Art, and more specifically, my own paintings, could be understood intellectually. My father, a painter of some expertize in his own right, was firmly planted in the schools of the masters: Rembrandt, Sargent and N. C. Wyeth. My efforts were criticized but I was encouraged to keep at it. My father gave me a cross to bear, that of creating "reality" in my work. Reality – a word that he hoped would call me back to earth from flights of conjured illusion. He wanted a reality concerned with a relationship to existence in my paintings. I countered with a statement that he should use a camera.

High school was a bore. My peers were jockeying for attention with expensive clothes, sports or cars. My academic record was non-existent – most classes were failures. Only one teacher from all the rest saw a possible talent within me.

I had been dating a girl who had been admitted to the hospital to have her appendix removed. So strongly did her surgery affect me that I used Picasso as a reference and did a cubist rendition of her operation. My instructor encouraged my effort to the extent that he adamantly insisted that I enter this picture in a statewide competition. The judging resulted in a second place ribbon. I felt my efforts as an artist were beginning to show results. But when I brought my prize painting home, it was scoffed at. It wasn't realistic. It would be shallow for me to think of my father in a negative manner now. But then, I was once more crushed.

A friend of my father's, an extremely talented self-taught artist, saw in my work what my high school instructor saw. This man's works were dark and moody things, full of pathos and agony, but they were realistic, which courted my father's approval. He worked as a commercial artist during the day and spent his nights at his easel, painting his personal pain, smoking cigarettes and listening to jazz music: MJQ, Chet Baker, Bud Shank or Shorty Rogers. Here was my exposure to jazz, as well as the Beatniks of San Francisco's North Beach, an area I would frequent a few years later. This man gave me a box of casein paints as an inducement to keep painting.

There are many people whom I have wanted to know, whom I felt I knew, even though I never met them. These people influenced my life as surely as my closest companions, but with their art and with their thoughts. Two such people were: Ted De Grazia and Walter Van Tilburg-Clark.

De Grazia goes back to my high school days. My art was beginning to play a central role in my life. De Grazia was, in great measure, a freethinking renegade, unfettered by convention. Many of his paintings dealt with the native peoples of Arizona. Rejected by most of his peers in the United States, he was accepted and accorded accolades by Mexico's most renowned artist, Diego Rivera. His style was minimalist in the extreme. Yet, through color and movement, his work was very much alive for me. He was unmoved by criticism. In the pages of *Arizona Highways*, his vivid art renditions were presented to the world.

He entered my life just when I was being vilified for my artistic efforts. I studied his drawing assiduously and the margins of all my class notes were filled with renderings of his illustrious paintings. Here was a person I could emulate, if not in style, then in the spirit of independent thinking.

In 1984, I was able to visit his home in Tucson. I came upon his grave near his Chapel In The Sun. I stood silently and offered a prayer of thanksgiving for this man whom I regard as a giant.

I became acquainted with the writings of Walter Van Tilburg-Clark at a time when I felt I needed grounding in who I was, a man born and raised in the West. The West, for me, is not merely a geographical area. It is a way of being, a way of thinking, a way of perceiving. Alkali runs through my blood stream. Sagebrush and piñons are part of my muscles and bones. To be absent from the spirit of the land can be as traumatic as the severing of a limb.

The force of circumstances found me in a forbidding city in the northeast United States. I felt utterly alone, with no relationship to the land. I felt no commonality even to the trees planted along the streets.

I paused one day in a used bookshop and enquired of the owner if there were any books to be had about the state of Nevada. She promptly handed me *The City of Trembling Leaves* and *The Track of the Cat,* by Walter Van Tilburg-Clark. The first chapters of *The City of Trembling Leaves,* a book about Reno, wrenched my heart. I knew this town. It was my hometown. The first school I attended in Reno, Orvis Ring School, is described, as is the candy store across the street, where I had often bought a penny's worth of candy or gum. I can still smell the distinct aroma of that candy store.

The place that I have always felt is my spiritual home, Pyramid Lake, Mr. Clark illuminated as graphically as an artist would with pigment on canvas. Over and again, as I read this book, I relived my experiences and his in the places he so vividly portrays.

I have never been interested in reading pulp fiction horror stories. I have found that living life has horrors of its own. Yet, the unseen, indescribable terror that wells up from within a tortured and inwardly longing soul is artistically and impeccably described in *The Track of the Cat,* one of my favorite novels.

I have always wondered about those whose deeds are

unforgiven. When the perpetrators of these deeds realize their grievous actions and flee to the Light, as Kurt does in *The Track of the Cat,* are they plunged to their deaths in the unseen chasm of despair? ... Or? The story was converted into a movie, and faithfully rendered.

Of equal importance to me, as much as people, are the places I have been, each with its own pulse of life, frequently now obliterated by black top and concrete. In many areas, the land is so domesticated with generations of cultivation and fences that it seems that the palpitation of the earth is non-existent. Life has ceased its rhythm.

Long ago, I realized that the land does speak in subtle nuances, rather like the heartbeat of a person that goes unnoticed until brought to one's attention. With this realization, I sought out the heartbeat wherever I could. The need to touch and feel that I was a small part of the earth seemed to be of grave importance to me. I often think of the life of trees, of stones, of mountains. I know of trees, yet alive, which once sheltered the starving Donner Party. I've held in my hand a pebble from the ruins of Casa Grande. The vibrations of these things resonate with life, with meaning.

Mountains, in their turn, silently watch the passing of the tribes of mankind as they slowly crawl across the face of the land, building and tearing down. Children of God: humble or haughty, arrogant or meek, they reach for the sky. All will crumble and dissolve back into the earth from whence they came. The living earth is but the dusty remains of all mankind.

THE SONORAN DESERT

There is a dark, magical past in the Sonoran desert. It is a part of the Ancient Ones who once walked here and who have left their traces. The wind is the breath of the cosmos, the motion of the power of all that is.

IMAGES

Between the mountains and where I am standing in the heated air, numerous images appear, seen like a mirage, materializing and dissolving. Refracted light from the earth seems to be like bits of the sun fallen from the sky.

DOVES

The heat from the earth rises to meet the heat that descends from the sky. This is Arizona in late June on an early morning. It is ninety degrees at 5:30. The heat creeps onto my skin with searching fingers. My shirt sticks to my back as I stand in silence.

From the corner of my eye, a movement turns my head. A skein of doves, sixty or so, rises and falls, turns and circles, in huge arcs, moving as of one mind, one body.

Some inner language moves these birds. They fly as one, not many. Is this flight to warm themselves from a night's rest, or is there some more subtle thing happening? Is this uniform flight of so many birds an act of gratitude for another day, a prayer, as they rise and turn in elegant sweeps?

THE DEATH OF A DOVE

A dove that was perched on a power line across from me fell to earth, dead, after one last breath. I watched it alive and as it died and fell. I, like that dove, will not be here after one last breath. Do the doves weep perennial sobs, for the one that I saw fall?

MONSOON RAIN

The monsoon rains have come, brought by the clouds and the winds. The first drops have arrived at their proper time, on the Day of Saint John, the baptizer of Jesus. Across the way, the mountains are veiled and pale pink snakes of lightning race from west to east. My hands are extended, palms up, to receive the blessing of the rain. Life on the desert is being refreshed and renewed.

THE CARNIVAL

The old man sat deep in thought, both of his hands on the table before him. A mug, half filled with beer was between his hands. A laugh from one of the men at the bar brought the old man's gaze to that direction. Once more, he stared at the effervescent bubbles slowly rising into the remains of the head in the beer mug.

"What would an old man who was obviously out of place here be doing in this dingy, riverfront bar?" I said to myself.

His clothes, though anything but new, seemed well cared for, and his over all appearance spoke of better times. The old man sipped once more from the mug, where the frosty ice had melted into a puddle that dribbled in a slow meandering, following the slight tilt of the table. Placing his elbows on the table, his long fingers came together, forming a tent.

"Old man," I asked myself, "why are you here? What deep thoughts have brought you to this place where the clientele feel they know all of the answers to life's mysteries? In time, any of the men sitting on those stools will confide some hidden secret that only they are privy to. Do garbage collectors and city maintenance workers know some truth hidden from the rest of the world? Is that why you are here, old man?"

As I mused over my own mug of beer, I couldn't keep my eyes from the old man. Was it a private hell that his mind was trying to free himself from? Or perhaps, some late life frustration over a long recalled, indiscriminate lover from his youth?

As I reflected over why this well kempt gentleman brooded, a peddler of worldly wisdom on one of the bar stools began to exert his formula on the eternal inheritance of the saints, like a fundamentalist preacher.

Again, the old man looked to where this distraction captured his attention. Slowly shaking his head, he massaged his beer mug, downing the remainder of the contents. He rose from his seat, and, with his cane in hand, he slowly and thoughtfully looked at the men on the bar stools and noted the inanity that saturated their conversations. The barkeep simply nodded to him as he left without closing the door.

I couldn't help thinking, after the old man had gone, that this was one more scene in the carnival we have come to call life, with side show barkers and cheap prizes for those who know no better.

TRANSFORMATIONS

None of my years have come easily. My extraordinary experiences have been cumulative and have been the keys to my personal transformations -- from a man with no name, a castaway who placed a message in a bottle and threw it into the sea – to a man witnessing the arrival of *being* in myself.

NEVADA

It is strange to me, how, when I was a young boy living in Nevada, I claimed certain places as mine, even though these places, in reality, belonged to others. These places rooted me and held me: Pyramid Lake, the old Franktown Road in Washoe Valley, Bower's Mansion, the old Winter's Ranch on the road to Carson City, even the State Historical Museum diorama of a cave, with gleaming eyes peering out at me. All these belonged to me alone. When did I grow up and realize these were no longer mine? Now, only the memories are mine.

THE ROAD

The heat in the tipi made it hard to breathe. It wasn't unbearable, but it was hot as hell!

"That's not what I'm supposed to think," Kyle Benson scolded himself. "I've got to keep my mind on God. That's what I'm here for."

The heat and the closeness of the people, the smells of their sweat and the smoke, and now the effects of the medicine – all were combining to wrap a quilt of mental lethargy around Kyle's mind. All Kyle could do was to stare into the ever-burning fire and watch as his friend, Carlos, continued to feed it long cottonwood limbs. Kyle watched as Carlos kept the limbs pointed into a V and how the fire's dancing, flickering fingers reached upward to the open peak of the tipi, where a vagrant spark was rising up and out of sight.

A nudge in his ribs from the man on his right startled Kyle from the drowsy trance he seemed to be drifting into. Slowly turning his head, he saw the man holding out to him the dish of medicine and a small, silver spoon. Kyle hesitated and then reached from beneath the blanket on his lap and placed the dish on his leg. Carlos had told him that the pieces of the sacred plant would become a part of him and impart the wisdom he was seeking.

This was the third time the dish had gone around the circle of people and Kyle took the silver spoon and placed a large piece of the medicine into his mouth and passed the dish to his left. As he chewed, the pungent juice dripped from his chin.

"Where are you, God?" Kyle asked in his mind from his heart. "Do you see me trying to reach you?"

Kyle's father, Karl Benson, had been a teacher for a couple of years up at White River on the Apache Reservation, which is where he had met Kyle's mother. After the wedding by a Justice of the Peace, the couple moved to Tucson and Kyle's father went to work for an engineering firm. The family lived near the University and Kyle progressed through the years in the Tucson Unified School District.

The problems that troubled Kyle were all inside himself. He knew he was troubled but he couldn't put his finger on what the trouble was.

Melissa Valdez was the same age as Kyle. They had known each other since the first grade. Now they were graduating from Tucson High.

Kyle walked up to the group of girls in the hall, who smiled at him but continued their conversation. As Melissa began to walk from the group with her books held to her breast, Kyle hurried up to her and asked,

"Melissa, will you let me take you to the prom?"

"I hadn't even thought of going to the prom, but," she paused as if gathering her thoughts. "Yes, I would like to go with you. It will probably be the last time that we'll ever see most of our friends. Thank you for asking me."

The two walked down the hall to the doors leading out

of the school and down the steps to the street. As they parted, Kyle said,

"I'll call you."

Melissa smiled and walked away.

Kyle believed that he was in love with her. He'd felt this way for a number of years, but he had never expressed his feelings to her. Perhaps, at the prom, he would tell her.

They danced every dance. When the lights began to dim, they left the gym where streamers and balloons hung from the ceiling. They passed other friends, who waved and laughed.

Kyle held the door of his mother's Pontiac as Melissa slid into the passenger seat.

"Would you like to go for a ride -- say, up to Windy Point on Mount Lemmon? It's still early. We can get something to eat, too, if you'd like."

"Windy Point sounds great. I haven't been up there in a long time."

Pulling into the wide parking area, the two got out of the car and walked to the stone wall. There, below, like jewels spread out before them, lay the city of Tucson sparkling, radiant and beautiful.

Kyle put his arm around Melissa's waist and said nothing, trying to come up with the right words. He had prayed for a moment like this for a long time.

"Melissa, do you remember when we were kids and the time I ran into you at Reid Park, about three or four years ago?"

"Yeah, my parents were taking me to the zoo."

"We played with a Frisbee. Remember?"

"I've never been able to throw one of those things right."

"But it's you laughing and running, and then, when we found a table and sat down to rest – that's what I remember most. Melissa, I feel that your eyes told me that you love me and, ah --" Kyle paused, "my heart met yours. I want to tell you that I love you. It was that day that my love for you began. You were not just my friend, but -- " Kyle paused, not knowing how to finished his thought that he had held within him for so long.

"Kyle, let's go back down. Maybe get a coke or something."

"Melissa, please, I'm sorry. I, I -- "

"Kyle, no more. Please, let's go."

Kyle did not try to see Melissa. What would he say? What could he say? It had all been said.

The fire that Carlos carefully tended began to move through a spectrum of colors. It was no longer simply orange or yellow, but violet and pink, purple and turquoise. Melissa's face smiled at him in the flickering flames, which danced in rhythm, now, with the rattles and the rapid beat of the water drum.

Again, the dish of medicine was passed around to the worshippers in the tipi. A girl across from Kyle suddenly vomited. Carlos left the tipi and returned with a small shovel and a bucket. He scooped up the expelled medicine, left and returned to care for the fire once more.

The man who was leading the meeting said in a voice that all could hear, "Our friend is not getting sick. She is getting well."

In unison, as if on cue, the people exclaimed, "A ho!"

Melissa's smiling face lingered in the flickering fire, her eyes in a steadfast gaze. She neither beckoned nor withdrew, her image intermingling with the now vibrant fire. Then, just as suddenly, she was gone and the flames took on the form of people dancing to the sound of the water drum. Faster and faster, they moved in scarlet, pink, mauve – never resting, reaching upward. The words of the road man came from far, far away, like an echo in a canyon -- faintly at first, then more pronounced, but not loud.

"Open yourselves to the spirit of Grandfather Peyote. Open yourselves to the fire, to the sound of the water drum, to the rattles. They are the voices of The Creator. Each of us has something to learn from Him. The fingers of our souls reach upward to hold the understanding, the love and the peace that will come to each of us when we walk out to greet the new day that will soon be upon us."

The fire became the fire once more. The people rose from their places and departed the tipi, shaking hands with each other. Kyle looked up at the morning sun over the Rincon Mountains. Liquid gold filled his head. Carlos walked to him and with a smile and a bear hug, and said,

"You okay?"

"Yeah, I'm fine. That's quite a ceremony."

"We call it a meeting. Hey, Kyle, when you get yourself together, call me and let's talk."

"Will do."

The people were visiting and waiting for the breakfast feast that was as much a part of the meeting as the more formal participation in the tipi. The men sat in lawn chairs or stood, smoking and talking. The women got the food ready and small children ran around, chasing each other.

The peyote meeting had been held on the O'odham Reservation out near the old Spanish Mission of San Xavier.

The smell of mesquite smoke drifted on the morning air. Tohono O'odham women were preparing fry bread near the mission in anticipation of the tourists who would be coming.

As he drove home, all Kyle could think of was Melissa's face in the fire -- that, and how sleepy he felt. He would put this experience into some kind of perspective later. He slept until noon. Even then, as he sat up in bed, he felt groggy. He lay back and the dream he had came back to him.

He saw himself standing near the palo verde in his backyard. Someone was standing near him. Turning, it was but his own shadow, but it appeared to be more than simply his shadow. It was something more, it was someone, someone who was trying to talk to him.

"I'll call Carlos tomorrow."

Carlos Nez was a Navajo and he had been Kyle's friend for some time, although he was older by five years. He was also a student at the University of Arizona. Kyle had confided his confusion about what he should do with his life and his feelings for Melissa to Carlos. Carlos was like an older brother and he listened to Kyle without passing any judgments. He only made suggestions.

Kyle had told Carlos that he felt that a major piece of his life was missing and that he didn't know where to look for this missing piece that would put a focus into his life.

Carlos told him, "Come with me on Saturday night. You may find a door you can walk through into a place of answers."

Jenny Benson, Kyle's mother, knew about the Native American Church. A few of her friends and even an uncle were devout adherents to this faith. So when Kyle said that Carlos had invited him to attend a meeting, she had no objection to him going. She had had her Changing Woman Ceremony as a girl coming of age. Since then, she had only occasionally attended a fundamentalist church when on the reservation.

When she married Kyle's father, Karl, and they moved to Tucson, the lure of city life and what it offered, attracted Jenny. She endeavored to fit into the social milieu of her husband. Kyle was born and life seemed good Karl and Jenny Benson.

When Kyle was three years old, his father was killed in an auto accident and Jenny had to make some decisions. Should she and her son return to the rez where life was lived at a much slower pace or stay in Tucson?

She applied for and was given a grant from the tribe to attend Pima Community College and she eventually received an Associate Degree in Medical Records Management. Soon after, she applied for a job and was hired by a local clinic. With this steady income and the investments Karl had made, Jenny and her young son lived well. They weren't rich but lacked little.

She knew that Kyle was troubled. She felt the same, at times. There was something missing in their lives. Perhaps his friend, Carlos, would help fill the void Karl had left.

The monsoons were coming and virga hung in the distance near the mountains to the south. Occasionally, a light shower foretold of more abundance that was coming.

Kyle sat in the shade of the palo verde tree, the same tree from his dream, where his shadow had seemed more than a shadow.

"What was it?" Kyle asked himself.

Jenny had taught Kyle a few words in the Apache tongue. As he questioned his dream, a small breeze caused the raindrops from a light shower to hang twinkling in the branches of the tree under which he sat. The sparkling orbs of water seemed to flash words and images through the leaves.

"What does this mean?" he asked himself.

The sparkling drops of water sang in the light breeze -- a song of a memory of something long gone, as gone as the now deserted breeze.

"Boy, what you have done is good. I am Ussen and I am speaking to you. I am your father, your brother who died before you were born. I am death and I am life, but I am also an old friend. What you have done with your friend, Carlos, is good. Now go."

Carlos Nez was always welcome in Kyle's home. Jenny made sure of that. She knew her son needed the guidance that only a traditional man could give him.

"Even if he is a Navajo," she said to herself with a grin.

Carlos walked through the front door with only a couple of slight raps for courtesy.

"Mrs. B, how are you? And I am hoping you are having a good day," Carlos said with his usual big grin.

"I'm fine, thanks. How was the meeting the other night?"

"Beautiful. I feel Kyle may find some direction, should he continue to come. Everyone there made him feel welcome."

"I'm glad. I appreciate your concern for him and your willingness to help him. He needs your friendship, you know."

"I like Kyle. He's like a younger brother to me. Where is he?"

"Out back by the tree he likes to sit under."

"Hey, cousin, how you doing?"

Carlos pulled up a lawn chair and sat by his friend.

"I'm trying to get my thoughts together about the other night and a dream I had." Kyle paused and said, "I don't know."

"Thinking about that girl you told me about?"

"Yeah, I don't know what to do about her, either."

"Let me tell you something, cousin. Everything in this universe was created to love and every situation sets its' own rules. What do you think you have to offer this girl? What is her name?"

"Melissa Valdez."

"You've only been out of high school for a few weeks. You have no job and nothing to offer her – no plans for your future. I don't blame her for putting you off. Wait. Get something going for yourself. Enroll in college. That'll impress her. Cousin, your life, what and who you are, what you have done so far has not been determined by yourself. Your circumstances have been shaped by a number of factors. It's time for you to sort things out. When you do, Melissa will still be there, maybe even waiting for you to make a positive move."

Kyle looked at Carlos. "Where do you get all of this? You're not that much older than me."

"Cousin, keep coming to meetings. Don't take any hopes or anticipations. Concentrate on the Grandfather Peyote that's at the top of the moon altar. It knows your heart, your life, your hopes – answers will come on their own. You don't have to ask."

Kyle could not take his eyes from his friend's face.

"Let me ask you this," Carlos said. "Has your mom told you the stories and the myths of your people there at White River?"

"Some. What's that got to do with anything? I'm here in Tucson, not out on the rez."

"Cousin, the myths and stories are continuous. They are the dreams, visions, the poetry and the drama of the Apache ancestors that live in your blood. They whisper to you and when you focus on Grandfather Peyote, they will speak to you, the same as my own Navajo ancestors do for me. Answers will come. Bet on it."

"That's pretty heavy, Carlos."

"It's real heavy, and cousin, it's all true."

"What stories from my mom's family traditions will tell me what I need to know about how I should live my life in the future?"

"There are many stories from many people that have come together in you. They are all available to you. Look within yourself for them. When you do, you will create your own definition of who and what you are. You are many people. Reach back and find who you are. You will find symbols you can relate to – they are all around you."

Kyle's eyes were riveted on his friend. His words struck a resonate chord. They made sense.

"There's a meeting Saturday night, same place, same people. You want me to pick you up?"

"Yeah, I guess so."

"Don't sound so positive, cousin," Carlos said, smiling

with a hint of sarcasm. "You know each of us has a spirit being who is always with us. It never leaves us. It's when we pay attention to that spirit that we begin to understand our lives and what is going on around us. My Grandpa told me the spirit can take many forms to get our attention – sometimes a bird or an animal, whatever. The way you describe your dream, I'd say your spirit is knocking at your door."

Kyle grinned, a little embarrassed. He felt naked. But what Carlos was saying was similar to what his mom had told him. He would make an effort to keep his mind open, as well as his eyes and ears.

"I gotta go. I have a biology class in an hour."

Kyle gave Carlos a wave as his friend walked around the side of the house.

"I don't know what to do," Kyle said to himself as he walked to the house. The moving grey clouds promised more rain. Walking to his room, Kyle stopped at the bathroom to wash his hands.

Pausing to stare at his face in the bathroom mirror, he said to himself, "If I never see her again..."

Dropping his head, he closed his eyes.

"How do I rid myself of my wish to be with her?"

With a clenched fist, he hit the wall.

A couple of days later, Carlos once more rapped at the front door and walked in with his usual grin. Jenny looked around the corner of the kitchen door.

"Hey there, Diné."

"Hey there, N'de," Carlos said in response.

"You want to stay for dinner? All we're having is fry bread, beans and ground beef."

"Better known as Indian tacos. Yeah, thanks for asking."

Just then, Kyle walked in the front door.

"Go wash up," his mother called out. "Dinner will be ready in about five minutes."

The three friends talked and joked as they ate.

"There's nothing like good Indian tacos to help a troubled mind," Jenny said, glancing at Kyle.

"Good?" Carlos responded. "Why that meal would have made Pancho Villa surrender his guns to Blackjack Pershing!"

Jenny almost choked, laughing.

Kyle and Carlos left the table and walked out to sit once more beneath the palo verde tree.

Pointing with pursed lips at the low-lying dark clouds that were being pushed by the wind, Carlos said,

"Those O'odham know how to pray for rain."

"Carlos," Kyle began, "I know kids from my class who know exactly what they want for themselves. Their lives seem planned out for them."

"Cousin, your life is a work in progress."

"So what's new?"

"The price I've had to pay for finding my own way in life has cost me much, but I'm achieving some satisfaction. I could still be up on the rez herding sheep or busting my rear at the coal mine up on Black Mesa. No way, man! I'm going into politics to help The People. And you know what? The answers I was looking for came from listening to the voice of Grandfather Peyote. This is what I've been trying to tell you, cousin."

"It's not just Melissa. Where do I belong? Here in Tucson or up at White River? I'm half Anglo, remember? Where do I look for me?"

"When a person feels at home, there is a feeling of everything being right. Your father loved your mom. He loved you and he provided for both of your needs. Your mom has taken good care of you. You've been up on the rez to visit. You know you will always have a place there. You belong to the land there and you belong here, as well. It's hard as hell to walk two roads. I know! But when you listen to the voice of the medicine, you will find that your spiritual center is a geographical one, as well. The earth holds you, cousin, like your mom did when you were a baby. Here or White River, it's all the same. Come to terms with it, cousin. You're not half anything. You're a whole human being. We are all people, you, me, your mom, Melissa and even all those whites out there. We all have to come to the realization that our blood is red. Cut out the crap about 'us' and 'them.' We were all created by the same sacred force.

Kyle walked west on Fifth Street, past the high school where he had spent most of every day for the past four years. At the corner of Fourth Avenue, he walked north to the small park where a group of what appeared to be homeless men sat or lounged on the grass. As he looked at these disheveled men, Carlos' words came back to him with clarity.

"You have no job, nothing to offer her, no plans for a future."

Turning on his heel, Kyle retraced his steps. A few blocks from his home, a girl approached him on the sidewalk.

"Hi, Kyle. Enjoying the summer?" Gail Vaca was a friend of Melissa Valdez.

"Hi, Gail. How are you doing?"

"Fine."

The two spoke to each other but didn't stop to chat. Gail was a few feet away from Kyle when she called back to him, "Did you know that Melissa's family has moved to Texas?"

Kyle came to a dead stop. "No kidding. When?"

"A couple of days after graduation. Her dad got a job in San Antonio." She grinned and shook her head. "Four years of everything the same, then, bam! Everything changes. What do you plan on doing now?"

"I haven't decided yet. I'll see you."

Turning, Kyle said to himself, "Not even a goodbye or anything!" He stood, in a state of total discouragement. He had no idea what to do next. "I feel totally useless."

Carlos had picked up Kyle and they were headed to the O'odham Reservation where San Xavier del Bac Mission glowed in the setting sun. The white dome with a cross appeared like a breast exposed to the turquois sky. The heat of the day would not relinquish its hold on the land and the people until after darkness began to creep outward from the western mountains.

Other than the initial greetings, little had passed between the two friends. As the old truck Carlos drove entered Mission Road, Kyle turned and said,

"Melissa moved to Texas."

Carlos turned his head and looked at him and then said, "You're now free to think about you. An emotion is something a person cannot always comprehend. Cousin, what you've been experiencing – call it love if you want to – is something you have imagined. It was and still is a creation of your heart and your mind. Now, all you have is her memory. And all either of you have is the past."

Leaving the truck, the two walked to the tipi where people were sitting in lawn chairs or standing, drinking coffee from a large can by a fire, smoking and talking.

"A ho, nephew. Ya-eeh-te," the man said to Carlos, with a handshake and a huge smile. "And here's your friend. Glad to see you, nephew."

Kyle shook the man's hand.

"Good to see you, too."

The man was Johnson Benally, the roadman.

As Kyle and Carlos waited for the meeting to begin, a man who had been the drummer on the previous Saturday arrived in a red pickup, with dual rear wheels. Leaving the truck, he nodded to Carlos and Kyle, shook hands with Johnson Benally and entered the tipi.

"You should see this," Carlos said to Kyle. "He's going to put the water drum together."

Carlos and Kyle entered the tipi and took places to the left of where the roadman, Johnson Benally, would later be sitting.

From a box he held, the drummer took a three-legged kettle, what looked like a deerskin, a large ball of leather lacing and a small leather bag. He sat silently in prayer, then took from the box a container of water and placed it with the other items.

Rising, he went to the fire, which had already been lit, and took a small amount of last week's crumbled charcoal. Returning to his seat, he poured the water into the kettle and added the bits of charcoal. The man thoroughly soaked the deerskin leather with the remaining water and placed it over the mouth of the kettle.

From the leather bag, he took seven small, round stones and placed them beside him. Unwinding the leather lacing, he laid that beside him as well. The man took a stone, placed it under edge of the deerskin and wrapped a length of the lacing tightly around it. He moved the kettle and repeated the same procedure until the kettle had seven knobs all around the rim and the deer skin was stretched tightly across the top of the kettle. He took the beater, gave the drum a few taps, turned the kettle to wet the skin, and tapped it again, alternating the sound.

Johnson Benally looked at the afterglow on the mountains behind him. It told him to prepare for the coming ceremony and he entered the tipi. Carlos was not the fireman for this evening.

When all had settled themselves, a folding lawn chair was brought in. This is where an old woman who walked with a cane would sit. Deep wrinkles lined her face and her eyes were hidden behind thick eyeglasses.

Once more, a large peyote lay at the top of the half moon altar, a sacramental medium for wisdom and understanding.

Tonight the medicine would be passed among those assembled in the form of powdered peyote, to be washed down with a cup of cool water. Kyle noticed that this seemed bitter, not like the pungent fresh medicine of the ceremony a week before.

The small fire in the center of the tipi burned a soft glow. The fireman stood with a long poker, slowly inching the cottonwood poles into the coals. The smoke rose upward to the open peak of the tipi in grey wisps.

The roadman had a blue and red sash around his shoulders, a symbol of the Gourd Dance Society. He now stood and addressed the people.

"Offer your prayers. We are here to support one another."

When he sat once more, he took a spoon full of the medicine and passed it to Carlos on his left. The medicine was passed to Kyle and then went around the circle. It was gritty and some of it stuck to Kyle's tongue. He closed his eyes and listened to the silence.

"Ussen," he said, using the Apache word for God, "help me find my way."

Cedar was sprinkled on to the coals and it's fragrance filled the air. An agave stock had been placed near the coals and it smoldered while a cigarette of tobacco, wrapped in a dried cornhusk, was lit from it. The cigarette was passed from person to person.

The chanting began with the rapid beat of the water drum and the gourd rattles. The chanting of the people echoed in Kyle's head and seeped into his body, filling his arms and his hands. A heaviness that quickly left him weak made his eyes water as he looked into the fire, now a bright violet. He felt that he was glued to the spot where he was sitting.

The chanting in his ears faded and dimmed and the silence, heavier than anything he had ever known, weighed upon his shoulders like a living being. Then, from far off, came a whisper. The whisper became louder. Turning his head, it appeared that no one else heard the voice. Looking once more into the violet flames that slowly became red as blood, the voice came once again.

"Time is forever, nephew, as it flows through the

mountains on the breezes of life. But to you, my nephew, it is but a blink of your eyes, and you are but a mirage, a dream. You are many times fearful that the people you care about do not understand you. Why do you hide your true feelings? You are traveling on an endless road. It is called understanding. You have taken my flesh within you. You will come to understanding now. You will never comprehend what is real until you realize your ordinary, daily life and the wisdom I will impart within you is a marriage of the two ways. This is the way of your ancestors, nephew."

The voice faded once more into the chanting of the people, the water drum and the rattles. The flames took on the color of flame once more. Kyle looked up at the opening above him. Day was dawning. There before him, the coals of the night's fire had been shaped into the form of the water bird by the fireman.

Carlos and Kyle rode in silence from the reservation. As they neared Kyle's home, Kyle said,

"Carlos, let's talk. You were right about finding answers. I think some came from myself, but most from the medicine last night. I seem to be seeing more clearly. I'm still a little unsure about what's in store for me, but I'm not scared any more. Did I ever tell you about my visit to White River last year?"

"No, I don't think you ever did. What happened?"

"Well, I saw a little kid walking with crutches. He was all crippled up. He was about seven or eight. Man! It was awful seeing him try to walk. I wished that I could do something to help him."

"Cousin, think about what you've just said. The University is only a few blocks from your home. The tribe will pay for your tuition. Go, cousin!"

That day, the monsoons arrived on schedule, the Day of St John the Baptist, and they washed away more than gathered trash and dead animals in the previously dry washes. The clouds, which had hung low for the few days before the first down pour, blessed the life in the city of Tucson and the Sonoran Desert with a cleansing clarity and freshness. Life was renewed and the world was full of promise. Babat Duag or Frog Mountain to the O'odham, quivered and burst with a vigorous energy -- an immutable kaleidoscope of emerging flowers. The doubts of winter were past.

SHADOW

On the desert, a shadow defines what is real and holds a truth of everything ever created. Yet reality has nothing or little to do with this plain of existence – God is at the absolute heart of it all. I believe that there is a place between the worlds, a place that is reality. It is the place of the ancestors and spirits. The Maya called it Xibalba, or "The Place of Awe," a place real and accessible. Dreams, perhaps?

HOME

From deep within myself, I've always thought of Nevada as my home. The superficial glitter of Vegas and Reno have always been just that – superficial and of no real consequence to me. It's the Nevada of the long, seemingly endless valleys of sagebrush, the alkali playas and the piñon hills, and the nearly eternally blue sky – that is Nevada for me.

To know Nevada's indigenous people and the evidence of their ancestors – this is Nevada. To taste the water of Pyramid Lake, to smell the wildflowers blooming in the Ruby Mountains – this also is Nevada for me.

To see the land slowly but surely reclaiming the ruinous efforts of mining, piñon grove deforestation by bull dozers dragging huge chains, and collapsing settlements – this is the Nevada I knew as a boy.

When the infrequent showers come and thunder crashes across the sky and the mountains are hidden in dark clouds, to feel the rain drops on my face – those same raindrops mingle with my tears of joy. Up in the Owyhees, mighty cliffs stand high above my head and are cut through by an ancient stream. Shadows stand starkly against the cliffs.

The sacred sage explodes its fragrance when the rains bless the land and I have stood long hours, dazed by the beauty that fills my senses. Subtle colors of tan, blue, rust and white form an exquisite palette to the eye. All these are Nevada to me.

THE WILD WEST

When I was a boy, I was totally engrossed in and idealized what is called The Wild West. Roy Rogers, Gene Autry, Red Ryder and Hoppy were all heroes of mine. Even the famous outlaws held a separate place in my imagination. I was ambivalent, although I didn't know that word back then, about the James boys and Cole Younger. Were they really bad, I wondered?

We in Nevada had no Dodge City or Laramie, no old Red River, but we did have Virginia City and Tonopah, Silver City and Goldfield. When my father would drive our twelve-cylinder La Salle up Geiger Grade to Virginia City, I was transported back in time instantly. The Bucket of Blood, the Silver Queen, the old Washoe Club, Piper's Opera House, the boardwalks, the Ormsby House, the Silver Stope – all transported me as easily as if I had ridden in on a Cob and Company stagecoach. To see the hearse that carried Julia Bulette to Boot Hill or the office in the Territorial Enterprise where Mark Twain was an employee, still moves my spirit.

THE RENO RODEO

Bunting lined the grandstand as the first riders entered the arena, bearing the Stars and Stripes as well as the dark blue Nevada state flag. The people cheered and the sun was hot that July afternoon. My excitement was at fever pitch. This is what I wanted more than anything else to do when I grew up. I wanted to ride broncs and bulls.

I didn't always have the admission price. Things were tough at our house. It seemed we never had extra money for things like rodeos. So I would walk the six or eight blocks from our home to the rodeo arena and sneak in by the bullpens. Those brahma bulls seemed gigantic and meanness seemed to permeate them like an aura of hate. Boy! Those cowboys had guts, I can remember thinking.

I once recall when a bull that had thrown a man, then tried to climb into the grandstand. How those people fled in all directions until that bull was contained and taken out of the arena. But this was rodeo days in Reno.

THE INDIAN CAMP

Pyramid Lake was the destination of every free weekend when I lived with my parents. And for every trip to the lake, my father would slow the car as we passed what seemed to be a geological anomaly, a plateau in northern Nevada. Plateaus and mesas are common sights in other parts of the southwest.

One day, he said, as he pulled the car off to the side of the road, "We should go and investigate up on the top of that plateau. Perhaps Indians had been up there for some purpose."

It was many months before we ever got to the top. Half way from the road, we discovered what seemed to be a permanent camping place of the Paiute people, perhaps for an overnight stay on the way to some trading venture.

A fire ring stood out in the wind carved bowl of sand, with a huge dune sheltering it. Almost immediately, my father found an arrowhead lying exposed to the sun. A close examination of the fire ring disclosed burned bone. This site lay about twelve miles or so from where Ormsby and his men were whipped by the Paiutes. So when a metal military button was found, we wondered if it had come off of a coat of one of Ormsby's men. On another day, I found, broken into four or five pieces, a large granite metate.

When I married in my early twenties, I left Nevada for

upstate New York, by way of southern Utah. I was gone for nearly thirteen years. When my marriage dissolved, I returned to Nevada. I was discouraged by the changes I saw – unrestricted urban sprawl. But one thing was clear to me: the desert doesn't change. I thought – it will speak to me and cleanse my spirit of the grime of the dirty old city I had left behind.

As I walked through the sagebrush toward the plateau, I stopped at what we called "the Indian camp." It had become desecrated by the tracks of all-terrain vehicles and the stones of the fire ring were in disarray. I cursed who ever had done this and continued toward the plateau. Then, there in the sand before me, where, long ago, I had found the metate, lay the mano or hand-held grinding stone. The desert had, indeed, spoken a welcome to me.

The spirits of those who had walked this very spot in ages passed, left their tracks in the sand. Their eyes searched my mind and touched me with their fingers on the wind.

I feel that I am an integral part of this land. I may never again live in Nevada, but Nevada will always be my home.

BOWER'S MANSION

The afternoon brings shadows from the sheltering, mighty Sierras, which somehow clearly define the history of this place that stands before me. The old, gnarled poplars reach like melted tapers and the zephyrs that blow off the Washoe are balmy and pleasant. They gather force and rustle the leaves in a chorus, welcoming the coming of autumn. The stoic pines of the looming massif stand in majestic splendor, swaying.

Standing and gazing at the house that Sandy Bowers built, my mind conjures images. The cupola on the roof must have been a haven of rest, where one was able to recline and look out upon the magnificent view of the lake and the tan hills beyond it.

I seemed to hear the shouts of glee from little Persia, with her dolls and her friends as they played near at hand. Did Eilley, Sandy's wife, stand and look through lace curtains and see her death? The opulence and glamour that was once a part of this place still persists in my mind's eye.

FORT CHURCHILL

When I drove out to Fort Churchill, after being in the east for many years, the green leaves of the cottonwoods daubed shadows on the car. Driving slowly up out of the canyon, the meandering Carson River cut deeply in the sand hills and flowed around fallen trees turned white by water and the sun.

I paused the car and reflected on everything about me. In my mind, I saw a train of Conestoga wagons with the sounds of creaking wheels, the cracking of whips and the shouts and whistles of the drivers. It was on the banks of this river that the sounds of hooves came to my ears. From around the bend, with pistol drawn, his head turned to see an enemy who seemed to be following him, was Pony Bob Haslam, bringing the mail to California.

The dun colored ghost of the old Fort loomed between the trees where dusty columns of blue coated horse soldiers paraded. The rumor of a Rebel victory somewhere in the south filled the minds of the men at Fort Churchill. Would the settlements in the Nevada territory fall next? Fort Churchill was small, not much of a protector for such a vast territory.

Now, only ghosts, lizards and small birds peer from windows, sightless eyes in the face of history.

MOSQUITO CREEK

Mosquito Creek was frozen. That small trickle that seeps over the hard packed sand and stones and sinks away, was now glazed glass. The small bed, through which the water flowed, though damp, was encrusted with crystals of silver. Strands of salt grass were stuck to the ice or were pressed flat and indented into the hoof marks of cattle. The salt grass was a pallid yellow on the grey sand and there were stones with frost on one side.

I piled rocks into a circle, scooped out the center, laid a tumble weed in the pit, added drift wood and a log, and soon had a halo of warmth radiating outward.

As the sun rose and the day aged, with lunch, I was

loosening the buttons of my jacket. I skipped stones on the dead calm lake. I ran my fingers over pieces of weathered wood and examined centuries old shells. I felt the land speak.

With a small shutter, the water from the miniature fall once more forced through with the help of the sun. It bubbled under the ice and small bergs jammed and then spilled out into the lake. The warming sun and the spirit of the land permeated everything about me. My soul sang out my joy.

THE OLD MINE

A cold wind blew through Gold Canyon. I parked off the road and started on foot up the winding dirt track. The only sounds were my own, the light wind and the faint hum of a low flying jet. It was an oxymoron to view the long con trail while walking this muddy mining track, now well over one hundred years old.

Piles of blue-grey ore tailings and broken, weathered wood stood in sharp contrast to the dark green piñons. I walked slowly up the hill, stepping over the crumbling rocks. The calm of the canyon was made more so by the furious activity which once had been a part of this landscape.

Within a short while, I stood before the opening, the hole in the mountain that had drawn men into the depths of the earth. No sound came forth, only a damp, cold whisper of air. Roots from a weathered piñon trailed near the opening and a large sagebrush partially concealed the opening, moving in the chill wind. Constantly changing cloud shadows passed over the land.

Turning to leave, I glanced at the stones at my feet. Stooping, I picked up a stone from the ground to examine it for mineral traces. It seemed to me that all the efforts that had been expended here had been for nothing. I tossed the stone aside and walked back to my car. I wonder if the ghosts of those miners watched me while I was there.

A Side Trip to Oregon

This place is not stagnant, not sterile of life, neither does it lack for beauty. There is a silence here, a silence when the earth does not speak. The breeze that softly blows is simply a breeze blowing. It has no voice for my ears. As I look around me, there is a meadow, all green with purple and yellow. It's an artist's setting, with abundant colors, but it has no voice for me. Black, shiny crows swoop and glide. Wispy clouds cast their shadows. I listen with ears tuned to another place. As I think about it, it was this earth that gave me life through my forebears. Somehow, I must still be a part of it. Why, then, do the voices of the ghosts of this place remain mute? The long dead roots of my family's past lie petrified in this land, even as my beginnings are in the hills and trees all about me. The voices of my family have become crystalized stones that gash and draw blood along this path.

A DAY IN THE HIGH DESERT

I stood alone on the plateau's rim with orange and rust colored stones all about me. I gazed down at the expanse of desert that blended into eternity. I could barely make out the far mountains where verdant piñons printed the hillsides, where lizards stared and mused as lizards do in the sun's hot glare.

The sun: the intense, brassy breath burned the air around me. The sun's white-eye center was like a god waiting, being neither good nor evil. The heat made me drowsy and I stood, seeing visions as I slid a stone with the toe of my boot. The stone rolled down and out of my view, perhaps to explode as a star in some far galaxy.

The wind's dry voice, the stillness about me, the view of infinity – all held me at the edge of the plateau. I gripped my walking staff tightly, lest I feel some pull to launch myself into the heated air. But no voice beckoned me to leap. I would live another day.

STONES

To pick up a pebble from the desert floor and to then break it open with a larger stone is to view, for the first time, a wonder.

THE WELL OF SIGHS

Mrs. Rosa Richards rose slowly from her comfortable chair, her back and legs creaking with audible snaps as she walked to the front door. The doorbell had rung again.

"Yes, may I help you?" she asked.

"I hope I'm not intruding," the young woman standing before her replied. "My name is Clair Scott and I'm working on a paper for school. I was in hopes that I could interview Mr. Richards. I was told that he has had many experiences in his life that need to be recorded and saved."

Mrs. Richards swept a loose strand of hair from her face and looked at the young woman before her.

Clair Scott had had her sleep disturbed for months with dreams. It was the same dream, over and over – she saw herself walking high above the floor of a large building that was strewn with broken glass. A low, barely audible sound drifted from the dark recesses of the room and she caught glimpses of a face here and then there. She saw a woman with tears cutting her cheeks, a man with a gold tooth sneering, a child, thin and wan, and an old man with sunken eyes.

Clair would awaken then, sweat soaking her bed. Rising, she would go to the toilet, exhausted, her throat dry.

"Who told you of my husband?" Mrs. Richards asked.

"The professor who teaches the sociology class that I'm taking at the college – Professor Lalo Alvarado."

"He was a close friend of my husband in the old days. Come in."

"Thank you."

"Ricardo, there's someone here to see you."

Richard Richards was not a Chicano, a Mexican or a Spaniard, but he had spent so many years in Mexico that he might as well have been a Latino. He spoke Spanish like a native.

Clair had found out as much as she could about Mr. Richards. She knew of the years he had spent south of the border.

"Does Mr. Richards speak only Spanish?" Clair asked.

"No, he will speak English if he has to."

Again, a lock of graying hair fell from the knot on the top of Mrs. Richard's head.

Richard Richards sat in a great, over-stuffed chair. A large calabash pipe that he held let clouds of smoke billow about his head.

Looking at Clair, he said to himself, "I wish I was fifty years younger."

"What brings a young woman like you to see a viejo like me?"

Again, Clair Scott mentioned Lalo Alvarado.

"There's one for you," Richards said, laughing until he choked, spilling ashes from his pipe. "I've known that vato nearly all my life. What did he send you here for?" he asked, settling himself once more.

"He told me I might hear of some of the adventures you have had – and that they needed to be put down for posterity."

"Are you an anthro?"

"I'm studying courses that interest me. I don't know

what I'm going to get a degree in as yet."

"You'll see." Richards said, relighting the huge pipe.

"I'll see what, sir?" Clair asked.

"Stay away from the establishment! You'll lose your soul, you'll be a robot."

Richards had thick bushy eyebrows and a slightly protruding brow ridge and deep, sunken eyes. As he moved forward in his chair to emphasize what he was saying, his face that had been partially hidden in shadow, now became visible. It was one of the faces Clair saw nightly in her dream. She stared at him, her breath caught in her throat.

"How can this be?" she asked herself. "I've never seen this man before in my life."

"So what do you want to know?"

"Tell me, if you would, about your time in Mexico, living with the Indians."

Clair took from her purse a tablet and a pen.

"Put those away," Richards roared. "Use the brain the Almighty gave you. Learn to recall if you want to learn anything. Perhaps somewhere there is someone who understands my longing and walks on stones of sadness."

He paused, looking at her, and then continued, "It may be you."

****

"My search as taken me many miles -- through deserts, pine forests, grey, decaying cities, and tangled, danger-filled jungles. For all of this, my heart still cries out loudly. My soul is not at peace. My heart is not still. I am yet an insatiable seeker. If I could leave this chair, I would be gone. Since you've come to me to hear my story, I would take you with me and we would find a new story for you to write."

Clair turned in her seat to see if Mrs. Richards had heard this outburst. But she was alone with this man and she began to wonder if he might be mad. Shadows hid the corners of the room, even though the sun shown brightly in the cloudless turquoise sky.

Clair began to doubt the wisdom of coming to see this man. To her, he seemed agitated and tormented.

"Mr. Richards, should I leave you alone? It appears I have upset you. I hope that I haven't stirred up bad memories by asking you to recall past events."

"Joven, do not be alarmed at me. I speak my soul, not because of any intrusion from you."

And so the stories began to trickle like a stream of snow melt. As The Great Sun warmed the withering soul, they became a thundering, crashing tumult.

"My early life," Richards began, "released me to think in my own perception, completely independent to a degree that few people are familiar with. My thoughts have never been imprisoned along institutional lines. Some of my failures were lucky breaks that allowed an escape from a trap that had been set to ensnare my thoughts. I was free, free to think my own thoughts. The life I was born into seemed to direct my path to ends other than the establishment of seeking personal truth. This freedom gave birth to a haunting question in my mind – are what I perceive and what I think separated by a deep barranca, a chasm?"

Clair stared in amazement at the old man. Who and what was he? His long hair and his face, free from wrinkles for one his age, made him appear as a wild man, a Messiah wanderer out of some heat-tortured desert.

"I must hear his story. Perhaps the answers to my dream may come from his lips," she thought to herself.

"Our Father, who art in heaven," Richards began once more. "Is He in heaven only, as some profess? Ah, no, He is everywhere. This I have found to be true. He goes by not only one name – He has many and He lives in all things. His breath instills life, even to the sacred stones at our feet."

"But," Clair started to say –

"You came to hear, to learn! Then, listen!"

Clair's mind became encased in a raging storm. She could not think, she could not move. She felt riveted to the chair she sat upon, chained by the force of the words that circled her like the circling of raptors seeking the ground-hugging rabbit that shivered beneath a bush. There was a terror, yet also a sense of calm in the room. She could not recall when she had entered and sat where she was. It was as if she had always been there. The voice of Richards was the unknowable forever.

"From the deep barranca that separates perception and thought, my real self emerged. It rose and left behind a shell, an old skin – like that which a snake sheds. I was free!"

Richards slumped in his chair. Ashes spilled from his pipe to the floor.

"Come again, if you wish, and I will continue, should you want to know more. Goodbye for now."

Clair walked to her car and sat gripping the wheel. "Is this man crazy, or am I for coming here? Is Professor

Alvarado playing some mind-game with me?"

Turning the ignition, she drove from the house out onto the street, turned off the radio and headed home. In her apartment, she put her coat on the back of the couch and went to the kitchen, with the mail that she held – bills, advertisements – nothing of immediate importance. She placed the mail on the counter.

Opening the refrigerator, nothing seemed appealing.

"Forget it," she said aloud.

In the bedroom, she undressed and turned on the shower. The hot water felt good and helped to wash away the confusion in her mind that the visit to Richard Richards had laid upon her. Flicking on the light over her bed, she began going over the notes she had taken in class. The words of Professor Alvarado once more hovered over her notes.

"I recommend an old friend who will, I'm sure, give you your master's thesis from what you can learn from him."

"I should have asked if Mr. Richards smoked marijuana, or was taking magic mushrooms," Clair said sarcastically to herself.

The dreams came to Clair once more. As vivid as they had been, now they were as real as waking. She was on the catwalk, high above the glass littered floor, the darkness, the emerging and disappearing faces – they were all there. Then they were gone. In their places, yellow autumn leaves hung wet on stark black branches and the wind sliced through the back of a slowly flowing, muddy stream. A flock of gulls glided white and grey against the setting sun. Clair reached with the tips of her fingers and touched a pool of blood, placing life upon her lips.

Outside her window, Clair heard the wind in the cottonwood trees. A voice spoke in her dream. It was not a voice ominous or harsh – it was neither loud nor soft. Spoken but not heard, only felt, as dreams and nightmares are often felt. There was an echo of Richard Richard's voice in the sound that she felt but did not hear.

"Is life but a seeking after dreams? Or is life but a dream itself, dreamt by us all?"

Soft laughter broke the spell of the dream and Clair sat up in bed, gripping the blanket that covered her. She turned on the light above her bed and looked about the room. It felt as though someone had been present in this room. But the room was as it had been when she retired.

"There is no one here – but, could there have been?" she asked herself.

****

Clair found an empty space in the student parking because she had arrived earlier than usual. She had to talk to Professor Alvarado about her visit to Richard Richards and her impression of his words. She walked through the campus, trying to gather her thoughts into a cohesive statement. She didn't want to sound like some disorganized undergraduate.

Opening the door of Professor Alvarado's cubicle that he called his office, she found the room was empty, except for the stacks of manila envelopes, class papers in piles, and heaps of books on the desk, the floor and on the small shelf that lined one wall. A large photo of Emiliano Zapata and Pancho Villa with their cohorts, hung on the wall above the desk. A computer screen saver showed a photograph of the huge calendar stone of the Aztecs.

As she turned to leave, Professor Lalo Alvarado approached, a smile on his broad face.

"Good morning, Clair, what brings you here so early?"

"I feel I need to talk to you – it's about Richard Richards. Is he – " she paused, looking for the correct word, "a little off? I don't mean crazy, but..."

Professor Alvarado's grin became a huge smile as he laughed. "Crazy? I should say not!" he said emphatically. Alvarado glanced up at the standard institutional clock that was clicking off the minutes. "Let me get a chair from next door, and then come in. I've got about an hour and a half before my next class."

Settling themselves after closing the cubicle door, Alvarado hit a button on a cassette player; soft Mexican guitar music swirled around the room. The eyes of both Zapata and Villa reflected some distant light and seemed to blink with life. Clair stared at the large photograph. Alvarado noted her gaze.

"There are heroes and there are also demons. At times, it's hard to tell the difference. My words don't tell of it. No words can or will. If you listen with your heart, all your questions will be answered in due time. Now, what is it you wanted to know about Richard Richards?"

"Professor Alvarado, you may not believe this, but you have just answered the questions I was going to ask you."

Alvarado smiled his broad smile and he rested his right elbow on his desk, his hand to the side of his head. He studied the face of the young woman who sat across from him.

Walking from the teacher's office down the long hall, students were walking in both directions, chatting or laughing. Clair walked to the student lounge, placed her books on an empty table, and entered the cafeteria, ordered a café mocha, and returned to her table. She sat, thinking about the circumstances that hovered around her. Snatches of last night's dream came and went in her mind.

The table Clair had chosen was near one of the huge windows that looked out onto the campus. Students walked from building to building, some in groups, some singly, some as couples. There were students throwing a Frisbee while a group of girls stood watching.

"How many times have I sat here, and how many more times will I sit by this window, looking out at the yellow grass that is waiting for rain to turn it green again? Seeing the same mechanically programed people with their mechanically programed thoughts?"

Richard Richards' words reverberated anew in her head.

"Stay away from the establishment, damn it! You'll lose your soul. You'll be a robot!"

Clair finished her mocha, gathered her books and walked to her car.

****

Richard Richards chuckled to himself. "So, you have come back. I'm not sure I know what you want."

"Mr. Richards, I'm not sure I know what I want from you."

"Now, that makes sense. We have a place to begin. If this is the time to speak my thoughts, then listen. I will take you to a place of truth and a place of lies, a place of incredible light, and thick, crushing darkness, a place where hearts and souls collide and stand naked."

Pointing to her, he said, "Inquire the meaning of a rose that speaks with its fragile fragrance and hue. Doubt the meaning of the sun's setting with a shout of triumph and glory and a hymn of victory, contemplation and repose."

Richards paused, retrieved his calabash pipe, filled it and lit it. A sweet aroma instantly filled the room. Clair's eyes began to water and she felt the smoke was suffocating her. With a wave of his hands, Richards cleared the air and smiled.

"The smoke liberates the mind of all extraneous thoughts. You will now be able to perceive more than you have known. Breathe deeply, close your eyes and stand a moment, if you must."

Clair stood on shaky legs and held the arm of her chair. The morning light cast long beams that caught and dispersed dust motes that floated in the air of the room like a rain gently falling in early spring.

"A serpent lives within the body of every person," Richards began once again. "We are the serpent. It is this serpent that is ourselves, that conjures the wizardry and witchery that pulls our thoughts like sticky taffy and molds our emotions. It then lets them lay at the bottom of our own devised hells."

He continued, "Far to the south, in the jungles of Mexico, are a people ancient upon the earth. They are known as the Maya. They know themselves as The People. It was these people who showed me the reflection of my own likeness, the likeness of the Feathered Serpent in a mirror of black obsidian."

Clair gave a gasp and gripped the arm of the chair she was sitting in.

"No!" she cried out. "You are not Quetzelcoatl! That was only a myth of the Aztecs."

"No?" Richards asked. "Then how is it you have lust in your heart to one day mate with some man and make a child, eh?"

"I have no lust in my heart for any man. I desire only to be a woman of integrity and to fulfill my destiny as such. I have no lust!"

"Lust, desire, want, it's all the same. But that is not all. You strive in another direction as well. You wish to understand and you question God. Is that not so? When the knowledge you seek is finally delivered to you, that deliverance is in preparation for more. Knowledge, like days of the week, comes on it's own. So how does one find one's way into tomorrow? Look to the heavens. Sublime halos circle the moon."

Clair began to cry. "I am so completely lost. How easy it seems for me to lose the path before me in the bracken that grows around me."

Richards blew a smoke ring and pointed a finger through it with a smile.

"You are the serpent – the same as I and, yes," he slapped his knee with a laugh, "so is Lalo Alvarado and all the rest of us, whether we want to accept it or not. We are made of spirit and we are made of flesh. That is the secret of the serpent, if you chose to call the metaphor Quetzelcoatl, Kukulkan or Gugumatz as the Maya I have known did, so be it. We mortals are, by our creation, polarities -- the eternal conflict -- and the spirits laugh."

Continuing, Richards said, "Deep in the selva, not far from the Lacandon Maya, the ones who hold the ways most closely, lived an old man whose name I cannot say aloud. To do so would bring his spirit here. He is long departed from this earth, but he was spiritually very powerful and he knew much. I met him in the old colonial town of San Cristobal de las Casas. In truth, he came to me. I did not search him out. I was in the main hotel at the time and I had come down to the restaurant for some rich Chiapas coffee, when this old man, dressed as a camposino, stepped to my table and addressed me.

"How do you know my name?" I asked him. I had never seen him in my life before.

He said he had been shown.

"By whom?" I asked.

"The rabbit on the moon," he replied.

I thought he might have smoked too much mota.

"Sit, viejo," I said, and poured him some coffee from the pitcher on my table.

After he had finished the coffee, he said, "We will go now."

"We?" I asked.

"Si, you and I. We have much to discuss."

We walked the cobblestone streets that led out of town. He then led me through the selva on a path that was barely visible. How long we walked, I could not tell. It seemed like all day. It was still daylight when we entered a clearing where a thatched roofed hut and a ramada were the only structures. Some hens pecked at the earth as well as a large, male turkey that kept opening and closing his tail feathers, strutting and making his call.

We walked to the Ramada where a table and two small stools stood. He motioned with his hand and we sat.

The sweat poured from under my arms in the heat. Suddenly, a young woman walked from the hut with a clay pitcher and two small cups that she placed on the table. I could not take my eyes from her. She was the most beautiful woman I had ever seen in my entire life!"

"She keeps me young," the old man said with a smile.

The woman said not a word and returned to the hut.

"You I have brought here to listen to my story and to remember," the old man said.

Richards continued, "It was four years that I stayed in that clearing in the selva while the old man spoke of the before times and the wisdom that the anthros say has been forgotten or lost in the burning of the old books.

"Not once did the beautiful woman address me. I never heard her speak. The old man said she was the reincarnation of the girls who had been sacrificed in the cenote, not far from Chichen itza. She had returned with the souls of all those sacrificed within her."

"What I have spoken to you since you first entered my home is what the old man, in part and in compliance with the spirits of the ancient ones, passed on to me."

There was a silence, thick and heavy in the room. The smoke from Richards' pipe curled in phantasmagoric plumes. Clair could not speak – it was too much to hold. She wanted to leave, to run from the words that resounded in her head.

"So, Lalo has sent you to me. I feel you came to me as I was drawn to the old man I knew in the selva of Chiapas. You are to hear, and take within you, these words, which you will then birth in time. The seed has been planted in the womb of your mind. Someday soon, we will fly, you and I, to the small clearing in the selva. Our bodies will be here, but our souls will leave this place and gather with the old man's and the soul of the woman who is the rebirth of knowing."

"No!" Clair cried. "I'm afraid."

Once more, Richards continued. "Long in the past, perhaps at the time of the previous Sun, the wise ones from the whole of what is known as the New World, gathered to speak of understanding. It was told that on a day, blood would run like a river and knowledge would be scattered like a broken glass, and lay forgotten but for a few. Those of the future would walk far above and look down at the broken shards of knowledge as merely myths and stories that have no meaning for those today."

"I've seen this – I've seen this!" Clair said with a sob. "My dreams. This has been a dream I've had for months."

"You have been blessed," Richards said. "It's taken me a lifetime to learn, to live this life I have been given. Come, mija, let us waste no more time. Let us walk together that borderless realm between spheres of spirit and matter. The construction of the cosmos will be shown to us, and the language of the crystal will be our speech. Our songs will be the poetry of the moon. Come, let us walk the line between heaven and earth, and hold the hand of spirit/ heaven and body/earth to support us and keep us in balance."

Clair rose from her chair and knelt before Richards. Looking into his face, she held his hands in hers.

"I will go – I have no choice now."

Richards smiled, rose from his chair and lifted Clair to her feet.

****

The two men and the two women sat in the hut in the small clearing in the selva. The small, smokeless fire smoldered before them. A woven mat hung across the door and moved slightly as a breeze blew upon it. An occasional vagrant gust would play upon the floor and stir the glowing coals to a momentary flame. Richards and Clair both shared in the telling of their journey. The old man nodded as if stirred by some long forgotten memory as the two spoke.

"You have brought the one who seeks wisdom and knowledge," the old man stated slowly, as if with effort. The statement was an affirmation of the two before him.

"You have choices to make, but I will assist."

Richards and Clair stood and gazed out on the horizon. The selva moved softly with hidden life. Far to their left, rising from the living green of the selva, rooted to the center of the earth, stood the temple palace, like a fortress, like a beacon. It thrust upward. It was the place of all knowing.

****

Days became weeks and weeks turned to months and Lalo Alvarado had long since decided that Clair Scott must have dropped out of school. He never gave her another thought. Zapata and Villa maintained their places and watched his goings and comings.

When the local newspapers told of the disappearance of Richard Richards and the discovery of his wife's body lying out among the gladiolas in their well-kept garden, murder was the first assumption. When the autopsy revealed no foul play, but only a heart attack, the mystery of where Richard Richards was only deepened.

Lalo had not kept in touch with his friend for some time. Due to his promotion as department head at the college, he had been over his head with his classes, student papers, faculty meetings, required cocktail parties, and appointments with students. It was when he heard the evening news as he was driving home, that he found out that Richards was missing and that his wife had died.

"Clair Scott," he said aloud. "Of course."

Lalo Alvarado drove a 1953 classic MG-TD that was in mint shape. It was his pride and joy. He had purchased it when he had accepted the promotion as a treat to himself. He drove it into his driveway and stepped into the rapidly falling dusk.

Once inside the house, he went to the frig and cracked open a Corona, and squeezed a lime wedge into the bottle. Loosening his tie, he kicked off his tassel top loafers and sat back in his favorite club chair.

"What was it she said that time?" Lalo asked himself, trying to recall Clair's visit to his office. He realized she really hadn't said anything. It had been he who had said something that she needed to hear. He was not able to bring back the conversation clearly, but he did recall Clair Scott's serious demeanor. Her attitude had given him the impression that she was on the edge of a nervous breakdown. He recalled thinking that she should lighten up – her studies were too much, perhaps.

The ringing phone made him jump.

"Yes, this is Lalo Alvarado. Who is this? The police? What's wrong?"

The voice on the other end continued. "We had a warrant to search Mr. Richards' home when we found his wife and discovered that he was missing. We found an envelope on his desk. It was sealed and on it was written – Give this to Lalo Alvarado."

"We have not opened it. We would like to have you come down and get it. We are hoping you can give us some information about where Mr. Richards might be."

Lalo stepped to the glass in front of the information officer. An older woman asked, "May I help you?"

"I'm Lalo Alvarado. Officer Davis is expecting me."

A buzz at the door on his left was accompanied by a loud click. The woman behind the glass pointed for him to enter.

Officer Davis was in civies. He reached out to shake hands. The two men walked to a room where half of one wall was glass.

"A one-way window, no doubt," Lalo said to himself.

The two men sat across from each other and Officer Davis took from his brief case an envelope, tapped it on his finger and handed it to Lalo.

"We would like to know what's in this. Would you be good enough to open it?"

"Sure, why not?"

Inside was a five by eight inch card on which was written: Oaxaca, Tepic, San Blas, San Juan Chamula, San Cristobal, and Kukulkan. There was nothing else in the envelope.

Lalo handed the card to the policeman, who asked, "What is this?"

"Those are towns in Mexico, except for the last one –

that's an ancient Maya god."

"You have any idea what this means?"

"I know that Richards lived for quite a few years in Mexico, but that's all I know for certain."

"You think he might be in any of these places?"

"I haven't a clue. I haven't seen Richards or talked with him for -- let's see -- about nine or ten months."

Lalo wheeled his MG back home, smiling to himself. Yeah, he did have a clue, but he sure as hell wasn't going to tell it to the cops. They would never understand.

Lalo Alvarado had the respect of his peers and he was not about to let that unravel after all of the hard work he had expended to get where he was now. Who would understand or accept today the months he and Richards had spent in Mexico, searching out herbalists, medicine people, yes, even brujos. This wasn't the sixties anymore. The society in the United States had developed a conservatism and a desire to somehow turn the page on all of the unrest and uncertainty of that decade.

Sitting in his favorite chair once more, he turned off the floor lamp. Darkness surrounded him, but for the faint glow from the street lamp out across his lawn.

"Richards," he said to himself, "why have you disappeared and left that card for me? Yeah, I have a clue, but who in their right mind would believe anything I could tell them about you, Ricardo? And Rosa -- why did you take her so soon after your marriage? I had a feeling about her from the beginning – that she would never be able to endure any discomforts or privations we would encounter down there. Now she's dead. That autopsy report! Boy! Did they get that wrong."

****

Richards and Clair walked along the crest of the bluff. They stopped to look down on the ceaseless embrace of the endless green of the selva below them. Clair followed automatically behind the man who forced his way into the tangle of emerald green. Somewhere within herself, she knew she would pass to the edge of her mind and perhaps beyond. Richards walked as one possessed, paying no heed to reaching brambles. Parrots and macaws of brilliant reds, blues and yellows passed overhead in flocks, squawking their raucous calls.

Pausing once more, Clair wiped her face with her arm. Still, Richards said nothing. He had not spoken for over an hour. Turning to her, he pointed. They had come to rest before a faint path that had opened before them from another direction. A few steps more and there, in front of them, was a pile of white, limestone boulders – or were they boulders? On the surface of the jumbled stones were carved faces of people. Clair instantly recognized them from her dreams.

She thought they would rest there. But, as they approached, out stepped an old man dressed in the ubiquitous white loose shirt and pants of the camposino. He had a straw hat on his white hair.

"So, you have returned, I see."

His eyes went from Richards to Clair and then back to Richards, who stood silent for a few minutes before answering.

"I can no longer stay where I have been. I had to return. Rosa is dead. The spirits told me to return."

"All of the birds and the animals of the selva told me you were coming. You have forgotten how to walk as a shadow."

The small clearing was but a short way. Everything looked as it had always looked. Richard took the pack from his back and placed it on the ground. The young woman emerged from the hut and strung hammocks from the rafters of the ramada.

"Rest yourselves," the old man said.

A storm slowly moved from the distant sea, and from the low, great cloud mass that was torn and furrowed, faces appeared and dissolved.

Swaying gently in the woven hammock, Clair closed her eyes and shooting stars fell around her. They showered upon the leaves and dripped to the ground. Light, brighter than any she had ever known, exploded and rolled away as crystal marbles into the foliage beyond.

"Shield me," she heard a voice cry out. It was her own voice. She wanted to be held, but there was no one to hold her.

Another voice spoke. Her mind trembled.

"This place is ancient where you are. Spirits move upon the air and have never left this endless verdure. These spirits will take on flesh once more and restore all to the First Time. Kukulkan will rule the land once more. Time waits to reverse itself."

The Well of Sighs was a gaping maw. Tendrils of lianas hung from the trees and sprawled, creeping down the edge of the cenote. Moss clung to the stony sides and ferns clung to crevices. A gangrous green scrum of algae and decaying leaves floated on the surface of the still water.

An air of silence held with its grasp the memories spent of the potency.

Clair stood on the brink of the cenote.

"My life is now over, but a new life awaits me. What I had hoped for is now mine, a life of new meaning. A new purpose is before me and I am at peace."

Clair was grasped by her arms and legs by Richards and the old man and they flung her into the abyss. Bubbles rose around her and her hair streamed around her face and neck. Through the tepid water, she slowly sank to the floor beneath her, where, partially buried in the slime and mud, were not only bones of other victims, but also carved jade figures, golden cups and highly decorated ceramic plates.

Clair Scott stooped to retrieve a small jade statue and a maskette of a human face with the mouth of a jaguar. She turned and slowly gazed at the remains of offered pleas for deliverance and hope. She felt no fear or sorrow. She reached her hand out to caress the form of a carved stele. She felt a confusing sense of contentment and happiness that dispelled any anger that had followed her as a shadow. The tattered remnants of long held uncertainties were washed away by the bubbles of light, which swirled around her. A floodgate spigot opened in her mind and her whole being was filled with light. The slimy silt at her feet oozed between her toes. An icy moon now hung over the selva and wooed the endless eternity of the sea. The pesadilla is dead. The penance is completed. Forgiveness rises with the Sun.

****

Richard Richards sat with his calabash pipe gripped in

his teeth. A grin slowly spread on his lips. Clair gave a startled cry and opened her eyes and looked about the darkening room. The paper she would write for Lalo Alvarado's class was written in her mind.

****

Lalo Alvarado sat back in his chair in the small cubicle he called his office and stared at the faces of Zapata and Villa that hung on his wall.

"It was my destiny to return to the place where I was born, but I could not linger there. I had tasted too much of the north.

SAND

I knelt in the sand and reached down and held a handful of the sun-warmed soil. As it slipped through my fingers, it was blown softly by the breeze. I grabbed again at it and found myself trying to hold myself in my hand – my life. The tiny grains flowed out of my fingers and became once more the floor of the desert.

OPINIONS

The opinions of the desert are the result of my personal experiences. My actions there are made from this basis.

FROM A NEVADA GOLD CAMP

The overcast rays of the sun squeezed beneath the cracks of the broken shade. They streamed diagonally through the upright spindles of the bannister and crept across the once polished floor, now covered with dirt and refuse. A dusty, defused sunlight barely lit the room through cracked or broken windows. Wisps of air, once inside, lost their force and eddied about the room. Small dunes of talc fine sand rippled in the corners of the old house. Each room kept small deserts within, while, outside, the desert of sagebrush and salt grass held the house in its grip. In time, the ever blowing, ever moving sand would engulf the old building and there would be no inside, no outside.

Even as I stood gazing about this musty room, the wind blew grit in around me. The faded print paper on the walls hung in tatters. From the ceiling, it sagged and bowed in loops. Cracked and pitted plaster showed beneath. I wished that I could know the history of this old home. The sensation of standing there crept over me and I seemed to blend with all that was around me.

ADVENT OF FREMONT

Was it blood that flowed within the banks of the river and streams? The wind bore a message of the destruction that was to come to the land and to the people of the land. Lupine, Indian paint brush, and waxy golden poppies nodded and wept at the wind's passing. The cottonwoods in the canyon quivered. The message on the wind swept across the desert and whispered of waiting death and transformation.

THE INDIAN CAMP REVISITED

The place is ancient, even sacred. The spirits of the ones who once walked here now move as wisps of dew on the morning air. They've never left this place of rocks, sagebrush and salt grass. They are still here in the pink and purple hills. They pass over the white playas. They prowl the shore of the great lake at the spawning of the cui-ui fish. Perhaps one day they will walk once more in flesh and bone and the old gods will be remembered.

THE CAVES

One event of my childhood stands out as though it occurred yesterday. When I was a small child, a door was opened which has led me down many paths. I've met people I never would have had the opportunity to meet. This one event has shaped my thinking, inspired interests and expanded my world.

The event began as a Sunday afternoon drive with my parents. On that day, I followed my father into the overhanging brow of a tufa outcropping. Even at that age, I was electrified. On the floor of the cave were teeth, finger bones, vertebrae, shreds of baskets and wooden implements. The cultural level had been disturbed over the centuries by pack rats and coyotes.

"People lived here once," my father said to me. "Look at the wall and the ceiling – they're black from cooking fires."

I had heard of cave dwellers, but here, all around me, they began to live again. From out of the heart of this cave, once more, these ancient ones walked again in the clear Nevada sunlight. It was eventually established that these people had lived here approximately three thousand years in the past.

I was with my father when he found the lower half of a person's body. The upper half had been buried under tons of rock when the roof of his home crashed down upon him in an earthquake.

Many times, I have retraced our steps in my mind and

pictured once more what lay in the accumulated dust of countless ages: a cape woven of bird down, a skull of an infant not yet knit together, the mummified remains of a small, wolf-like dog, a desiccated fish in the cooking area, a callous from a human hand, fire sticks and darts. The bow and arrow had not yet been invented.

Two items were found that fired speculation. My father placed them in my hands -- what were perhaps representations of spirits or even totems. We never knew.

As an adult, I often wondered if it had all been a dream. But no, it was no dream. I know that laughing children played there once. Women cooked over fires and went to the lake for water. Men fished or hunted there and gathered bird eggs. This was home to them. This was the center of the universe.

I wonder now when and why they decided to leave and move – was it because of the earthquake? It's hard to leave one's home, no matter what the reason. Did they look back as they left?

I recall that a few years ago, I was terrified by a dream. In it, I was standing near the cave with the sun shining brightly. As I stood gazing at the cave, in a depression beneath the stone mass, partially hidden, was the prone figure of a man. Only his head and the upper portion of his body were visible. His hands were at either side of his head and he was clutching arrows or darts. His eyes followed my every move. I recall my body going as cold as ice. It was then that I awoke.

The time at the cave has become ingrained into the core of my being. For a brief span of time, the cave of the ancient ones was my home, as well.

PYRAMID LAKE

Walking along the beach, where bluffs frown out upon the ever changing colors of the lake, the sun casts rays upon the pyramid. The pinnacles shine like ivory and I am wrapped in shadow. The flames from my fire down the beach have beckoned to me, so I will rise with a shiver and walk into the night.

LIFE IN A SHACK

Silver, icy fingers reached half way down from the low side of the roof. Snow blew through the cracks of the wall in small, fine drifts. The cold wind breathed on my face and puffs of steam issued from my nostrils. The newspapers my mother stuffed into the cracks did little good. The wood-burning stove threw warmth only a few feet into the one room we lived in. The small shack seems to be always cold – even in summer, there was a feeling of chill about the place. Nights in winter were bitter. The bed clothes would be frozen to the board walls when I awoke in the morning. Rather than pajamas, I would bundle in a heavy green and black buffalo plaid hunting shirt when I slept at night.

Having little, and trying to make do, was a state I experienced frequently in my childhood. But our family always felt that someday, things would improve. There was always hope.

My parents had not always been forced into such circumstances. And this converted chicken coop was simply a step to something better, because "God won't let us down," my mother would say. It seemed that God was forced to play a bigger part than He might have chosen for Himself in those days. I learned many lessons about living then and know more now, for that time of hardship.

UNIONVILLE

The two men who had been working steadily on their claims on the outskirts of the rapidly growing settlement of Unionville stopped and rested their hands on their tools. Shading their eyes with their hands, they stood and stretched their aching backs. One of the men walked to a large rock and sat down; he then filled a pipe he took from a bag at his feet.

"Look at the horse that man is riding," he said, pointing with his pipe stem.

Riding slowly up the graded road that wound through the piñons and junipers growing in the hills, came a rider on a grey and white horse. He was a stranger in a community of strangers.

Unionville was not much different from any of the gold camps in California, Nevada, Arizona or Montana. But the amount of gold coming out of the mines around Unionville appeared to rival the diggings in Placer County, California. Silver had been found further up the canyon and the talk was all of a load to rival the Comstock. One more stranger was nothing to bother with.

And so the man rode steadily up the graded road of Unionville, his eyes searching, not knowing what he might see but confident in their steadfastness. Both miners noted the shiny brass breach of the rifle in the scabbard that hung from the saddle horn of the rider.

Pat Taggart tied his horse to the rail and stepped to the boardwalk. He turned and looked all around him. Men crowded the dirt streets, vying for information about the latest strike or failed hope. Wagons came and went, pulled by teams of sweating horses. The sounds of building could be heard and shouts filled the air. It appeared that Unionville was going to have some permanence. It was no longer simply a cluster of miner's shacks and tents.

Taggart slid the 44.40 Golden Boy from the sheath on his saddle and walked through the door of the Esmeralda Saloon, glancing around at the sparsely filled room. A few men stood at the bar. They glanced at him from the mirror hanging above the bottles lining the long shelf behind the bar and went back to their conversations. Most of the tables around the room held no customers. The stamp mill rumbled up in the canyon. Most of the men were working in the mine. When the shift changed, the room would be filled once more.

The bartender, a middle aged man whose bushy eyebrows made his eyes seem hooded, stood waiting, his arms folded across a brocaded vest. The flesh beneath his eyes sagged like pockets. Under his nose was a pencil thin mustache.

"What will you have?" he asked in a gravelly voice.

"Your beer cold?" Taggart asked.

Without answering, a mug was brought from beneath the bar and filled from the long handled drought. Frost slid down the side of the mug. Laying a coin on the bar, Taggart turned and walked to an empty table near the corner window. He could see anyone coming in the door or passing outside.

The bartender picked up the coin and glanced at it. With a grin, he placed it in the box behind him. He was pleased with the tip.

Taggart would sit and wait for the incoming men when the shift at the Pink Lady Mine changed. The Golden Boy lay on the table. Removing his hat, he ran his fingers through his long hair and finished his beer.

"Say, Mister," the bartender said, as he walked up to the table, "I hope you're not here to start a ruckus with this here piece."

"I won't start nothing, but I may finish something. I'm waiting for whatever law man this place has, sheriff, marshal or constable."

"We just got a sheriff a few weeks back. Before that, the 601 took care of problems."

"Vigilantes, you mean," Pat Taggart replied as a frown darkened his face.

"Sheriff Tanner ought to be wandering in any time. Another beer?"

Taggart shook his head as the bartender picked up the empty mug.

****

Sheriff Will Tanner was a man slight in build, but he walked with an effortless, quiet power. His reputation for upholding the law was well known throughout Nevada. Before coming to Unionville, he had cleaned up the small town of Pioche, a place filled with lawless troublemakers. It was once rumored that Bodie had a reputation equal to Tombstone down in the Arizona Territory, but Sheriff Tanner had put that rumor to rest.

The shifts at both the mine and the mill had changed when Sheriff Tanner walked through the door of the Esmeralda Saloon. He stood with both hands on the swinging doors and gazed at the now crowded room, raucous with loud talk and laughter.

Walking to the bar, he said to the sad faced bartender, "Anything I need to know?"

"There in the corner," the bartender said, moving his eyes in that direction. "That gent says he's waiting for whatever law we've got here."

Tanner turned, leaned back and put both elbows on the bar and surveyed the room. Walking slowly, picking his way through the crowd, he stood before Pat Taggart's table.

"I understand you want to talk to me," he said.

"Yeah, Sheriff. Pull up a chair." As the sheriff eased himself into a chair opposite the long rifle, Pat Taggart pulled open his buckskin jacket. There, over his heart, was a badge, Arizona Ranger.

"You're a little out of your jurisdiction," Sheriff Tanner said. "But if I can be of help to you, I'll be more than willing. Who you after?"

"He goes by more names than a Mexican. But he's known by most as Three Fingers Joe George."

****

Joseph George Starr had developed a reputation in the Arizona Territory. Though handsome, witty and dashing, he was as dangerous as a Gila monster. He seldom walked faster than his normal, leisurely pace. Even when he held up a stagecoach or an isolated ranch for a horse or two, his getaway was at a slow lope. Everyone knew that his skill with a pistol was deadly.

He had developed the moniker "Three Fingers" from an incident back in his teens. He had been working on a cattle drive, bringing steers up from Sonora, Mexico. As they approached the old presidio of Tubac, the herd began to stampede for the Santa Cruz River. It had been a long and very hot trip up from the hacienda where the cattle had been purchased.

As Joseph let fly his lariat at one of the lead steers, somehow a loop caught his left hand. The fast running steer and the slowing pony caused enough tension on the rope that two fingers were ripped from his hand.

Joe George did a lot of thinking while his hand was healing.

He said to himself, "There are more and better ways of making a living, besides getting beat up by a bunch of beeves."

With not much to do with his time during the healing of his hand, he began to improve his skill with a Colt .44 left to him by his father. He had a natural aptitude and his aim was soon deadly.

Joseph George Starr did not initially intend to become an outlaw, but circumstances sometimes have a way of changing a man's thinking, especially when gold, silver, lead and copper were making mine owners rich. Fate, like blind justice, hung in a balance for Joe George. That balance tipped and a new course was laid open for him. It came in the form of one more tragedy.

Joe's father was returning home from a business trip in a coach that also carried bullion in the boot. Somewhere near the small settlement of Elgin, three men with flour sacks covering their faces relieved the stage of its gold.

The passengers were also told to hand over their valuables. Joe's father pulled a revolver, but a shotgun blast killed him before he could fire a shot.

Joe and his friends tracked the men when the affair became known. The trail the three men left was easy to follow. One by one, Joe George got his revenge. He never rode on a cattle drive again. But because Joe George had revenged himself on his father's murderers, rather than let territorial law mete out justice, he, himself, became wanted by any lawman that might want to apprehend him.

Joe George knew the country well and was able to avoid any posse that might be searching for him or any bands of Apache raiders out to terrorize the settlements. It was here that his reputation began as one of the most feared outlaws in Arizona Territory.

The commanding officer at Fort Bowie had been notified and his patrols were told to watch for Joe George or any Apache bands. It was then that Joe George decided to move to Nevada.

****

"You been a ranger for awhile?" Sheriff Tanner asked as they walked up the hill toward the sheriff's office.

"Circumstances have shaped me for what I'm doing," was Taggart's reply.

Tanner glanced at the ranger and got no impression that the man beside him felt himself too good for what he was doing, or that he disliked what he did. The two men entered the office, removed their hats and sat back in the chairs placed near the roll top desk.

"What makes you think your man's up this way?" Tanner

asked as he took a meerschaum pipe from a rack over the top of his desk and began to fill it.

Taggart removed his jacket and took out fixings and rolled a cigarette.

"The town of Bisbee looks like it may be one of the biggest copper producing spots in the whole of the west," he began. "A lot of speculators and influential and important men from back east have moved in. We, that's the Rangers, got word that some gent from a consortium of investors had opened an office and influenced most of the respectable citizens to try and make Bisbee the county seat."

He continued, "All of these mining camps that are springing up, both here and in Arizona, bring in every trouble seeking rough, and Bisbee's had it's share."

Sheriff Tanner leaned back in his chair. As Taggart continued, he rubbed the back of his neck and relit his pipe.

"It seems one such who had been hanging round town for some time decided to put the squeeze on this gent from back east for some easy cash. Well, the ploy didn't work. He was refused. Why the law wasn't notified, no one knows. All anyone knows for sure is that a bullet in the head sent the businessman to the other side. This rowdy had two compadres with him when the killing occurred. Men in the street, who saw what was going on, opened fire. Two of the men got away. The other was wounded and couldn't get up. He died two days later. Before he died, he identified Three Fingers Joe George as the leader and said that Joe George was planning on heading up this way. The captain of the Rangers assigned me to track him."

There was silence for a few minutes.

Taggart continued, "This Joe George Starr has become a real bad one. He'll kill a man who even dares to defy him."

Sheriff Tanner blew a stream of smoke. "That's interesting what you said. A wire went out a few days back about a holdup of a stage outside the town of Belmont. The stage driver told the sheriff that one of the holdup men had what looked like a mangled left hand. No one was shot, though. I was called to serve here in Unionville because an unarmed man was shot in the street a few weeks before I got here. I'm wondering if this man with the mangled hand is connected to all of this and is the one you've been looking for."

****

The dark night carried no moon. Only the stars and the lights from the mill illumined the upper reaches of the canyon. Taking advantage of the shadows, two men walked slowly toward the mill and smelter where the gold that was being torn from the earth was melted into ingots.

"There's a watchman making his rounds somewheres round about," Three Fingers Joe George whispered to his companion. "If we watch to see the order of his circuit, we might be able to get the drop on him. I'd just as soon not have to kill him, if we can keep from it. But if he gives us any trouble..."

He never finished his sentence. The other man understood. Keeping to the shadows of the wagons and the other machinery, the two men waited.

In some strange way, there was a feeling in the citizens

of Unionville – attention was focused on the toughs that were drifting into the little but growing community. The feeling most people had was that they wanted life to go on peacefully, not like in Pioche or Bodie or Virginia City, for that matter. The unpleasantness had been heightened by the recent killing of the unarmed man right in the street in front of the saloon. The killer had escaped capture, or so everyone thought. It was the killing that brought Will Tanner to town. In its own way, it also brought Pat Taggart.

The man who had applied for the job of night watchman at the mill had convinced the owners that he could use both pistols to effectively make a point. He blew the ace of spades that had been nailed to a tree squarely in the middle, at twenty feet.

Three Fingers Joe George and his companion had set fire to some of the hay wagons as a diversion with the intent of drawing out the night watchman. But an alarm had been given from people down in the main part of town. The people were shouting and a crowd began gathering with buckets of water. With the racket, the night watchman appeared with a pistol in each hand. He had just turned the corner of the building when he saw the two men fleeing from the burning wagons.

"Stop or you're both dead men," he yelled.

One man turned and fired, missing the watchman by inches. His partner fell in a heap, with his hand on his gun. The fleeing man made use of the darkness, reaching his horse and riding into the night.

When Sheriff Tanner arrived at the mill, the crowd had finally extinguished the burning wagons and the group stood before the dead man.

"It appears you were doing your job," Tanner said to the night watchman.

"Do you recognize this man?" Tanner asked Pat Taggart, who had walked up as he turned the body over.

Taggart chuckled softly. "Yeah, I recognize him. Look at his left hand. This is Three Fingers Joe George."

There was a silence between the two men as they stared down at the body of the man on the ground. Taggart looked at the crowd of men milling, talking, some out of the sides of their mouths as they watched the sheriff.

"When there's a killing, there's no way to go back. It's done," Taggart said to everyone and no one. "Joe George Starr's troubles are over."

The murmuring of the milling crowd was but noise, with no meaning other than a stark realization that a life had been taken. It was a life that, but an hour earlier, had walked and breathed.

Pat Taggart was walking to the livery as Sheriff Tanner approached out of the shadows.

"You can stay over to the jail."

As the two men walked down the hill, there was a weariness between them both. The milling crowd was breaking up, talking among themselves – about killing and being killed.

The next day, Pat Taggart, Arizona Ranger, rode his grey and white horse down the graded road of Unionville through the piñons and junipers that grew in the hills.

THE LAND

I journey, guided by the spirit of the land. I only stop to rest at those places of solitude which shelter and cause a quiet, a calmness. This is a land of the nativity of my perceptions. It is my starting point, a place that birthed my thoughts. This land is protected by spirits and they watch as I cross this frozen lava field before me. A slight breeze stirs the sagebrush and junipers.

Thoughts rise from the depths of my mind like crystal orbs of dew, bursting upon the surface of my imagining. Will my bleeding feet come to rest upon the black sand of the shore of the great lake, where pelicans and cormorants glide, and cui-ui swim in the depths? My life celebrates even death here in this land of primal beginning.

THE STONES OF MOSQUITO CREEK

The wind blew steadily in gusts over the sand. It blew the fine, grey sand into long, searching fingers that snaked around stones and clumps of salt grass. As I stood watching the effects of the wind, I paused and looked back. There was the uncluttered fullness of the desert valley -- a completeness. Turning, I walked slowly to the ridge of the box canyon and stopped on the rim. Green cottonwoods below me reached deep into the sandy soil and swayed in the wind. The green was contrasted vividly with the grey and tan beneath my feet. There before me was the blue-green gemstone, with its placid, even surface. To my right were the sparkling silver slivers of Mosquito Creek. It was then that a cricket chirped and spoke.

"You walk with gasping breath and faltering steps upon the stones and struggle into the brassy sun. Will you be charred or purified? Will you become an ember or burnished gold?"

WHISPERINGS FROM A TWILIGHT BREEZE

While hiking in the mountains, I had stopped to rest, when, suddenly, I heard a voice speaking to me. I was so stunned, my breath choked in my throat. The voice seemed to come from nowhere and everywhere at once.

"Who are you?" I asked.

"We are spirits – that is, if you were wondering what type of creatures we are. This land in which we live is inhabited by many fantasies such as we – But what, you may ask, are we doing in this book you are writing – a book about life? But don't you see? We, too, are life. Actually, a very large part of it. Whether you admit it or not, we are the ones you come to when life weighs heavily upon you."

"The desert in which we live is a very magic place that charms your life. Who are you, you have asked? We know who we are. We know who you are and why you need us. We are not God. Think of your childhood to understand who we are. Remember the stories told by your mother, your father or whoever. I'm sure, at that time, we were real to you. We became a part of your life for a while. We made your life a joy. You had a private friend, remember? And you had a secret place, as well. We may be but illusions to you, but we have been around for a very long time. We will be here longer than the moon, longer than you, my friend."

As quickly as the voice had come to me, there was

stillness once more. Had I dreamed this or was I suffering from heat stroke? The words linger clearly in my mind and do not dissolve, as in a dream. I know what I heard – there's no denying it. There's no more to add.

A GHOST TOWN IS NOT A GHOST TOWN, BUT ONLY A SHADOW

Stopping by the shell of a home in an old mining camp, I paused by the weathered wood and bricks that had once been a home. The wood was as hard as stone from the many years of buffeting by the elements in east central Nevada. I ran my fingers lightly over the wind-smoothed surfaces. As I looked at the remains of this old home, a yellow jacket seemed to hang suspended where the wall and what was left of the roof met. It bounced gently on the air, pulled by invisible strings like a marionette. The strings would jerk and it would bounce again. The yellow jacket seemed to be looking for a way into the mortar of the wall of bricks. As the insect bounced, it found the crack in the mortar it remembered was there and entered it. Its wings caught the sunlight which flickered upon its back, a momentary rainbow of color. Then it vanished.

A ghost town is a misnomer. How can the place be a ghost with this little creature so much at home there?

A Desert Litany

If a person sleeps out in the desert with only the stars to light the night, if he listens, a voice may come and whisper a secret or a truth.

Your salvation is in the wet, heavy wind that blows through the sagebrush valleys.

Your help is in the cry of the hawk that glides on the summer air above the plateau.

Your protection is in the ancient stones that time has covered with green, brown and grey lichens.

Your path to solace is in the tracks the lizard makes in the sand.

Your still waters are pools of steaming sulfur that are the essence of the earth who bore you.

Your valley of death is a valley of life, where death and life become one.

Your dreams of contentment are visions that speak and are cloaked in stardust.

THE BLOOD LETTING

He sat among the rocks that had been thrown up from the center of the earth eons ago. They were now covered with lichens. He sat with his gun gripped between his knees, with his hands tucked under his arms, hoping to get the blood circulating into his fingers. The exhaustion of the climb is what had brought him to the shelter of these stones. He sat, blowing into his hands, and then he placed them again under his arms. The wind whistled through the cracks and ridges of the rocks as he looked about this side of Peavine Mountain. The valley that he had left earlier in the morning lay far below him. The sparse green of the trees there had given up the effort to reach up the mountain. They climbed only to the low hills below him. He huddled the gun closer, as if the blue metal and polished wood could warm him. No thoughts crossed his mind. He simply sat. Clouds of steam from his nostrils surrounded him. A small bird flitted from stone to stone and then to a thorn bush. Raising the .22 to his shoulder, he watched as the bird hopped on the bead at the end of his gun barrel. Rising stiffly, using the rifle as a help, he walked to the thorn bush. The little bird lay in the crotch of three branches. Blood oozed on one branch and one was shattered where the bullet had entered. He held the bird in his hand. It's life slipped between his fingers and soaked into the sand. It left small, dark holes that looked like burn marks. He placed the bird where it has fallen and turned and walked down the mountain. Salty tears cut paths into his dusty face. A cold wind entered him and froze his soul.

SPIRIT OF THE LAND

There is a spirit of the land, one who lives in the mountains, the streams, the tan desert hills and the blinding alkali flats. One whose abode is in the piñon groves and the endless valleys of sagebrush that reach into eternity.

When I have walked the sandy desert in the searing heat of midday or beneath the massed stars of the night sky, seeking answers, it is only myself that I discover.

THE TUNNEL – SOUTHERN UTAH

I came to the job on the tunnel after the project had been underway for almost a year. I knew no one and no one knew me. For about a month I was concerned only about my wages. When I returned home, it was just about my wife and I together, since we had been married only a few months.

One day, an incident occurred that cut an already established thought path in my life a whole lot deeper. Though many years now in the past, this incident still sends shock waves rippling in my mind. It has held my thoughts like an almost divine commission – that of extending kindness and the effort to understand another to the utmost of my ability. Jesus accepted the unacceptable and loved the unloved. This incident would solidify this example for me.

The sun blazed down on our sunburned necks and the aches in our bodies had long ago given way to muscles like iron straps. Our dust covered faces were crossed and re-crossed with streams of sweat. Our metal helmets weighed like lead on our heads. Five days a week, we worked laying railroad ties and rails or shoveling blasted rock down a cliff from the mouth of the mountain, where men worked like moles in a half-light of dust, dynamite fumes and sometimes, darkness.

The respite of our midday meal meant time to joke or lie in whatever shade was available. I knew no one, so I spoke very little, other than to offer a morning greeting. One day, it seemed like a day for talking. My companion was an exceptionally dark man of Mexican heritage. His crooked teeth were very white when he smiled. His name is now long forgotten. His working life had been spent as a hard rock miner, a laborer and a crop picker. He seemed to have an inborn sense of awareness about his life and his place in it. I viewed him as a man of perception.

One day, as we sat eating our lunches, with no warning of the coming statement, he said to me,

"Tell me. You seem to have no concern with eating,

talking or working along side a Chicano. Why is that?"

I was amazed. Reassuring him that my prejudices ran along individual lines, not racial ones, I tried to state my feelings as clearly as I could. We soon returned to our work and did not mention the subject again.

About a week later, I received a knock at my door. It was my acquaintance from work, with some of our fellow laborers. I invited them in and he came directly to the point of his visit. His family lived half way to Salt Lake City, in the town of Price, and he wanted to bring them to Moab, where he was living.

Uranium had been discovered, as well as oil deposits, along with the world's largest potash deposit – all of which had turned Moab into a boomtown. It was no longer a sleepy little Mormon outpost. Construction crews were frantically working to create housing.

"Where do you live now, that you can't have your wife and children?" I asked.

He paused and there was dead silence in the room.

"I live in a tool shed. I sleep on a seat from a car. I have no running water, only an outhouse. I pay $50 per week for that."

I was stunned.

Lord, have mercy on such as these.

Life was tough in Moab. Working in the tunnel presented many dangers.

Among them were rocks falling from the ceiling of areas that had been newly blasted out. Had I not been wearing a helmet, I would have been killed when a rock as big as a dinner plate fell and hit my helmet. As it was, it felled me and laid me out on the ground.

One incident magnified the dangers for all of us. It was well known that a man would be instantly fired from the job if it was noticed that he was carrying a pack of cigarettes in his shirt pocket. We were employed in what was known as a high danger area. Under no circumstances was an open flame allowed anywhere inside the tunnel.

One night, my wife and I were at home and suddenly, a huge boom echoed and re-echoed from the direction of the tunnel. We all knew that there had been an explosion of some kind. On the following day, everyone learned that a woman had lost both a husband and a son in the explosion. The only physical remains that were ever found were the two hard hats and one boot with a foot still in it.

The consensus of opinion was that one or both of the men had lit a cigarette.

SILENCE

The desert is quiet as the sun begins its climb. The wind moves with a sigh.

CANYON LANDS

I was standing not far from Dead Horse Point near Arches National Monument in Southern Utah. Around me, the towering rock thrust and jutted upward out of the earth. A feeling of suspense, something indefinite, held me to this spot. Brick red cliffs and pinnacles looked down on me from heights far above the uppermost tier of my imagination.

SMOKE CREEK DESERT

I walked alone with my memories into the heart of the Smoke Creek Desert. The spirits of the ones who once lived here appeared. They didn't speak but hung as if by nails on the blue expanse of the sky. The strength of the desert has allowed my soul to listen and to see.

Who is it that knows where the mystery of the ancient past lies hidden? Who knows the secrets of the people who once lived upon this earth and now reside in song or myth? Who can speak of the intangible something that binds a people to a place? It is a bond that no tongue can accurately name with a certainty.

WANDERING

Inill-ah-ah-doo-ii is the Achomawi word for one who has "gone wandering." This describes both my own travels across the country and the restlessness in my soul. My life is an ephemeral illusion, in perpetual transformation.

HEAT

The sun has locked up the land with dryness and it cracks open. The heat makes the land shimmer in this light and the horizon dissolves in the line of earth and sky. There are few details – only the mountains and the openness of the desert's pale tints. The wind blows it forever clean.

THOUGHTS ON THE FIRST ONES

I've thought often of the First Ones, The People of the land and what it was like before the first invaders arrived. The words of The People tell it clearly – how their villages sprouted near the waterways and how the land gave willingly. The smoke from the fires became the web of imagination. Imagination took form from the tales of the before time. Imagination became exquisite baskets, cradleboards and winnowing trays. And so The People lived, generation upon generation in this desert, this beautiful and mysterious place of spirits. The People remained. They remain yet.

THE PATH OF THE MOON

While camping at Pyramid Lake one night, I watched the moon rise slowly from behind the black mountains. It seemed to be a light hole in the sky behind the thin, scattered clouds. As the moon started following the path where the day had gone, it laid a path across the waters of the lake, beckoning me. When my ashes are placed into this lake, will my soul travel up this path to the moon and beyond?

BELMONT, NEVADA

Scorching in the summer sun and shriveling in the winter cold, the old buildings crumble. The town is dead.

THE SIERRAS

Often, as a child, I would pause for an instant to stare up at the Sierras. Their blue and white immensity would someday symbolize for me all of my wondering. One thing I've come to realize – I feel my spirit at times is as faded as my Levi's.

THE CAIRN

I followed a path that led and opened to me up the gradual inclined slope of crumbling granite and lava. Around me was the natural separation of the distributed, life hoarding sagebrush. I paused before the ragged edge of the mountain. From this location, it appeared as a plateau. I climbed to the summit. Walking to the edge of the cliff face, there before me was a pile of stones, precisely piled in a tapering cone. I picked up a stone at my feet, turned it in my hand and placed it on the pile. I thought of the Buddhist monks of Tibet who do the same thing in their peregrinations through those mountains of hidden secrets.

METAPHOR

A desert is a fairly simple thing to understand. It is a metaphor for life, where one's awareness is measured in space and time.

The Portal

The sun was turning the Santa Catalina Mountains fiery orange, pink and then violet – as the shadows spread slowly across the expanse of the valley of the Santa Cruz River. Lights from the city of Tucson began to twinkle on.

My Yoeme friend, who had been sitting with me in our patio, had told me on other occasions, stories of his family, both in Arizona and in the state of Sonora, Mexico. He told of his grandfather, who had ridden with Pancho Villa in the Revolution, and how his family had crossed into the United States after the fighting had ceased.

On this particular evening, as the stars began filling the night sky, our conversation turned to more esoteric subjects. I mentioned that I had recently read a book by the well-known writer, Louis L'Amour, on the subject of portals into other dimensions. I asked my friend if he had ever heard anything about this subject.

"Oh, yes," he replied. "I was told by an elder in my family about two portals here in this area."

Without directly asking him, I waited for him to continue if that was his intention.

"A number of years ago in our village," he began, "an elder who was a contemporary of my grandpa, was the last of his generation still alive in the village. He had no family of his age or any friends. All of them had passed on – he was the last."

"This man," my friend continued, "spoke only our Yaqui language, although he could understand Spanish to some extent. He knew no English. The young children in the village attended the public schools where English was the only language being taught. Some of the children still understood the Yaqui language that was still spoken in their homes, but they did not use it in public."

My friend paused in his narration, sipping from the coffee cup he held in his hands. It seemed he was either debating with himself as to whether to continue, or perhaps, he was searching for words.

Setting his cup on the table, he turned to me and said, "I must be careful what I say to you. Although you are my friend, I am not at liberty to speak openly – I can say only so much. I hope you understand."

I told him he could say whatever he felt he should say, and not to worry about anything.

"Thank you," my friend said. "This elder's life was being made miserable by the young boys in the village. They mocked him if they saw him out and about – or they threw stones at his house. Some of the boys even called him a witch."

"This elder had a nephew who ran errands for his uncle and who looked in on him periodically. One day, the old man asked his nephew to take him out into the desert, out beyond Old Tucson Studios into the Altar Valley and clear across to the far mountains. He told his nephew he wanted to be alone to breathe the air away from the village and feel the spirit of the desert. This the nephew did, telling the old man he would return in a few hours to drive him back to his home."

"When the nephew returned to the exact spot where he had left his uncle, the old man was not there waiting for him. The nephew parked his truck. Seeing the old man's footprints in the sand, he followed them. He walked quite a ways up into the foothills. Suddenly, the footprints stopped. The nephew searched the whole area. He even returned with friends who helped in the search. The old man was never seen again."

"That's quite a story," I said to my friend. "So, you believe he entered a portal into another dimension," I asked.

"Yes," my friend said. "I was told that the portals in this area sometimes move from place to place. I can tell you no more."

We both sat without speaking. The moon slowly rose in the east and the stars filled the sky.

A LIFE FORCE

In my wandering in the desert, far from any other person, I have found that a life force (I call it a spirit) exists and frequently manifests itself. This spirit becomes noticeable for those who seek it, because all else is absent. In the presence of this spirit, my mind becomes empty. As I pick my way through my own debris, the skeleton of a cottontail rabbit bleaches on the sand and I am aware that life is a finite resource and only renewed in death.

IDENTITY

I am once more standing in this living, yet frozen in time spot, in the great northern desert of my childhood. An avalanche of memories, loosened by the jolt of the sun, begins to sweep away the current reality I have been living. How many of my memories define my identity?

THE SUN

The sun, which has been shining on the mountain before me, now comes blasting on to my head from behind a scattering of ephemeral clouds and out onto the valley beyond me. The refracted light hangs the far mountains in a shimmering curtain of air. Times in the past, I watched storms pass through those mountains. This spot, really no different from any other place on this desert, has always held my spirit. I've always returned to it, if only in my mind. I sometimes feel my life really began here.

THE BOULDER

Over the years, I've noticed an indestructible sameness in the desert, a place where the natural changes are so minute as to be nearly imperceptible. The desert is an ecological niche unique in the evolutionary cycles of the planet, and people respond to it intensely – there's no ambivalence.

To most, the desert is a place of fear. To some, it is a sanctuary of serenity. To all who come, it is a place of awe. This is a place where a person must come to terms with himself. I've spent years wandering in this desert. One spring day, I was in a nameless valley of sagebrush and rock outcrops, with the hills around me dotted with piñons. I paused beside a large boulder to rest for a spell. But long after the need to pause had passed, I felt held there by the solitude of the place. Leaning back upon a large stone, I took out my pipe and felt myself melding with my surroundings. I began to meditate upon the reflections of meanings. I've learned to listen, especially when I'm in the desert, and to listen with my mind open, with no desires, hopes or plans. I've learned to listen to the voice of silence, to the echoes of all that may be around me.

The image of an abandoned claim marker that I had walked passed a few miles back returned to my mind, and so also a piece of worked obsidian that I held in my shirt pocket. What had these people thought out here? How had they faired?

A desert landscape, more than any other I have found, forces the mind to question what is real – contemplating how the bizarre craziness of mankind's modern technology seems artificial and transient. Perhaps it is because the desert is so still and, in a way, empty of all but the essentials. Whatever is heard or whatever one sees is perceived with a sincere clarity.

Sitting on the boulder I had been resting on, I noticed a column of small black ants in their unwavering single file march to or from some destination known only to themselves. I saw my own life as a series of wanderings, though perhaps not as uniformly true as those of the ants near me. The goal of my peregrinations has always been for personal growth. I've held the place I happen to be in as sacred or holy ground. In so doing, the place has responded to me. My migrations have been my education.

The people I've met over the years have come from all stations in life and they have shared their diversity, their richness or their poverty, and I have been enriched and rewarded by having their lives touch mine.

I walked from the boulder out onto and then beyond the barren salt pan, the far mountains yet shimmering on a curtain of air, floating in the hot, brassy sky like a fairy castle. The shining mirage lakes appeared and then dissolved back into the earth. The mountains settled back into their original places and I walked on.

IN THE BABOQUIVARI MOUNTAINS

Creosote, mesquite and smoke trees stand rooted deeply where marks carved on a basalt cliff face weather and darken. Echoes of a flute and a drum drift on the air. Spirits dance in the semi-darkness and log bon fires reach upward to the Pleiades and the Dog Star.

SAN XAVIER DEL BAC

Thoughts ebb and flow around your mind at San Xavier. The sightless eyes of the Santos seem to follow my steps. Rusty, joyful ringing issues from the bell tower and angelic voices of a children's choir sing a hymn to San Francisco Xavier.

Since time began, the sun has embraced this land called Bac "where the waters come together." A deep peace long ago settled on this land. I know. I feel it.

THE SANTA CRUZ RIVER VALLEY

The mountains are torn from tan paper and are glued to a blue gossamer background. Feathery palo verde trees and fuzzy cholla crowd the foreground.

COYOTE

The exploits of Coyote, "who once lived here," are well documented. He's always been spoken of as living in the past, not the present. To many, he's only a myth. But Coyote still lives. His trickery, perhaps more subtle now, is yet very evident, as is his sometime cruelty. Coyote can show you both great beauty and at the same time, frustration to the point of despair. The essence of Coyote is the essence of the desert.

HIDDEN MEANINGS

The Sonoran Desert has begun to open to me all of its hidden meanings and treasures: the bones of a jack rabbit, a woodpecker burrowing in a saguaro, a pottery shard. The cry of a hawk, silhouetted on a palo verde tree, brings a pause and the wind stirs the mesquite near me. The hawk takes flight and the wind blows again and half a mile is covered in three seconds.

The Santa Catalina Mountains loom in the back of my mind, somewhere on the horizon, rooted to the core of the earth -- quiet, impassive, but in the corner of my eye, in my peripheral vision.

A barrel cactus, three feet high and over one hundred years old, spirals with the sun and dead blooms from last season hang on its thorns – crucified, beauty will be reborn. A wash cuts a swath in the sand where delicate, purple and yellow flowers pause and bloom for the season along its banks. A spider's web clings to waiting moss and time etches lines in the stones.

WATCHING AND LISTENING

While standing this evening in my small patio, the wind is blowing hard and dust flies across the Santa Cruz River Valley. The mountains have been hidden since sundown and the air is thick – no stars are to be seen. Coyotes and desert big horn sheep, as well as bobcats, range the Santa Catalina Mountains. Rabbits and squirrels must be wary of all sounds. Was that the wind or death on four feet? I know spirits are up there as well. I feel their solemn, steady gaze while hiking. Resting near an old saguaro once, I saw a vision of an old man, sitting on a rock, his long grey hair streaming from his head. He was staring down into the valley below. He hummed the ancient creation hymn of the Tohono O'odham. The grit in my eyes burned.

The Catalinas are a screen that hides secrets and wonders deep within the shadowy folds of grey and blue. I may find answers someday. The beauty and awe, the mystery of the Pimeria Alta will sift into my heart and mind and my life will be overcome by the strength of the desert.

One day I sat far above the valley, on a gravel slope. A sentinel quail watched me warily, ready to cry a warning to the small flock down under a stand of palo verde and brittlebush. The sun was bright in the crystal air. A haze in the valley gathered at the base of the far foothills. The saguaros held their places in the earth, noting the centuries. I sat, not so much for rest, as for my throbbing leg. The band of quail moved further down the slope, which dropped sharply away. Shadows were sharp edged and the palo verde and the brittlebush gave a hint of softness and a tender beauty to the contrasting jagged boulders and fractures in the earth. On a ridge below and across from me, cut through by an arroyo, stood the soul of the mountain. I had been noticed and watched for some time.

As I sat on the slope, enjoying the beauty and serenity around me, I saw one of the boulders move. The large brown body was as brown as the boulders around me. I thought that it was the heat or the sun playing tricks. It was no trick. It was no rock. It was an old stone ram, the ancient symbol of the desert. My breath barely moved from my body. My tongue was as dry as a dead leaf.

The ram stopped and turned to look up at me with yellow eyes gleaming and flecked with gold, shimmering like amber. His moist nose flexed and flared for some scent of danger. He did not leap and run but turned and walked slowly a narrow rock ledge and then turned and looked at me once more. He stood beside a saguaro and gazed with golden eyes.

As he moved away, the sun turned his body to polished gold and he bristled with rays of brightness. The sun seemed to concentrate on a spot between the ram's fore legs, like a disc of brilliance, a medallion of honor and glory. Walking slowly to a bend in the ridge, he glanced once more across the arroyo and vanished into the heated silence.

THE SUN DANCE, BIG MOUNTAIN

Standing beneath the arbor, I looked at my friend. His pain was etched upon his face like time lines upon a rock. He moved calmly to the rhythm of the drum, his feet barely lifting. Has it been four days or four thousand years that you have hung skewered to the sacred tree of life?

One will was joined with many and a voice was sent in silent suffering, as life was renewed. He prayed his supplications – that were escaping between dry and cracking lips. His eyes have glazed and darkened to the piercing point of light that has cut him to his soul.

The same eye that stared down at you, stared at me, that same ancient spirit. Our hearts and the hearts of all creation, merged to the unifying beat of the drum. The ancient and ancestral chants, the voice of the earth, unite and cover the tracks of the bear and the flight of the butterfly. The red tailed hawk cries out --

"They suffer for us, their relations."

PASCUA PUEBLO DURING LENT

The breeze gave rise to dust that swirled in eddies, and columns of sparks spiraled upward from great bon fires of mesquite logs. Small groups of people clustered and talked in faint whispers. Some sat staring into the night. The opened capilla threw light into the blackness. Children ran in and out with shouts and a lank mongrel sauntered in to lie in the broad aisle of packed earth before the altar.

The dust mingled with the smell of the fragrant smoke, the food stalls and the people. It became the matrix that glued the spirit of the people into a cohesive whole. Participants and visitors were wrapped in an aura of antiquity.

At a right angle to the capilla, a long row of glowing coals at their feet, sat musicians preparing their instruments. Suddenly, at a seemingly unspoken moment, the soft music drifted on the night air. It was at first unnoticed, but it permeated in a soft, throbbing heartbeat. Everyone in their own time became aware of the strains of the music. Hearts and heads turned to the sound. The Matachines were preparing to dance their prayers. Their tasseled hats fluttered in the wind. The rattles that they carried kept time to the violins and the harp. Lent in Old Pascua was a time to reflect.

DREADFUL BEAUTY

The Sonoran Desert is at once beautiful and dreadful. It holds life and death in the same hand. The hot wind that blows across the immeasurable solitude is like a fever burning. The desert can make a person crazy and the madness of the man walking the wide land can lead him to be a lover of the desert forever. The madness comes from the silence, a vast desolation where far mountains enclose emptiness. It is a sprawling wilderness of tenuous life and peril. It is a land of horizons as varied as hopes. It can mirror success as well as failure.

The broken land will part and close behind you and the wind will whistle in your ears. Mirages flood the land before you and cat claw bushes tear your flesh, but you feel no pain. The Sonoran Desert is luxuriant with mesquite, cholla, prickly pear cactus, animals and reptiles and the remains of the ancient ones. The small villages of the people are miles apart in the solitude of who they are.

MEETING COYOTE THE TRICKSTER FACE TO FACE

I was standing in a picnic shelter as the sun began its descent behind blue and purple mountains. Out of the corner of my eye, I detected movement. A coyote was chasing a jackrabbit.

Coyote was a massive, handsome male and he quickly seemed to loose interest in the chase. He loped silently through the brush, his nose to the ground. His gate did not slacken until he was about twenty feet from me. Then he stopped and looked at me with yellow eyes. He stood for some minutes, neither afraid nor challenging, then turned and walked back down the gentle slope on which I stood. He turned once to look over his shoulder at me. Was he grinning?

CASA GRANDE MONUMENT

A thousand years of wind blows around crumbling foundations of melting adobe bricks, near where multi-colored corn, the fat of life, grew in rows. Lifeblood no longer flows in the hand dug, bleeding ditches, grown over now with creosote and mesquite. I can see traces of a hand on the mud wall and there, a shattered fragment, a broken shard burnished by wind and rain. Your days have unraveled and lie tangled and broken in the cotton blossom fragrance wafting on a thousand years of wind.

BABOQUIVARI PEAK

The Elder Brother, I'itoi, the hero, once walked in this desert and these mountains -- I'itoi, the monster slayer, the man in the maze, the shining one. Traces of his passing are evidenced in the deep shadows cutting blue and purple into the living mountains and into the silent desert.

The top of his mountain glows magenta as clouds lift long enough to let the setting sun shine upon it. The whole mass of the mountains breathes with life as the color goes from pink to orange. The light glows and reflects into the air around me and the mountains tremble and hold me in a trance. These mountains unfold with movement and ancient power that mingles with the dying rays of the sun.

SUMMER SOLSTICE AT ZODIAC RIDGE

Dust swirled in clouds as I drove down a dirt road. My headlights were gyrating with the hill's contours. When I finally pulled off the road and parked in the mesquite and cholla, the silence of the desert settled rapidly around me. Standing in the pre-dawn blackness, I stared in amazement at what I felt was a portent, which burned blue in the sky, flames wafting from it. I thought it was a meteor, but when it struck the mountain before me in complete silence, I knew this could only be one thing: a spirit manifestation. This didn't fit with even my many years of wandering in the lonely places of the mountains and deserts. I was stunned, speechless.

The sun would soon show from beyond the high mountains to the east, which loomed black as I walked toward the oval of standing stones overgrown in yucca and ephedra. I stood and waited for the sun.

When the sun's face began to crest the far ridges, shimmering light moved as dancing figures. I did not move until the sun had cleared and began its course across the sky.

For thousands of years, the ancient ones had come here to this place of healing and rejuvenation. I had been told that a village once stood a few miles away near where the light had hit the mountain when I arrived. The ones who were responsible for maintaining this sacred healing place had occupied this village.

Looking to where the sun had risen above the mountains, a shrine showed clearly upon the far ridge, placed by the ancient ones of this land. It was from behind this cairn that the sun came up. The hoary age of this place was evident. The sun now rose slightly to the right of this rock pile on the summit, rather than directly behind it. The earth's precession established the deviation to be about 4,000 years off from the center of the shrine.

I experienced that day what many in the ages past have also witnessed. Was it a few days ago or centuries ago, that I walked the sacred oval of standing stones and viewed the sun's rise behind the cairn on the distant mountain. I stepped back, through long gone days, and yet, I am here. There is no past, no future, no space, no time in this place, only the eternal now.

MORNING

It was yet night in the folds of the mountains and the darkness was reluctant to relinquish its hidden secrets to the searching, fast approaching day. The sun increased its intensity and its light once more dispersed the stars. Cactus wrens called from a creosote bush and a faint breeze moved the leaves on a low growing mesquite tree. Day had now arrived in the Sonoran Desert.

STANDING STONES

In the southwest, history is written on the standing stones that the First Ones carved, within the rock shelters that they lived in, on the sacred shrines that they placed on hills or near watercourses. Their spiritual resources were mined from the desert heat, the wind in the creosote, the mountains and the river valleys. History here is not dead or long gone. It is the heartbeat of experience. It is a past/present that will return to life from its cyclical dormancy. History is the realm of legends and myths. Beyond history lies the world of the Tohono O'odham. It is a land less dreamlike than real. It is a land of spirit and substance.

A MAN OF MYSTERY

The desert breeds people that city dwellers can never understand. This is especially true of native people who live in the Sonoran Desert or other areas far from the influences of the dominant society. Their whole mindset appears to be at odds with what urbanites would term "normal." Occasionally, city life can be a curiosity for them,

I suppose. From out of the reservation, a brave soul will wander into the maze. I once knew a man who was, in his own way, one of the most powerful yet singularly strange people I've ever known.

This man's power was a spiritual force imbued by a lifetime of living in reservation isolation. His traditional elders were a major influence on him, as well. This, I am sure of. His antecedents also instilled within him a wisdom from countless ages of life from the deserts and mountains of Arizona: he was Yavapai/Apache and Akimel O'odham.

At all hours of the day or night, I could expect a knock at our door. There he would be, a huge grin on his face. I never asked him why he always wore a Rastafarian T-shirt with Bob Marley's image on it. That really wasn't any of my business. He had a few quirks that were intimidating to most people, although he never gave me the impression that he was in any way malevolent. He simply had his own ways about him. But, don't we all?

The monsoon had come almost with a vengeance. The humidity was high, like a sauna. The moisture hung in the air when it was not coming down in buckets. Through the rain came my friend, water dripping from his hair that hung to his shoulders.

"Got any coffee?" he asked. He was totally comfortable in our home.

"Let's drive up Mount Lemmon and get out of the heat," I suggested.

"Sounds good to me," he replied.

The Catalina Highway is a spectacular drive. Saguaros climb the foothills as the valley falls behind you.

The ecological zones are prominently visible as the road climbs and turns ever higher. The Catalinas are called Sky Islands as they rise steeply from the desert floor into the cool ponderosa forests, where black bears and mountain lions roam in the shadows. To the Tohono O'odham, who are one of the indigenous people of southern Arizona, Mount Lemmon is known as Babat Duag, Frog Mountain.

Summer Haven is a respite for the people of Tucson. There are cafes, gift shops, summer homes and even a ski lift – the furthest south in the country. This is a beautiful spot.

Driving up the mountain, thunder roared and lightning flashed in long, snaking streaks, from horizon to horizon, across the sky. The clouds had settled all about us. The temperature was at least 40 degrees cooler.

We sat on the deck of a favorite establishment, drinking coffee and eating chocolate chip cookies, enjoying the time together. My friend never went anywhere without his backpack. It lay beside him on the floor.

"On the way back," he began, "let's stop somewhere and smoke the pipe."

When and where he became acquainted with the tradition of the Sacred Pipe Ceremony, I never knew. This is a ceremony from the People of the Great Plains. But I've always felt that this coming together in a spirit of peace and camaraderie is what binds people together in friendship.

Driving down the mountain, the weather had increased in intensity. Rain was falling heavily in the valley. We could see it through the breaks in the clouds. The mist at this elevation was almost like a solid wall. I pulled off to the side of the road. A spur of the mountain rose for 500 feet or so to the right of us. My friend said we were to climb to the top of this spur for our ceremony.

"This is going to be something," I said to myself.

He charged up the rocks like a mountain goat. I followed at my own pace. When I got to where he was sitting, I couldn't believe where we were. The top of the spur was just a little bigger than a manhole cover. My wife had followed slowly up the climb, wearing flip-flops. I don't know how she made it, but she did.

There we sat on the top of this solid rock pinnacle. The drop off was at least a thousand feet on three sides of us. Thunder was crashing so loudly around us that we could not hear each other speak. My friend filled his pipe as if nothing was more natural. Sulfur smell filled the air, held by low, swiftly moving clouds. Lightning, blindingly bright, flashed all around us. When he put the match to the pipe, a crack of thunder, louder than any I've ever heard, resounded directly over us. The flashing lightning seemed to be only a few feet from us.

We smoked the pipe, said our prayers and returned to the car.

MONSOON SEASON

When the monsoon rains arrive in the Sonoran Desert, the entire country is transformed. The rains fall in a solid wall and the wind is a force to reckon with. The storms are a major blessing in the desert. Life, the very essence of being, is renewed. But the blessing is two-sided. A genuine danger hangs about the edges. A few years ago, a catastrophe occurred that still burdens the hearts of many people.

The Santa Cruz River, which, up to about 75 years ago, ran flowing all year, is now as dry as the floor of the desert. When the full force of the monsoon brings flash floods into the normally dry washes feeding the dry riverbed, the water flows in a brown torrent. It brings with it all that was in the way. It is not unusual to see the bloated corpse of a cow, old tires, household refuse – all swirling in the khaki colored water.

The riverbed flows along the eastern edge of the O'odham Reservation for a few miles. One summer, as the river crested in this area, some children ran along the bank. Suddenly, earth, which had been undercut by the waters, gave way. The children were swept away. They were never found. They were buried beneath the earth. Their loss is still mourned in the community.

MONSOON STUPIDITY

Arizona has enacted what they call "The Stupid Motorist Law." A fine is levied against anyone who has to be rescued, and they also have to pay for the cost of the rescue. Any roadway that passes through a normally dry wash has a clearly posted sign in both directions with a printed warning not to enter when flooded. Anyone stupid enough to try and cross during the full force of a flash flood, is risking death. But there are always those who try.

I knew a man who gave every impression of being in full control of his senses. He was a man of above average intelligence. But one day, he gave me cause to wonder.

He was coming home along a three-mile dirt road, which was crossed by a number of normally dry washes. As everyone in this area knows, during the monsoon season, nothing is taken for granted. This man was driving a jeep similar to a four-wheel drive military vehicle. He must have thought this conveyance was indestructible. A microburst of intense rain had hit about half way down the road and visibility became nonexistent. Instead of stopping when the storm hit, he continued to inch along the road. He attempted to ford a wash that cut across the road in front of him.

Why this man is still among the living is a miracle known only to God Almighty. The force of the water, which hit the jeep when he was half way across the wash, flipped his jeep over, as if it was a tin can. He was able to climb out the passenger side door and walk home.

The next day, the sky had cleared as if no storm had passed only 24 hours previously. He walked from his home to try and rescue his overturned vehicle. If it had not been for the aerial protruding from the sand, he would have had to look hard to find the completely buried car. One doesn't fool around with Mother Nature.

THE DESERT RAT

When I was a boy, my father knew a man who could be called a real desert rat, a man who spent more time out in the desert than he did at home. What made this man unique for me was the fact that he had learned many of the secrets of the desert and could relate stories that captured my attention.

It was after I returned from a long residence in upstate New York that I re-established contact with my father's friend. We spent a long evening drinking coffee and talking about times when he and my dad would wander off into the sagebrush.

This man had educated himself about the history of the native peoples, both the Paiutes and the Shoshones. He could identity projectile points with the classifications assigned by archaeologists. This man had one of the largest collections of projectile points of anyone in the state of Nevada at that time. His interest appeared to be almost like an addiction.

As we talked that evening, he told me some stories that, to some, would appear to be untrue or at least fantastic, almost beyond belief.

An archaeological anomaly found usually beyond the Rocky Mountains, out on the plains, has been designated by the term -- banner stone. To my knowledge, its use has never been established with satisfaction by archaeologists. Banner stones are bow tie in shape and range in size from a few inches to a couple of feet long. A hole usually has been drilled through the knot of the bow tie. Some have suggested that they were used as atl-atl weights. But one measuring two feet long could only have been used for some ceremonial purpose. My friend found one in eastern Nevada, partially buried in the sand. At the time he found it, it was the only one ever found west of the Rockies.

TSABITS

The Shoshone people tell a story about a cannibal giant named Tsabits, who ranged the area of northeastern Nevada not far from the Idaho border, near the Owyhee Mountains. According to the Shoshone, this giant was eventually subdued by their people, who came against him in a force.

In this area of the state is a small settlement called Jarbidge, which is a corruption of the giant's name. The settlement, sitting in a small valley, had a brief history of mining activity in the nineteenth century. The traditional Shoshone people will go nowhere near this valley. They say that the giant's spirit lives on. They call the whites who venture into this area crazy.

My dad's friend said that when he was up in the area, one day, as he crested a large dune, there below him, partially covered in sand, were the remains of a large human skeleton. He picked up an exposed femur and held it against his hip. This one bone was the length of his whole leg, from the top of his hip to the sand.

"This SOB must have stood about eleven feet tall," he said to me.

He had found Tsabits.

MORE FROM THE DESERT RAT

Another story he told me is almost fantastic beyond belief. But I believed him as I would believe my father. He was once again in the northern part of Nevada, wandering out among the sand dunes. There he found what he first said looked like a puddle of blue water. Walking down to it, he said he saw a sizeable handful of blue beads. The string that they had been strung on had long since turned to dust.

He said he lay flat on the sand and proceeded to collect all of the beads and carefully placed them in an envelope he had in his shirt pocket. The beads were wind and sand worn but he said he could tell they were glass trade beads.

When he returned home, he notified an archaeologist he knew from the University and an appointment was arranged. On the appointed day, he said he poured the beads on the professor's desk. The professor stared at them and said not a word. Rather, he went to a bookcase, drew forth a volume and turned to a page with a color photograph. There, in vivid color, was a photo of trade beads found in the Caribbean that had been brought from Spain by Columbus. The beads my friend had found were identical.

How these beads had traveled from hand to hand all the way to this spot is once more one of the greatest mysteries of the desert.

I have no idea what happened to my friend's collection of artifacts after his death. I no longer lived in Nevada and was not informed of his passing until many years later.

ANOTHER TALE FROM THE DESERT RAT

North and a little east lies the dry lakebed of the once sparkling Winnemucca Lake. This lake was fed as Pyramid Lake is still fed by the Truckee River. From high in the Sierras, this river flows down from Lake Tahoe, or Lake Bigler (as it was once known). Early in the twentieth century, the Newland's Reclamation Project went into effect. Water was redirected out to the Fallon area for agricultural development. Winnemucca Lake went dry. During exceptional wet winters, the lake would glistened with a thin sheet of moisture, never more than just a few inches of water. For all practical purposes, Winnemucca Lake was dry, dead.

Back in the eighteen hundreds, when the lake received a continuous flow from the river, it held a substantial amount of water. The beach levels can still be seen in the surrounding hills like rings in a bathtub.

A number of years ago, a cache of trapper's tools and fishing gear was found in a rock shelter above the shore. There is plenty of evidence to show that, in the past, the shore was lined with willows in places, which provided refuge for the mink and muskrat populations that also abounded in the area.

Knowing that trappers as well as fishermen once haunted the now dry lake, my dad's friend set out to find whatever might be left from their endeavors.

He told me as we sat drinking coffee at his kitchen table, that in the past, he had found fish hooks and other pieces of equipment on the dry lakebed. On this particular day, he said that a shiny glint had caught his eye. When he walked down to pick it up, at first, he thought it was a quarter – George Washington's face was on one side. Lettered around the edge of the opposite side of the coin were the words 'One Half A Cent." In the middle of the coin was the name of an establishment in Tonopah, Nevada.

When he returned home a few days later, he did some historical research and found out just what the establishment was – a bawdy house. Roaring with laughter, he slapped his hand hard on the table, jolting the coffee mugs.

"What the hell can you get in a cat house for half a cent?"

I never was able to understand what George Washington had to do with a brothel, either.

THE WALK FOR LIFE

During the decade of the eighties, and then picking up momentum in the nineties, the attempts being made by people fleeing their homes in Latin America had become a torrent. The civil war in Guatemala was a blood bath -- the extermination of the indigenous Maya. Many people all over Central America and Mexico were willing to make the effort to cross the length of Mexico to take whatever chances they would face in the United States. None of the border crossers were aware of the incredible brutality of the Sonoran Desert for anyone who did not take precautions. Death was the final destination for nearly all who attempted the trek from the US border to Tucson, Arizona in the summer. The statistics printed in the *Arizona Daily Star* or broadcast on radio and TV stations were staggering. On average, five to ten bodies a day were being discovered. They were placed in body bags and brought to the border patrol headquarters. These statistics were mind numbing for those who cared.

Incredibly, there existed for some time, a vigilante organization who patrolled the borderland, enforcing their own interpretation of the law. This group was heartless. A church in Tucson that subscribed to the sanctity of human life placed 100 gallon tanks of water spaced along the border between Mexico and Arizona. The word "agua" was painted prominently on these tanks. When church members drove out to refill these tanks, they often found them empty and riddled with bullet holes.

The statement of the vigilantes was, "Let the bastards die. They belong in their own country."

Another church denomination had recently elected a new bishop who was of Mexican heritage, for the area of southern Arizona. This person was very aware of the horrendous loss of life and, working with the church, devised a plan that was widely advertised through all of the various media, requesting people of conscience to come, regardless of religious affiliation, and join them in participating in a "Walk for Life." The reason for the walk was to bring to the awareness and attention of the community, the state and the nation, the almost insurmountable problems facing indigenous peoples fleeing their homes in Latin America. A five mile walk each way, the starting place for the walk was the sponsoring church in the center of Tucson and the destination was the largest cemetery in the city. To help everyone better understand and comprehend the suffering of those making this trek across the Sonoran Desert, the walk was held in the middle of summer, with temperatures well above one hundred degrees.

At the farthest edge of the cemetery, where no grass grew, no trees stood, away from the eyes of the city, lay a potter's field among the cholla and prickly pear cactus. There, where the creosote grew, were the graves with no names. Small white crosses stood in rows. No one had any way of knowing which country these people were from. There was no way to notify anyone.

No one arrived en masse – people came at their own pace. When my friend and I got there, the Bishop was there and a prayer was said for respite from this horrendous situation and for the families and friends of those deceased.

I knew I would have a hard time making this ten-mile walk, especially in this heat. I have a gimpy leg and a cane and I struggled. When I finally made it back and was able to take my boots off, my feet were swollen and purple and the pain was terrific. But it was small or insignificant to the pain of those who had lost their lives crossing this desert.

It has always been my way that if I say something, I stick with it – if I'm going to do something, I do it. I have a hard time with hypocrites. I believe life is sacred and should be protected at all costs. This is the way I was trying to walk my talk.

My Dakota friend, who had walked with me, turned, when we got to where we could sit in the shade, and said, "I'm proud of you, uncle."

The whole time I was walking, I kept turning in my head the phrase I had heard at the Big Mountain Sun Dance years before:

"We walk on the prayers of our ancestors."

THE DINÉ WEDDING BASKET

You might wonder why I am including a story about a wedding basket in a book about the desert. The Navajo or the Diné are a desert people. The basket is a classic example from a people who have created a tangible concept of their spiritual walk through this land. This basket expresses without words the Diné concept of Hodzo or, "to walk in beauty."

Quite a number of stores in Tucson carry arts and crafts from the Native Peoples of Arizona. Many of the stores carry fine quality, high-end merchandise. From a store owned by a friend, I purchased a Diné wedding basket.

It was shortly thereafter that a Diné friend dropped by

and I showed him my acquisition.

"Do you know what you're looking at – the design?" he asked.

My pause told him what he wanted to know.

"The white represents the dawn, the opening of the basket and it is the doorway of one's thoughts. The center white designs are the sacred mountains. Some baskets have six points, some have four. If there are six, Mount Huerfano, the doorway, and Gobernador Knob, are the sunlight opening. The red part of the basket represents the sun's rays. The black part is darkness and clouds. The edge of the basket is the Diné "roots" finished off with prayers, thoughts and values. The basket holds the life and the thoughts of The People.

What a valuable lesson, so full of beauty woven into this basket that I hold in my hands.

TEACHING

Once long ago – I don't even recall how long ago it was now – the desert opened to me a lesson, a teaching and something for which I was in need. I recall that I was sitting in the shade of a rock outcrop on a warm day, holding in my hands what appeared to be a piece of worked obsidian. It was not quite an arrow point, but it had been obviously worked. The edges were knapped uniformly.

As I looked at this piece, I gradually became aware of the spiritual essence in the heart of this worked stone. As this dawned on my thinking, I gazed around from where

I was sitting and realized that all around me – the stones shading me, the wind blowing softly, the sage brush scenting the air – all of these have an inner meaning, an inner form and a spiritual power.

SAGE BRUSH

I read recently that biologists feel they have discovered that sagebrush, *artemesia tridentata,* originated in northern Asia when the land masses were contiguous. It is not surprising that many indigenous people consider sage to be a sacred plant.

GOING WITHIN

The man had never been to the red rock country – the huge expanse of what seemed to be endless plains of undulating hills, all dotted with juniper and piñon, with pillars and monoliths jutting upward like reaching fingers. He had read often of the ones the travel books identified as Anasazi, who long ago had built impregnable villages high up in well fortified and sheltered naturally hewn caves. He was going into their lands.

He had followed the dirt track after leaving the highway a few miles to the east, and now he sat and turned off the car motor. He let the silence overtake what had been, a few minutes before, the steady sound of the car's engine. He felt an excitement about being there.

Stepping from the car and closing the door, he stood and gazed at the uncluttered sky. He felt it was the deepest blue that he had ever seen. The faint aroma of the sagebrush drifted to him and he breathed deeply of its fragrance and started walking.

As he followed the water-cut arroyo, sand leaked into his shoes, but he paid no attention, he was so filled with the wonders of this place. An hour's walking brought him to the entrance of a narrow gully cut by eons of occasional flash flood runoffs from the summer monsoon cloud bursts. The arroyo he followed led like a natural path directly into a cleft in the soaring cliffs.

The man paused to gaze up at the cliff's face, rising precipitously up toward the sky. He was overwhelmed by the stark beauty of the place.

It was when he stopped to rest in the shade, that he realized he had been following the random meanderings of the different channels that fed into the main ravine.

He had been walking for hours when, leaning back against the rock wall, he became aware of the pain in his feet. Removing his shoes and emptying the sand from them, he looked at his swollen feet. He paused and remembered reading about a man who, while walking in Death Valley, had dug deep into the sand and buried his aching, swollen feet.

As he dug, the sand was hot on his hands until he reached the cool moistness below.

"Oh God, it's hot," he said to himself, as sweat trickled from under his arms.

The wind began to blow.

"I should get back but I need to rest my feet."

The trembling leaves of the quaking aspens danced before his eyes. So, too, the gentle swaying of the tall pines on the hills about his home, now far away. The cool breeze that blew gently though the trees that he now recalled – now became the breath from hell.

He felt his mind lurch as the stinging sand, the miniscule pieces of the great cliffs that now surrounded him, stung his flesh. The breeze abated and stillness pressed in around him, holding him in a grip. He dared not move. The effort was now more than his painful feet could muster.

"Why? Always, the questions. Have I no answers?" he thought to himself.

A breath like a furnace swept through the dry channel once more, carrying stinging sand. As he asked himself why he had come here, his skin began to prickle, as if he were chilled.

He drew his feet slowly from deep in the sand and he knew he would not be able to walk any further at this time. His feet were swollen, a mottled purple. If he wanted to leave this place, he would have to crawl on his hands and knees. His tracks had been wiped away by the wind.

The wind, ah yes, the wind, once his friend, was now his enemy.

"If the wind has become my enemy, how am I able to explain this? How am I able to defend myself?"

It was painful to move his head, but he did so. Looking up, he stared at the figures and designs carved upon the rock face far above him. His eyes, lacking moisture, were struggling to focus. The figures began to dance to a rhythm he felt, but did not hear.

How long he had been sitting he could not remember. It was painful to even try to recall when he had left his car and walked into the labyrinth of channels cut into the rocks. Again, he asked himself, why? It was better when he closed his eyes against the wind and the heat.

Turning his head slightly, he looked toward the mouth of the canyon. The heat brought shimmering mirages and he wondered if, perhaps, he might be a mirage as well.

Awaking suddenly from his musing, what was it that had startled him? A stone, no larger than his fist, lay a few inches from his legs. It had not been there before – this he was sure of. He recalled a childhood thought: he had wished that he could see a stone fall from the bluff near his home onto the talus of ages -- a stone called forth by the hand of God, not by an animal or a person; a stone whose time had come to lay at the base of the bluff rather than being a part of it. He tried to laugh at his foolishness, but the only sound he could make was a feeble croak.

Other memories began to pass before his mind's eye. Once more, he saw the face of his first love. She had been unsure of love and so their love story, barely begun, had ended rapidly. The agony of their parting was, he recalled, more painful to his youthful longing, than the tortures of this oven of red, reflected stone where he sat.

He remembered standing, holding her photograph.

"I know I will never see her again."

In his memory, as he stared at her smiling face, it was as though she came alive in his hands. Her smile widened slightly. Her lips seemed to open to him as he touched her face. It was not soft flesh he touched, only the cool, smooth surface of the photo. Once more, she became a frozen image. Sighing deeply with regret, he placed the photo into the envelope she had sent and put it into a book on his shelf. He would never see her again.

The girl in the photo now seemed exceedingly remote, a love he had imagined, a creation of his heart and mind, a desire from his soul. As the heated air blew around him, he was amazed that he had even known the girl.

With a nostalgic longing, his mind now sought meanings. In truth, he knew deep within himself that they never had had anything in common except a past that they could never discuss. He saw the distance between them with clarity. It was the beginning of forgetting.

The carved figures on the stone's face above and

away from him began to dance once more. The rhythm brought another memory from long in his past – a church with organ music and people singing –

"Amazing grace, how sweet the sound, that saved a wretch like me."

"What have I been saved from? To die, here, in this lost and lonely canyon, burned by the heat of hell?"

His head dropped to his chest and he let fall a trickle of sand from his hand.

"Perhaps I will die here," he said to himself. "This is a good place to die."

Forcing a grin, the man continued, "Or will I live to see another day? I guess I should consider why I chose to drive out here. What was the reason for my first love returning to my thoughts? Was it simply to torture me in this place? These and other old thoughts must go. I only burdened my mind by holding them. What is the point?"

He raised his eyes and slowly shook his head from side to side the erase the cumbersome burden that had weighted upon his mind for years. Another thought now filled the void left by the previous images. He remembered a time when he was a young boy. He was surrounded in the playground by a group of boys from more well to do families. He felt the taunts and threats clearly once again.

"You're nothing but crap," one boy yelled in his face, his bad breath stinging the air. "How come your old man don't provide better?"

The man's father was lying in the hospital, dying, but that didn't seem to count for much. He recalled the slaps in the face and the mocking grins of his assailants.

"Yeah," he said, in whisper to no one but himself, "we were poor.

We were on the outside, but we knew, or at least we hoped, that we were people who had family and friends who loved us. Damn it to hell!"

He slammed a fist into the sand.

"Is it because of these thoughts that I am now facing that I have come to realize that I have never felt at home within society? I've always been an outsider. I've got to overcome society's contradictions that have marginalized people on the fringe. I have been saved from myself, so it seems -- saved from my own weaknesses and foolishness.

The words of the old hymn returned to his mind –

"I once was lost but now I'm found, was blind, but now I see."

"I have been lost within the maze of my passions that have held me with iron fetters. I have been blind to the warnings, the small white crosses, that have been placed before me on my life's road."

He recalled his frequent feelings of uselessness and a deep loneliness that had plagued him for years.

"The errors of my past have brought me to this point."

He wanted to weep at these thoughts that tortured him within as the wind and the heat – always the wind and the heat – tortured him from without.

Far away, a low rumble caused the man to painfully lift his head to listen. It came again. He saw a stream of water begin to flow from the high hills beyond him. As he watched, the stream became a chocolate covered torrent, fed by rivulets that increased its force, bringing rocks and small plants torn from the banks. The debris tumbled, turning and twisting, carrying dead branches. The man sat beside the rushing water. Only a few eye blinks before, there had been nothing but dry, hot, burning sand before him.

"Will this be the end, or will I now be able to return to life?"

The warm, muddy water swirled around his legs and it felt good on his swollen feet. Black spots darted before his eyes like hungry gnats. As the water swirled about his feet, he reached for and grasped a floating gourd. Placing it to his lips, he recalled another time.

He had been in his mother's kitchen. With care, he placed a watermelon on the table. He took a knife, longer than a Bowie Knife but shorter than a machete, and touched the striped skin of the melon. With an audible crack, it split in half, spewing the sweet juice like blood from the heart of an Aztec sacrifice.

Not knowing whether the gourd he held in his hand was poisoned, he sucked at the moist pulp and once more, a memory came to him. He stood as a child in a Sunday school room.

"We are reading from Isaiah," the teacher said. Opening the Bible, she read, "O God, you will keep in perfect peace those whose minds are fixed on you -- for returning and rest we shall be saved. In quietness and trust shall be our strength."

The man said to himself, "I have completely rebelled against the experiences that were forced on me by my own ignorance, my family and my society. When first I abandoned this legacy, I remember that I was overwhelmed with rage. But now, I am able to replace in its stead, an acceptance of contentment and an intriguing realization that something more exists – something more than I have ever been shown before. All I need do is to grasp it and make it my own."

When the man left the canyon, the carved figures on the cliff face no longer danced. He walked and crawled, but he had found himself. He was a traveler on an endless road who had sought and come to accept his past. He could now embrace the future.

JARBIDGE

"Look, it's been nice seeing you again. If you have any questions on your policy, you have my card. Take care of your leg. And don't let any more trees fall on you."

We waved our goodbyes and I walked around the shiny black and white eighteen- wheeler in the front yard. I thought to myself about the guts it took to be a logger and drive one of these rigs.

Pulling out of the driveway, the radio announcer stated the time was 12:13 pm and I remembered that I hadn't eaten lunch. I glanced at the brown paper bag on the seat next to me.

I have a spot that I call my own, though it's accessible to everyone -- a small pond rimmed with fir, hemlock, dogwood and pine. It's was only a short way from there and that's where I would eat.

When I shut off the ignition and walked toward the pond, the air was crisp and cool, but rather mild for this high altitude. I spotted a pile of old boards near the pond's edge. Wading through nearly knee high grasses, I sat down. I just sat for a while, letting the beauty of the Oregon woods surround and soak into my being. This, I thought, was the most peaceful spot I had ever seen. It was too late in the year for butterflies or dragonflies, but the birds circled and darted, singing their songs in a harmonious chorus. The sun reflected on the water, making golden ribbons. As I watched them play upon the water's surface, I noticed, partially hidden among the grasses growing into the water, a large rainbow trout. He looked to be the king of the whole pond. He watched every move I made and somehow, I suppose, he knew I didn't have the equipment to catch him with me. I wondered if he knew how much I would have liked to catch him. I wondered about his age; because he was so large and I realized that he was scarred by life. He had fought many battles and he had survived. Who was I to catch him? In some way, he wished to live, just as I did.

I took my lunch from the bag and threw crumbs into the water. Somehow this old king, mantled with the knowledge of time, knew they were safe. He knew that no hook was hidden in this offering.

It was late afternoon when I returned to my office to ask if any calls had come for me. As I passed through the outer office, the secretary, Miss Stevens, said, "Andy, your wife has been trying to get ahold of you all afternoon."

"Did she say what she wanted?" I asked.

"Yes. There's been a death in your family. Your nephew was killed."

"Oh, God! Did she say how it happened?"

"In an automobile accident. I'm sorry."

I walked into my boss's office and he looked up and said, "Hey, I'm sorry to hear about your nephew. If you need a few days off, you have them."

I was rather shaken at the news, so I said simply, "Thanks."

Leaving the folder of papers on his desk, I added, "Oh, by the way, here are the papers and the policy I delivered up in Wolf Creek. Look, I'm going home. I'll see you when I see you."

On the way home, I began to remember things I hadn't thought of in years. I remembered my nephew Ross's christening and how happy my brother Clayton had been. Clayton, there's one! I wonder where the hell he is? He probably doesn't even know this has happened.

I've always thought it somewhat strange that people you think you know well can keep you guessing. Who would have thought that Clayton would give up? My brother was kind of a late starter by today's standards. He had been very idealistic, or at least he had been once. He was the knight on a white horse who would save the world and right all the wrongs.

After an arduous time at a university, he graduated and became a doctor. I guess it was because of his easy-going personality that he had a large practice. Inside, he had a boiling interior. Big brother was pretty well off there for a while. His wife was the center of social functions in their town and things seemed to be going well for them. But, obviously, that wasn't the case. In one of the few letters Clayton ever wrote to me, he said he wanted to give up his practice and go to a mission hospital in South America. He confided that his wife had told him she would leave him if he did. So, for a couple of more years, he lived a lie. Then, one day, a little girl was brought in by ambulance. She had run out into the street and been struck by a truck. Clayton couldn't save her. I can only imagine what happened when the child died, because he turned and walked out and never came back.

I didn't hear from Clayton for a long while. Then, when I least expected it, I received a short note, postmarked Elko, Nevada, which stated simply, "I've come home. God bless you and your family. I wish them well – Clayton."

That was the last I'd ever heard from him.

****

The long drive was almost over, or so I thought at the time. There, on my right, were the signs advertising all the local service clubs. I'd already been passing signs cajoling tourists with the tarnished gilt of the casinos for some time. Soon I was in one of the West's last old-time towns, Elko, Nevada.

I had childhood remembrances of overhearing conversations about the fantastic hunting found here – both big game and birds – but, although I hunted both, I had never gotten over to this part of the country. Now, here I was, hunting a different game – my own brother, whom I hadn't seen in years.

My mind was anything but anticipating the thoughts of having to try and find him and tell him the news I was bringing. But someone needed to tell him, I thought, and who better than myself.

I fingered in my shirt pocket for the rumpled paper with the only address I had for him. It had been read many times – Silver Star Motel, Interstate 80, Elko, Nevada. I was on the Interstate, so it wouldn't be hard to find.

The gaiety and excitement that had made Elko the hub of Eastern Nevada for the last 100 years was mirrored in a hollow way in neon. Hanging over all the gaudy little casino hotels there were neon cowboys or billboards with Indians beating on their mouths with a tomahawk in one hand. I couldn't help but think of the beauty of the desert I had just driven through. And now, here was the feeble attempt to draw in the unlucky person, either coming into or leaving the state.

On the far outskirts of town, set back from the road, with three huge silver fuel storage tanks for neighbors on one side and railroad tracks behind, was the Silver Star Motel. Pulling onto the wide, graveled area that served as a drive and parking lot, I stopped the car at the office and got out. A pink sign buzzed and blinked by the office door. The doorbell was obviously out of order and hung out from its hole, but my knocking was soon answered.

A short, fat woman with thin black hair and a mustache stood blinking, with a cigarette in her hand. She said, "Yeah, can I help you?"

"Yes, do you have any rooms for a few nights? Your sign didn't say whether you had any vacancies or not."

Taking a drag on her cigarette, she said, "That damn thing only works half the time. My old man never seems to get around to fixing it. Yeah, I gotta room."

The cigarette had grown into a long, grey worm that hung limply from the stub as she took another long drag.

"You got business up here?" she asked as she handed me a key with the name of a hotel in Las Vegas on it.

"As a matter of fact, I do, and maybe you can help me."

I took a ballpoint pen out of my jacket pocket and signed the register card and then continued, "Do you know Clayton Larson?"

"I don't know no Clayton nobody," she said, squinting at me and taking another drag on her cigarette.

"Look, I'm his brother. There's my name, Andrew Larson. I have a slip of paper with this address – I assume this is where he gets his mail.

I held out the paper and she took it, still squinting at me and then at the paper.

"I know a Desert Larson. Lives up around Jarbidge somewhere."

I didn't know Clayton was going by any aliases or nicknames, but somehow I wasn't surprised. I said, "Yeah, that's him. Can you tell me how I can find him?"

"No, I can't. He never said anything about a brother, but then, he never says much about anything. One place you might try is the Ophir Hotel down by the rail yards."

"Why would he get his mail here and stay in another hotel?" I asked.

"That ain't no hotel, mister. That's a cat house," she said with a laugh that lacked any humor.

"Thank you," I said, turning out the door toward the car to get my things.

Dusk had fallen and the last gleams of the sun showed on the mountain peaks on the other side of the valley. I stood looking out for a long while until it was black, with only the sounds of the night. Out on the highway, the large trucks were roaring, changing gears for the trip into the blackness -- into a cavernous black void where only the constant white dashes on the pavement surface marked any trace of man's passing.

****

After breakfast the next morning at the diner across the way, I drove to a service station for gas. As the attendant was filling the tank, I asked him directions to the Ophir

Hotel. He was stretching across the hood, wiping the windows with blue paper towels.

He said, "I believe it's closed this time of the morning, but it's down this street," he said, pointing over his shoulder with his thumb. "Two blocks, turn left for one and it's on the right, in the middle of the block."

I paid him, thanked him and left.

The Ophir was old and dingy, with years of train soot covering the surface and fire escapes hanging from all the two story windows. As I walked up the sidewalk, three men were talking in front of the entrance. I mistook them for Mexicans, but on passing them and overhearing their speech, I recognized the complexities of the Basque tongue. I remembered the Basque boy I had gone to school with as a child and how intelligent he had been – Alvarado Navarro or something like that. In the reflection of the door, I saw them stop talking and watch me walk in. They looked at each other in surprise.

The air inside the building smelled like a just cleaned rest room and the lobby was decorated in well-worn 1940s style furniture. As I walked up to the desk, an old man with a long, bony neck and arms sticking out of a faded plaid flannel shirt said, "We're closed, mister. Come back about four o'clock."

"Could I speak to the manager? I need some information."

Setting his pail and mop down, he said, "She ain't here right now."

"Look, it's important..."

"Get rid of the son of a bitch," came from somewhere in the interior of this decrepit old building.

"You heard the lady, mister. Move out."

"Look, do you know Desert Larson?"

"Who wants to know?"

The owner of the voice was a middle-aged woman with her hair in curlers. She wore a loose fitting sack with huge blue and white flowers on it.

"Excuse me, ma'am. My name is Andrew Larson. I'm looking for my brother, Clayton... I mean Desert Larson. Can you tell me where I can find him?"

"I never knew old Desert had anybody but himself, let alone a brother. Slim, bring my coffee in here. You want some?"

"Yes, thank you."

"What's he done you want to see him for?"

"I've got some bad news to tell him. His son is dead."

"Well, I'll be damned. A son?"

I could see that she was more than half right on that statement, but I said nothing.

"What! Is he married, too?"

"No, he's been divorced for years."

Slim handed me a cup of black coffee, turned, shuffled to the counter, left another cup with a lipstick smear on the rim and then moved off into wherever the door behind the counter went.

"I don't know where he lives. All I know is, he has a special friend who lives here -- he comes to see her whenever he's around. Her name's Wink. I don't know how she got it. Here, I'll buzz her and you can talk to her yourself. Maybe she can help you."

The woman moved around the counter to an intercom system, flipped the switch and then she leaned over and spoke into the box.

"Wink, there's a man down here, wants to talk to you about old Desert Larson. Says he's his brother. Maybe you can help him track him down."

There was no sound from the box but she jerked her head toward the stairs.

"Room 23, down the hall."

As I walked across the lobby and up the stairs, I began to be more aware of the time that had elapsed since I had last seen Clayton and how much I had never really known him. I began to feel lonely and I missed him now. All of these people, even though they knew only a little bit about him, knew something about him that I didn't. It made me feel sad.

"Why was it," I said to myself, "that we were never close, never got to know each other as friends?"

I knocked softly at Number 23. After a pause, the door opened a crack and then opened wider. Wink was about 30 years old, with long dark brown hair, almost black, which hung to her shoulders. She seemed neither friendly nor hard, neither attractive nor homely. She was just any girl.

"Come in," she said, dropping her eyes.

"I'm sorry to bother you, but I'm looking for my brother, Clayton. Can you help me?"

"He lives about 90 miles from here, up towards Jarbidge, back in the hills."

"Can you tell me anything about him? You see, I haven't seen him in quite a number of years. I never really knew my brother very well."

"That's too bad, but I can see why. Old Desert is a little strange – I don't mean crazy, just odd in his thoughts.

Here, sit down."

We walked around a large double bed, neatly made up, to a divan that was placed at the end of the bed, so that it looked out on the railroad tracks below.

"Old Desert comes in about once a month to get his mail and any supplies he needs. When he does, he comes down here to see me. We mostly sit and talk and he stares out of the window at the tracks," she said, tracing the design of her dress with a finger.

"I've come to tell him that his son is dead. He was killed in an auto accident back east."

"Oh, God! That'll kill him. He loved that boy more than life itself. I know all about Ross. He always talked about him and he always sat staring at those tracks going east. When was it?"

"A week ago," I replied.

"How'd the boy's mother take it?"

"I don't know. She sent me a telegram telling me about it. That's all I know. Is there anything you can tell me about him that might help me understand him better when I see him?"

"I'll tell you this – he's more Indian than white," she said.

"We have no Indian blood in us," I said, frowning. "I don't understand."

"I mean he's Indian in his thinking. He's become an Indian. He and a medicine man from up at Duck Valley are friends, sort of. They go out and talk to the spirits for guidance."

"You're losing me. Doesn't Clayton believe in God anymore?" I said, lighting a cigarette.

Wink handed me an ashtray that I put on a small table beside me.

I continued, "This sounds crazy."

"Crazy or not, I guess Desert does believe in God, but not the way you do, I mean. He feels he has the power of his own life hanging around his neck."

"Meaning?"

"Old Desert and this medicine man matched wits one time a while back. I guess some pretty strange things took place. Desert was walking around out in the hills one day and he came upon this old man kneeling on a blanket, praying. Before he could turn around, the Indian called him and started in on him. Called him every name in the book. Desert went to leave but got frozen in his tracks. The old Indian laughed at him. Desert said he just couldn't move, like something was holding him. Well, he told me he had never been so scared, when suddenly, the Indian kicked a sagebrush and old Desert could move again. Desert said he apologized for interrupting the old man's prayers. And then he walked off back to his cabin."

She continued, "Well, about a week later, Desert told me he got a knock at his door. It was the old medicine man. How he knew where he lived, Old Desert didn't say. Anyway, the Indian told him that he was chosen to be his brother. Desert invited him in and I guess they really had a conversation. Desert is known to the Indians as Horned Toad, because he lives all alone. Well, Old Desert showed him an arrowhead he had found lying on the ground one day. The medicine man told him it would be his death. He reached into his pocket and took out an amulet, and he told Desert to wear both around his neck, because they represented life and death."

Wink stopped and looked out the window. "Other than

his deer hunting trips or when he talks about back east with his boy, he doesn't tell me much more. He mostly sits, staring out of the window here, like you're doing now. I guess I'm the only friend he has, except for the old medicine man. Old Desert calls him Rabbit."

I thanked Wink for her time and her information and walked out to my car. The woman and Slim were not to be seen when I passed through the lobby. When I reached the car, I was confused, to say the least. Was this my brother, or some man I'd never heard of?

****

Highway 51, north out of Elko, is a narrow, two-lane road that starts climbing as soon as you leave town. Although the climb is gradual and seems slight, it draws you steadily into higher elevations. The next morning, as I started on this lonely road, I felt like I was being drawn into another time – not just simply another physical location.

During the night, the sky had closed in on the landscape. Elko was cool and damp when I left and the mountains were hidden from view by the clouds that sat upon the land. My car radio said that the area was expecting snow and traveler's advisories were in existence on all highways. The land around me, as I drove, was wet with rain, which had stopped shortly before dawn. A mist still hung in the air.

Sometime around noon, I saw before me the main body of the storm cloud, like some huge animal that had eaten the road and was following it, sucking it up as it went along. The wet on the earth from the rain gave way to snow and the sagebrush was heaped high, looking like shrubbery in full bloom with a burden of white blossoms. The hills near the road, the sky, and this entire scene resembled a lithograph on grey and white paper.

Now, I drove seemingly into the very heart of this living, clinging thing. It seemed that it would devour me alive if I didn't turn and flee back down into valley once more. The snow fell wispy and at random, blowing over the front of the car, catching and building in a tiny drift in the corner of the windshield.

I drove, hypnotized by the swirling flakes, buffeted by the wind. I was weary to my bones. The land changed rapidly as I drove higher. The snow that had covered the mountains in a belt now only clung in small windswept piles at the base of the sagebrush or on one side of the fence posts I passed. Above my head stood monolithic stones that were scattered at random like a collapsed Stonehenge. Chartreuse and rust colored lichens covered the north side of these ancient monuments, giving an indication of the extreme age of this area – so little touched by man's advent on this globe or his effect upon the face of the earth.

The canyon seemed to close in over my head, with only a wide band of light grey showing above me. I slowed my car to a wide place in the road and stopped. An oil drum that served as a trash receptacle stood as a reminder that somewhere there were people.

When I shut off the ignition and got out, the silence was as loud as any noise could have been. But slowly, my own sounds accustomed my senses to reality once more. I was able to shed the feeling that I was being absorbed into another being. I was here, searching for my brother, somewhere in the high desert of Nevada. The Owyhee River flowed beneath the ice and through scrub willows. I wondered if I would find Clayton, and if my news would kill him like Wink had said.

The road to Jarbidge is rough graded with washboard stretches for miles on end. The turn-off from the main highway had a faded sign – Jarbidge 45 miles. It made me wonder if my car would be in one piece when I returned.

Wink had said she thought the road going up to Clayton's cabin was either the last or next to the last road on the left before you reached Jarbidge. She said that she remembered Clayton saying something about having an old tire on a post next to the road that went to his cabin as a marker. I remembered from years ago that there are roads all over Nevada that just end out in the desert at mining claims.

After passing a number of roads, I began to wonder if I had passed the right one. The road dipped sharply and then, to my left, there was a two-rut dirt track cut into the sand and up and out of sight. A weathered post stuck into a small cairn leaned badly to one side and there was the tire hanging on the post.

My wheels slid on the graveled surface as I braked the car to a stop, put it in reverse and slowed to see this marking. I turned the car on to this dirt track and started up the small, sandy knoll. Tracks had been worn deeply in spots, which forced me to drive the center ridge and off to one side of the road.

All the way from Elko, as I absorbed the scenery about me, in my concentration on both my task and the skills needed to drive this road, images of all that had transpired since I had arrived were taking shape in my mind.

I wondered about Wink's comments about Clayton and God and how it seemed to me that he was somehow being held in some barbaric superstition. I couldn't help but think back about when Clayton and I were children, going to church with our mother. She would lecture us on how to be good Christians. Now, he was apparently involved in some weird relationship with an Indian medicine man. And he was out here, all alone in this desert, coming in, like some crazy old rat, to sit with a prostitute.

"Man," I said to myself, "I've got to get him out of here before he winds up in an institution."

The sudden lurch of the car brought me out of my thoughts and I scraped the side of the car with the ragged branches of a large sagebrush.

"There goes the paint job," I said aloud.

I took a cigarette out of my pocket with one hand, and held tightly to the wheel with the other. I drove around a huge pile of solid basalt covered with lichens. Piñons crept down from the foothills. I was wondering what I would do if this was not the right road. I began to feel as though unseen eyes were watching me. The feeling of complete solitude, coupled with being watched by perhaps the spirit of this place, made me aware once more of the feeling I had had as boy while tracking a deer I had wounded. I remembered how alone I had felt at that time; how, even though I was in no actual threat of danger from any seen source, I had wanted to go home -- to be once more before our fireplace, tying fishing flies.

This same feeling, that I had felt then, was once more a part of me, as if it had been waiting for me all these years

-- as if it had been patiently waiting for the time when I would be alone in the wilds at this time, this place.

"This is stupid," I said aloud to myself once more, simply to hear my own voice and to know that I was still awake.

"This is Nevada, one of the fifty states. It's cold out here. It's raining and snowing and overcast. Don't let your mind go wandering. Don't be like Clayton. You're the smart one, remember?"

The huge boulders I had been driving around opened into a small valley, and there was the cabin. It had once been part of some long forgotten mining operation, from years ago. The tunnel was surrounded with ore tailings of yellow and pink, as if some gigantic mole had started a hole there and never returned.

I slowed the car even more and stopped near the cabin and got out. I could hear no sound but my own -- no wind, no overhead jets, simply a stillness that entered my soul through the pores of my skin.

"Clayton," I shouted. My voice bounced off the hills like a pistol shot and came back in my face. "Clayton!" I called again.

Stillness.

I banged on the weathered door, but no answer came from within. Wiping the dust from the window, I peered into the gloom. It took a while for my eyes to adjust to the dark interior, but I knew that the cabin was obviously being occupied. Going back to the door, I turned the knob and it opened.

A dank, musty odor filled my lungs, an odor of stale wood and tobacco smoke and the smell old desert houses seem to accumulate over the years.

On a table in the center of the room was a photograph in a dime store frame of my nephew Ross when he was a child. It had been the right road.

I went back outside and called again. Still, no answer came from the hills. I glanced up into the sky, which looked ominous. Perhaps it would start snowing again tonight. It looked as if Clayton's valley got mostly rain, with the snow falling on the ridges around him.

I went to the car and got my flashlight from the glove compartment and returned to the cabin. The shaft of yellow light in the almost total blackness made me think of myself as an archaeologist entering a newly discovered tomb. A kerosene lamp stood half full on a shelf. It took a flame readily. In a lean-to at the side of the cabin was a pile of small logs. I brought some of them in and soon had a fire blazing in the open-faced stove. It sent a glow of warmth into the room and filled the air with the pungent smell of piñon.

I said, "I can't return to Elko and come back tomorrow. I'll stay the night and maybe he will be in later this evening. He's probably shot a couple of rabbits for dinner or something."

I found some coffee and some canned food and fixed myself something to eat. I threw some more wood onto the fire to keep my spirits up and the chill out. Having eaten, with Clayton still not back, I sat on his bunk and began to take notice of the interior of this small cabin. The rough walls were lined with shelves, jammed with books. Where the shelves stopped, he had all forms of artwork he had collected in the past – oils, watercolors, lithographs.

"Old Clayton still loves the arts, anyway," I said to myself, drawing on a cigarette. "Why did I say 'old'? He's only four years older than I am. Was this because everyone I had spoken to recently also called him Old Desert?"

I snapped the cigarette into the fire and walked like a person in a gallery, looking at his pictures. They were mostly Indians or they portrayed old west subjects. Turning, I was again in front of the photo of Ross, a smiling little boy with blond hair.

"He was a good kid," I said to myself, "a little spoiled, but a good kid." I picked up the picture. "Too bad he's dead."

I stretched out on Clayton's bunk with my clothes on and fell into a sleep filled with dreams with Clayton and myself as kids again. In the dream, we were running in the park across from our house. Suddenly, it wasn't Clayton I was running with, but Ross.

In the dream, the picture of an old Indian woman, done in pencil, by his window, suddenly came alive and walked into this room. She worked at the table, blinking blankly with an old scarf on her head....

My dreams warded off rest.

The next morning, after some coffee, I walked out of the cabin. During the night, a faint dusting of snow had covered the piñons and sagebrush on the hillsides. On the ground in front of the cabin, there were animal tracks that appeared to be either coyote or dog.

"It must have been too dark when I arrived last night for me to see them," I mused to myself.

The tracks led up through the narrow end of the little valley and over the ridge between two large boulders. I thought perhaps I could see something from the ridge that might tell me where Clayton had gone. Going to the car, I got my overcoat and started up the gentle slope, following the tracks.

I was blowing steam in clouds when I reached the top. There before me was the vast expanse of the high desert, powdered with snow. I could have been on Jupiter. It seemed as if no other man but myself had ever seen this view, had it not been for a bundle which lay half concealed by a large sagebrush.

I took a cigarette out of my pocket, lit it, and breathed deeply of the smoke.

I stood staring at the bundle. Suddenly, I shuddered, because something within me was telling me that I did not want to walk to it. I ground the cigarette out with my foot and started down toward the slope. There was Clayton.

I remembered seeing once a picture of a dead Indian after the massacre at Wounded Knee, where rigor mortis and freezing temperatures twisted an old chief into a grotesque posture. After years of not seeing him, this is how I found Clayton. I squatted down beside him. Snow had drifted in to the creases of his clothing and into the lines of his face, hiding his eyes. His hair had grown long and was bleached by long exposure to the sun. His complexion had taken on a bronze hue for the same reason. He did resemble an Indian.

In his hand, twisted in his fingers, was a chain with an arrowhead hanging from it, clotted with blood. I couldn't see the wound readily, but when a breeze blew his hair, there on his throat was a black gash. He had killed himself.

Wink's words came back to me.

"He thinks he holds his own life around his neck."

Turning and walking heavy-footed back up the rise, my mind was stunned by the sight of Clayton's body. I felt I was intruding upon the remains of an act that had been done in private and should have remained unseen.

Stumbling through the waste high sagebrush, I began to question myself -- why, after all these years, had he had killed himself and why had I been the one to find him? Why had he died in such close conjunction with the death of his own son? The events of this whole trip were deeds done in a paperback novel, not real life. But they had happened. Lying out there was the body of my brother.

Snow was sifting down from the clouds that were now moving directly into the little valley when I reached the cabin. The piñons on the hills were slowly fading into the wall of grey and lightly dancing white. Walking to the lean-to for wood once more, the stark white weathered form of a skull was hanging on a peg on the side of the cabin. Close inspection revealed that it had once been a mountain lion. Its large canine teeth were yellowed and lined with cracks. The whole thing was finely pitted and worn smooth. In its stark lines, it became the beauty of a piece of sculpture. Protruding from its eyes were pieces of twigs and bits of dried grass, where the continued use by a family of small birds had now made this a home....

The snow fell quietly. The wind blew gently and the stars circled somewhere above the clouds.

SKY

I am a desert person in need of the sky.

I'ITOI'S CAVE

"According to some, it is said ...."

"When they emerged into this land known as Pimeria Alta, I'itoi was, for the Tohono O'odham, the clarifier of the mysteries of everyday life, of harvesting, hunting, illness and health, as well as being the instructor of ceremonies."

To the traditional Tohono O'odham, the world in which they live is alive and imbued with a sacredness that is especially concentrated at special places like mountains and caves. Within this sacred landscape are the communities and the abode of the ancestors.

In the beginning, The People lived in the underworld, successively emerging from one world to the next. Coming forth from the last world, I'itoi, the Elder Brother, was there to direct them, to show them, to teach them and to help them.

I'itoi's Cave is a deep cleft in the mountain's sheer face, hidden from below by the talus of eons and thick undergrowth. It yawns, impervious to time and change. We squeezed with effort through the womb opening, awestruck. The cave interior is a world of prayer and sacredness. The sandstone and basalt massif wherein is hidden the cave is a twisted, folded and compressed layer thrust up from some long ago eruption of the earth. Within the cave, as I stood mesmerized, I felt the drumbeat, the pulse of eternity, the scrutinizing beat of life. I feel I'itoi's Cave may commemorate a long forgotten but original sacred entrance to the underworld, in the manner of the cave beneath The Temple of the Sun at Teotihuacan.

Our eyes quickly became accustomed to the dim interior, the only illumination coming from the entrance. The shock of my surroundings left me awestruck. All around me were offerings of every conceivable object imaginable – what appeared to be prehistoric pottery, ceremonial rattles, eagle and hawk feathers, photos, rosaries, even gum wads. Hanging from the ceiling was a t-shirt, which, in the half-light, resembled a floating spirit. My Dakota friend took from his shirt a smudge stick of mountain sage. The pungent fragrance billowed in clouds around us. As I took my small pipe and slowly filled it, my O'odham friend rolled a cornhusk cigar, the traditional smoke of his people. Tobacco smoke blended with the fragrant sage smoke and prayers were begun spontaneously. The lady in our party knelt, weeping. I placed two pouches of tobacco in a declivity in the wall. A rosary and pristine eagle feather hung from a slight projection near at hand. With no word from any of us, we instinctively knew when we should leave.

Once again in the bright sunlight, we stood for long

moments in silence, our eyes slowly readjusting to the glare of the sun in an uncluttered sky. Although we had no drum, I felt compelled to sing The Four Directions Song of the Lakota Inipi Ceremony. As I addressed each direction, we all moved slowly in a sun-wise direction. My O'odham friend said that I should begin the descent and that he would follow directly behind me should I fall.

Half way down the mountain path, most of which had been washed away by recent rains, there was a small desert tortoise, slowly working its way up the steep incline. I stooped and picked it up. Its small, reptilian eyes blinked at me. I mentioned to my companions that this was my relative through my association with the Mohawk Clan of the Turtle. Placing it gently on the earth, I sprinkled a pinch of tobacco on its shell and it continued its arduous climb upward.

We stopped to rest at a spot that overlooked the entire vista. A low, horseshoe shaped wall enclosed a cleared space, enough to sit comfortably. My friend said that this spot had been used by the Ancient Ones for vision quests. I again left tobacco pinches in the four directions. While resting in this ancient vision quest site, the place of the Ancient Ones, my spirit touched the ebb and flow of all things.

Once more, far below in the valley oak trees, I gazed to where we had been. No trace of the cave showed. A light breeze cooled our sweat soaked clothes. The rains of the season had allowed a small, crystal clear stream to flow down from the heights of Baboquivari. Tannin from the oak leaves prohibited drinking, but we liberally splashed our faces and arms.

Resting my back against a live oak tree, my eyes focused on the cliff's face. When did I'itoi walk this earth? When had my friend's people arrived? He told me he felt they had been here four thousand years, five at the most.

As we headed back to the main paved road, which is in a north/south direction to and from Mexico, my O'odham friend asked if we would like to see some petroglyphs. A huge wall, perhaps a thousand feet high and slightly more than a quarter of a mile long lay to the south of where we were driving.

Two thousand years, five or even fifteen thousand? How can we measure the depth of spiritual perception of these great and beautiful petroglyphs, the ancient marks upon the stone that state: I have been, I am, I will always be?

I'itoi's Cave has become for me a metaphor for the narrow places that I have moved through in my life – of having to move through times of trials and fears, tears and uncertainty. It seems that as soon as I am able to squeeze through one tight spot, when I then take a step forward, my own self-doubt narrows my path and I am forced to squeeze, shaken and battered, through one more tight spot in the tunnel leading to eternity.

The awareness of my limitations at times consumes my spirit.

PEAVINE MOUNTAIN

When I was a boy, I would frequently spend the day climbing Peavine Mountain northwest of Reno, where my family lived. I loved to sit beside the yawning mouth of an abandoned mine tunnel. A trickle of water, I assumed was laden with arsenic, leaked out from somewhere within. I would sit for hours and let my mind wander at will while the theme music of my favorite show, "Gunsmoke," floated in my brain.

I could look down at the valley and the bustling craziness of Reno. I wondered what the valley had been like when it was known as Truckee Meadows. Or, what was it like before when only the Paiutes knew of the place?

One day, when I was hiking with my brother and one of his friends, from out of its hole, charging like a mad lion, came a large badger, hissing and growling loudly. I thought my brother's friend was going to wet his pants, he was so scared. We left Mr. Badger alone and he did us no harm.

ALONE WITH THE SUN

Many days and nights were spent on the beach at Pyramid Lake, alone with the sun, the stars and steady lapping of the small waves upon the shore. The solitude was complete, idyllic and beautiful. It was only there, in this ancient place that the confusion in my head dissolved into nothing.

GONE WANDERING

When a person walks out into the desert, whether he is at one with himself or a mass of jangling confusion, he walks with aloneness. He will come face to face with himself and discover who he really is. I have found myself by standing, touching, smelling and tasting places like Wounded Knee, Zodiac Ridge, Pyramid Lake and Cahokia. In so doing, I have become one with all that is around me and I have felt the spirit of the place touch me.

NEVADA DESERT

The deep, abiding spirit of the Nevada Desert so insinuated itself into my soul that when I was a young boy, growing up there, amid the sagebrush and piñons, that the sun-dominated desert subjected my nature to frequent changes: some willful, frequently stormy and often sudden.

PEOPLE OF THE PAST

The people of the past who lived and worshipped at the sacred sites that I have visited, have left their traces: a broken piece of pottery, an etched form on a rock face, a fragment of worked stone. These are all part of a mystical past.

THE FEATHER

A story was related to me recently that once more speaks to the mysteries and spiritual insights gained from life in the desert. In this particular instance, the situation related to the death of a native man who had lived his entire life in the Sonoran Desert.

The man, during the course of his life, had risen from relative obscurity to a position of prominence and importance both politically and ceremonially. He was well respected by both his own people, as well as the dominant society. Seldom had anyone ever heard a disparaging word uttered against his name.

This man had worked hard maintaining a strong hold on the traditional ceremonies of his people. He was looked to for stories of the past, as well.

The practice of cremation of the dead had always been a part of his cultural tradition. When he died, his wife had his body brought to the crematory at the funeral home.

When his wife came to receive the urn of her husband's ashes, the owner of the establishment stood before her as white as a sheet and asked if he could speak to her privately. As it was told to me, after retiring to another room, the conversation went something like this:

"Something occurred which is so extraordinary that I am at a loss for words," he began. "When I opened the container to place your husband's ashes into the urn I've just handed to you, there, on his ashes, lay a pristine eagle feather. I have no idea how it got there or why, if it was already in the container, it was not incinerated."

My thought, when I heard this story, was simple -- he was being honored by the Creator.

THE DRAGONFLY CLAN

He knew what he had seen. He knew what he had heard these many weeks before he had seen them. And now, everyone in the small pueblo said he was crazy. The younger ones all said they knew he was weird. Some of the older ones suggested that he was going loco.

"My eyes don't lie," he grumbled to himself. "I know what I've seen."

It had been mid-morning, a couple of days after the summer solstice. He sat on his porch, waiting for the heat to overtake the day and rest its heavy hand on the earth. Now, it was merely warm. The dogs had begun to pant, their pink tongues lolling out the sides of their mouths. He sat dozing, not really sleeping, listening to the sounds of the cactus wrens in the palo verde and mesquite trees. A slight movement toward the base of the hills brought him fully awake. From his porch chair, he could see the open expanse of undulating country. There was no mistaking it – something moved in the distance, on the slight ridge between himself and the base of the mountains.

Walking to the edge of the porch, he squinted, trying to get a sharper image. People. The number suggested a hiking club, perhaps.

Turning, the man went to the top shelf in his closet and reached for his binoculars. Returning to the porch, he focused the glasses.

For weeks now, he had heard the drum. The sound came at irregular times of the day and night. It didn't sound like a dance band drum. It sounded more like a taut skin stretched over a wooden frame, an Indian drum.

He had stopped the occasional neighbor who passed in front of his house, but, no, they had not heard the drum. Word must have gotten around the pueblo, for now, when someone passed, they no longer hailed him or looking his way.

As the green and brown of distant rocks and shrubs came into view before his eyes, he moved his head in the direction of the hikers. The people were not members of some hiking club.

"Who are they?" he wondered?

As he watched, the small group moved from the shadows of a mesquite tree. Both men and women appeared to be dressed in skirts. Some of the women carried small children on their backs or on their hips. Taking the glasses from his eyes, the man wiped his face and once more peered into the binoculars. The men and older boys carried spears or bows and arrows.

He hadn't heard the young man walking toward him on the road until a greeting was called out. Taking the glasses from his eyes, he recognized the son of a family who lived a short distance from his home.

"Joey," the man called. "Can you spare a moment?"

The young man turned into the small yard and stepped onto the porch.

"What do you see in the glasses, Paco?"

"That's what I wanted you for. Here, take a look," he said, handing the glasses to Joey. "You see that ridge between us and the mountains?"

Joey nodded.

"Can you see the large pile of boulders and the mesquite tree near it?"

Again, the boy nodded.

"Slightly to the left, near that old saguaro, do you see any movement? I saw something moving and I can't make it out." Even without the glasses, he could still make out the slowly moving figures.

"I see nothing there, Paco," the boy said.

The man took the binoculars from Joey's hand. "They're still there. Can't you see them? Paco asked impatiently.

"They?" the boy asked.

"I mean it – it's still there."

"Let me see once more. Maybe I was looking in the wrong place." Joey moved his head from left to right and then back again. "Paco, there's nothing there. Perhaps it was a dust devil," the boy said, handing the glasses back to Paco and stepping down from the porch. Waving his hand, the young man continued down the road.

"A dust devil," the man grumbled, "does he think I'm drunk? I know the difference between a dust devil and a group of people!"

Returning his gaze once more to the spot on the ridge, he looked through the glasses again. The people appeared to be resting. They sat or lay on the ground. Some of the women nursed their young. An old man seemed to be talking to them. His grey hair flowed to his shoulders.

Glancing at his watch, Paco saw that it was 10:00 o'clock. Placing the glasses on his chair, he went inside. From the closet, he took a canteen and filled it with water.

Picking up his hat, he said to himself, "I should be able to walk to where they are by noon. Who can they be?"

Crossing the dirt road before his home, he looked both ways to assure himself that no one was coming in either direction. He then carefully lifted the strands of barbed wire fencing and eased himself between them. Once on the other side, he turned and began walking toward the slight ridge, no more than a mile and a half away. The walking was made difficult by the clinging cat claw bushes, the cholla and patches of prickly pear cactus. The temperature began to rise noticeably. He paused beside a mesquite tree and wiped his face with his arm.

The people rested on the earth, moving occasionally to stay within the shade. They would walk no more this day until the sun was behind the jagged mountains and the elder gave the word.

He had led them for uncounted days in their search for the place that the Creator would show to them. Long in the past, when they, the Dragonfly Clan, emerged into this world with the other clans, they were told by Masau'u to cover the whole land and leave their marks upon the stones as they passed. They walked yet, though their numbers had greatly diminished over the many changes of the seasons. Yet the old one, the one born with the mark of the dragonfly on his arm, led them over the land. Many of the older ones believed that their leader could not die, that he had emerged from the world below. They all knew him to be ancient, yet he never aged beyond what they knew him to be.

This old one, whose name was They-Lived-In-Stone-Houses, dozed lightly, always aware of the sounds of his people all around him. Long ago, the people of the Dragonfly Clan had ceased calling him by his name. Affectionately, they called him The Old Man or Our Father. On this day, his people were resting from the heat. Some had asked him why they couldn't rest down in the shade of the cottonwood trees near a small trickle of water, so they could refresh themselves.

"We are close by the Others," the Old Man replied. "We must not be caught unaware. We are few and they are many. Down in the trees is the obvious place to look for us if we've been seen."

The people could see the logic in this and they were satisfied. The heat of the day intensified and soft snoring was heard from around the encampment. They-Lived-In-Stone-Houses dozed with half closed eyes. All was still. Only the insects moved.

A sentinel quail gave its warming call, then again twice more. The Old Man slowly stood, supported by his stick. The young man who had been keeping watch from the pile of boulders nearby came to the old man.

"One of the Others approaches us," he said, with a note of apprehension in his voice.

"I will handle this as I have always done in the past. Quietly awaken the people. Let no infant cry."

Paco stood by the rock outcrop, removed his hat and wiped his face. Taking out his pipe, he filled it, lit it and slowly walked, looking at the ground. There! Footprints! But not made by shoes or boots.

"Moccasins?" Paco said to himself. "Are these Indios?"

He hadn't heard the old man approach. The two men stood staring at each other in silence. Only the cicadas buzzed, a cactus wren called and a slight breeze could be heard.

"Jesus, Maria y Jose!" Paco whispered.

Two years in the past, Paco and his friend, Ezekiel Juan, had attended the big Christmas pow-wow at the Convention Center. Ezekiel had run into an old friend from South Dakota and introduced Paco to him. During the introduction, Ezekiel had handed the man from South Dakota a pouch of tobacco. Later in the day, Ezekiel explained to Paco that his friend was an elder or medicine person and that tobacco is always given to such a person as a sign of respect.

Paco stood looking at this elder dressed like an illustration from a book. He extended his hand and said, "Do you speak English?" No reply.

"Do you speak Spanish?" Silence.

His extended hand was not accepted, only glanced at. Instead, the old man seemed intensely interested with the pipe Paco held in his teeth. He sniffed the smoke as it was carried off by the breeze. Remembering what his friend, Ezekiel, had said, Paco offered his tobacco pouch to the old man. Slowly, the old man reached out and accepted his offering. The pouch opened, spilling some of the tobacco on the ground. Holding the pouch to his nose, the eyes of the old man never left Paco's. Then he motioned for Paco to leave, waving him away with his hand. It was then that Paco noticed the two men crouched behind the shrubs, drawn bows in their hands.

"Okay, old man, I'm going," Paco said.

There was no indication that his words were understood. Turning, Paco began retracing his steps.

When the man from the Others disappeared, They-Lived-In-Stone-Houses turned and walked back to the waiting people. They emerged from their hiding places to gather around him. They all wanted to know what had happened.

"We heard words," one of the women said. "What did he say?"

"He spoke words unknown to me, but I was given this." He held the pouch out for all to see. "It is the sacred herb I use when we pray for rain or guidance. Perhaps this one of the Others is one with power."

The afternoon wind began to pick up and it blew the heated air until it was like the breath of an oven. The only movements were the scurrying ants and a red-headed vulture sweeping the sky in huge circles.

Paco was nearly to the barbed wire fence across from his home when his foot caught on an exposed root. Fighting to keep his balance, pebbles rolled beneath his boot and he fell heavily to the ground.

****

The people of the Dragonfly Clan sat for the rest of the day and into the night, discussing the encounter with the one from the Others. Eventually it was decided that They-Lived-In-Stone-Houses would climb alone to a nearby hill and go into the silence of his mind, to the place of misty dreams where Tawa dwelled. There he would find the other part of his soul, the compassionate part that cried at suffering and loved life. There was also the place with no barriers, where the soul of the one from the Others and his own spirit could sit and converse. There answers would be found.

****

Paco could not move. Never in his life had he felt such pain. He had tried to move, but spears of hot agony rushed through his whole body. Moving his head slightly, he found he could only open his right eye. Focusing, he realized that it must be near dusk. What had awakened his senses more than the pain was a sickening smell. Moving his head ever so slowly, he saw a vulture sitting not ten feet away from him, apparently working up the courage to investigate.

"I'm not dead yet, cabron!" Paco yelled. The vulture jumped back and again settled its wings. It would wait and see.

With all his effort, Paco tried to stand. The pain in his arm nearly made him pass out. His leg was swollen and his head pounded. Once on his feet, he looked to see where he had fallen, then toward his house across the road. He heard someone calling his name. With the last of his spent strength, he yelled, "Help me!" and collapsed into darkness.

Throughout the night, he saw images and faces. He heard voices and saw lights come on and off. Paco imagined that someone was working on his bruised body. He also saw the face of the old Indio. It was if the man was speaking to him, but how could that be? Oh God! The pain! Again, the darkness came to him.

When he awoke, Paco found himself in his own bed, propped up with pillows. His arm was in a cast and he felt a bandage on his head.

"Aiii, Chihuahua! I'm too old for this nonsense!" he said aloud. His voice brought a sound from the other room.

In the door, Joey stood looking at him.

"Aiii, Paco, what you do out there? Lucky I heard you yell. I see this old buharro flyin' low to the ground, then you yell."

"Gracias."

"You are awake, so I must return home. I will return in an hour or so and stay the night. I'll bring my bedroll and sleep on the floor. That way, if you need anything, I can get it. I'll be back soon."

When Joey left, the quiet of the night settled on the room, the half-light of the dying moon shining through the window. Paco put his head back to sleep, when, from the shadowy far corner of the room stepped the old man, They-Lived-In-Stone-Houses. He walked silently to the injured man's bed, reaching his hand out to touch the white cast. Just then, Paco moved his head. Giving a startled yell, he tried to pull away.

"Do not move, my friend. You will injure yourself more."

"Who are you? What do you want? Who are those people you were with this morning?"

"I am called They-Lived-In-Stone-Houses and I and my people are the Dragonfly Clan. We seek our home place that Masau'u will show us. We have journeyed for many turnings of the seasons. I feel we are the last clan still in migration.

"Are you.... Hopi?" asked Paco.

"That is our word for peaceful. We seek to harm no one and we avoid conflict when we can. We will defend ourselves when threatened. But tell me how you came to offer the smoking herb. To us, that is a sacred plant to be used prayerfully."

Paco explained what he knew about offering tobacco to elders. Suddenly, it dawned on him that he and this man were talking to each other.

"How do you know my language? Are you from a reservation up north?"

"I don't understand your phrases. All I know is, when we emerged into this world, we were told to disperse across the land. This is what we do. My spirit visited you earlier. I know much about you that your spirit told me. I sense your pain from your fall. I will assist in the healing."

So saying, They-Lived-In-Stone-Houses touched Paco's arm. The cast split open and fell to the floor. The Old Man placed a hand on Paco's head and on his foot. Lightning flashed in the Old Man's eyes. Paco sat up. The pain was gone. He moved his arm.

"You are a medicine man!" Paco said in amazement. "I thought that was just an old superstition.

They-Lived-In-Stone-Houses pointed to Paco's bare torso and said,

"You are one of us."

Tilting his head, Paco looked at the birthmark he had carried all his life. It did seem to resemble a dragonfly.

When Joey returned an hour later, the cast from Paco's arm lay shattered on the floor and Paco was gone.

A Strange Life

I've been told frequently, that I lead a strange life, spending days in the desert where no one goes. But life is rushing by me, they say. In truth, I have found true companionship in all that the desert has shared with me: the fossils I found in a side canyon while boating on the Colorado River near Moab, Utah, and the petroglyphs I saw there, as well. I've heard the echoes of abandoned hopes in the old gold camps of Nevada and have then examined my own hopes and found them worthwhile. I have felt the gaze of The Elder Brother, I'itoi, in the burning Sonoran Desert mountains, in the company of an O'odham friend.

My real self is a wanderer, a vagabond who has nothing, or at least, very little to do with what others may call life or reality. Many times, I have been assailed by fears and wished that I could share other peoples' daily affairs, to take some part in them, to enjoy and live as they do, instead of being only an onlooker. But then, when I lay before me all that I have been given, all that I have been shown – do I really want what they want? No, definitely no! I bow before the Almighty and say from my heart,

"What's next? I'm ready. Let's go."

SEARCHING FOR AMBROSE

It had begun a year and three months earlier. He was sitting in a posh San Francisco Hotel, reading the morning newspaper, where fog in the streets reached like phantom fingers searching for a victim. The main article on the front page of the newspaper was titled "Bandits Raiding." Pancho Villa had raided a small town on the US border in New Mexico, and Black Jack Pershing was giving chase somewhere in Chihuahua.

"I wonder what makes Pershing think he can catch Villa? With the support of the people, he'll never find him. Once they taste blood, those peons can be cunning," he said to himself as he turned the page.

Months would pass and he would find out just how difficult it is for one to find what is being sought in the backside of the desert, in a land of bones, tequila and rattlesnakes.

A disturbance at the entrance of the hotel caught his eye. A striking woman arrayed in black, with shiny beads on her short jacket, and an ostrich plume askew in her hat entered the lobby. She carried a cage in which was a raucous parrot. A bellhop struggled with her luggage.

Returning his gaze to the newspaper in his hand, his interest was held by an article with a heading in large print.

An American journalist had disappeared somewhere in Mexico – that journalist was Ambrose Bierce. After reading the article, he laid the paper on the polished mahogany table, sat back in his comfortable chair and placed his now warm coffee to his lips.

"Pardon me."

He hadn't noticed the man emerging from behind the potted palm and who now stood beside him.

"May I present my card?" the man asked. It read: Ezra Quackenbush, Pinkerton Detective Agency. The man was small but burly. He wore a dark suit with a bowler, bushy mustache and gold rimmed glasses in front of piercing, menacing eyes. A cloak of subtle intimidation surrounded his presence.

"You are well known to our agency. I have been commissioned by my superiors to request that you undertake an assignment, if you are willing to do so. It could prove to be lucrative if you accept. All expenses paid, by the way."

"How do you know who I am, and how did you know where I was?"

"May I just say we have our ways."

"Fair enough. What, may I ask, is the assignment?"

"As you know, the famous journalist, Ambrose Bierce, is missing. He is known to be in Mexico. We know, as well, that he had been with Villa on a number of his, shall we say, engagements with the government forces. We think that he is no longer with the insurgents. He may be trying to reach Zapata, but that is doubtful. Bierce has information useful to our government. There are some in Congress who are suggesting that the United States annex Baja,

California. But no one knows yet how that wind will blow. In any event, we want Ambrose Bierce.

The man finished his coffee and returned his cup to the saucer.

"When would you prefer that this exercise in diplomacy take place?"

"Your choice of words emphasizes the confidence we have in your abilities. Tomorrow."

****

It was the first week of May. The dust, the smell of sweating horses, sweating people, mixed with the animal dung in the streets made the air almost unbearable. Buzzards sat on the roof peaks of houses and businesses, in the border town of Nogales when he stepped from the stagecoach. The white heat bore down on the land with a hand of cast iron. Graffiti, bullfight posters and revolutionary manifestos plastered the walls of many of the buildings. Villa and his army had been there but two days in the past, scoffing at the gringo general who thought he could take the man who was leading Mexico into a new future of blood. The stones upon which this revolution was conceived was the blood of countless centuries of just such promises of glory and death. Many were the martyrs of defeat.

It would take nearly a century for the world to believe that Bierce had, indeed, died. Many continued to doubt it. That he had only sequestered himself to ruminate on the follies of existence in some hidden hamlet far from questioning eyes was the speculation of many conversations. Some questioned if he had been shot by either Villa's men or by the government forces.

Had he been thrown by a horse and died in some hidden canyon? He could not have had a heart attack – heart attacks weren't romantic enough. But these and other thoughts about Bierce would come months and years later. Coyotes and javelinas know secrets no human ear has ever heard.

An old Indian woman stood looking at him as he stood on the walk, jostled by rowdy and untamed men with their huge sombreros that appeared as sails on boats with no rudders, cast upon a tempestuous, anarchical ocean. The old woman stood unnoticed, a tin cup in her hands. Her face was lacerated by years of deprivation and the blight of warfare raging in the country.

The man dropped a few coins in her tin cup and walked to the Hotel Santa Eulalia. The window near the door was gone and the rough wooden door was wracked with bullet holes. A food hawker passed, stopped, turned and looked with anticipation. Then he continued down the walk.

The man entered the building, whose dark interior smelled of death and stale decay. The dry, cracked wooden beams overhead looked as though they would, at any time, give up the effort of holding the roof. A cockroach ran from a crack in the wall, paused at a respectful distance, and then retreated across the floor into the dark shadows of the far corner. A silence of desperation and dejection lingered in the room, concealing some hidden horror and nights of purchased love.

A man with a mangled and withered arm and hand stepped from behind a dirty drape that was a cover of privacy, screening whatever lay behind him. No words passed in greeting between the two men, only their eyes met and reviewed each other with skepticism.

"I am seeking Senor Armando Gavilan. I was told to ask for him here."

The man with the impaired arm turned and withdrew to where he had just emerged. Cobwebs wafted in a vagrant breath of air overhead. As the man waited, he glanced around the room's dismal interior. There, on the floor, was what he felt was the cause of the smell of death – a large, black smear which also outlined a human hand.

He had not noticed a door on his right when he had entered from the street. It now opened on well oiled hinges.

"I am Armando Gavilan," said a tall man whose dark skin spoke of Indian antecedents. "Who is it that asks for me?"

"I am seeking the Norte Americano newspaper man, Senor Ambrose Bierce," the man said, without answering the other man's question. "I represent the United States."

"Your words are meaningless. Any can make such a claim. Spies of our rapidly dissolving government have taken many disguises."

"Do you know the name -- Senor Ezra Quackenbush?"

"Come this way," Senor Armando Gavilan said, stepping to the side of the door. With his hand, he motioned entrance into the room beyond.

He was ushered into a dark room with two chairs and a small table on which an oil lamp gave off a feeble glow in the otherwise mournfully empty room. A thick curtain covered the only window.

Senor Armando Gavilan, with no further inquiry, said indifferently, "He is dead and has been for some time. I can only tell you where his bones lie."

"Who or what killed him?"

"That I cannot tell you. In war, who can say?"

"I must have proof of what you say. Where do I go to see his grave?"

"He is buried on the Hacienda Dulce, beyond the town of Creel. Tarahumara Indians found his body and buried him.

"How do I get there? Are there roads?"

"If you can call goat paths roads."

"Can I hire a guide?"

"If you pay well. You must be aware of bandits who pose as Villa's men." Pausing, Senor Armando Gavilan continued, "You could make it to Hacienda Dulce in – let me see – a week, perhaps ten days."

"Get me a guide." The man placed a small stack a gold double eagles on the table. The reflection by the oil lamp on the coins brighten an area of the table.

Senor Armando Gavilan stared at the man before him, then at the coins. Without counting them, he placed them in his pocket.

****

The journey through the heartland of Mexico was fraught with ruthless danger. No one was ever quite sure of who it was one could trust. There were many who were shot simply because they looked like they could be on the other side.

As he skirted the immensity of the Sierra Madre, the Mother Mountains, the spine of the continent, twice, small guerilla bands stopped him in his travels -- the first, but three men, the second, four. All seven men verified the accuracy of the man's 44.40 Henry repeating rifle with its polished, shiny brass breach. At the first encounter, though wounded, the guide turned the mule he rode and galloped back the way they had been traveling.

The Sierra rose to his left with mysteries of its own. Far to the west, the deep and forbidding barrancas lay, exposing the ligaments of the earth, crystal splashing rivers and streams racing there, the blood of the planet flowing deep in these immense cleavages. Around him, scrub oaks, Spanish bayonet, yucca and clump grass grew beside and around the narrow goat path he was following.

Soon the land opened to a broad plain, where, before him, a growth of uncared for olive trees struggled amid deep growing chamisa and wild flowers, nodding sentimentally as if mourning over numerous graves.

As the man topped a rise, in the distance, a number of white washed buildings with dark tiled roofs stood baking in the opaque sunlight. Pausing and looking in all directions, he saw no moving thing but a redheaded vulture, a harbinger of death, seeking to feed, gliding in enormous circles over the cluster of buildings.

Giving his horse a nudge with his heels, he slowly approached what he hoped would be his destination. The horses that he had taken from the dead bandits fell into line behind him with a tug on the rope. Two rifle shots blew a blast of earth around his horse's feet. Tightening his grip on the reigns, he did not slacken his pace, but slid the Henry from its scabbard.

From the doorway beneath the overhang of the portal, a heavy set man emerged, a rifle in the crook of his arm, a large, upturned sombrero on his head.

Descending the steps, walking with economy of

movement, never taking his eyes from the man on the horse, he now stood in the shimmering sunlight. Hooking the thumb of his left hand into his belt loop, he held the rifle aimed at the man on the horse.

"Norte Americano?" he asked.

"Ambrose Bierce," was the reply.

With a loud guffaw, the man with the rifle replied, "That cabron is dead, gringo. Dead like you will be."

He raised the rifle but, before he could pull the trigger, the Henry 44.40 blew off the top of his head.

The rider dismounted and picked up the Winchester that lay beside the dead man, who was what the ominous vulture had been waiting for.

As the man slid the Winchester into a pack on one of the horses, a girl of about fifteen or sixteen years entered the shadow of the portal and stood looking at the dead man on the ground. Blood pooled around his head. Already, two hungry ants were investigating.

The young girl, dressed in a long, dark skirt and a soiled white over blouse, gazed up at the man, now on his horse once more. She walked out into the humid sunshine. Stepping to the body of the man on the ground, she spit on it.

Looking up at the man on the horse, she said with a rigidity as hard as granite, "Gracias."

She moved toward the man on the horse, reached up and held the reigns in her hand, shielding her face from the sun with her other hand. Reaching down, the man took her arm and swung her up behind him. Turning the horse, he retraced his way back the way he had come. Now, all of that was passed thinking of.

The girl said she knew of the Hacienda Dulce. It was but a few miles to the south and west. But she cautioned, they must hurry lest someone find the body of the evil man who had stolen her from her village of Belem in the Rio Yaqui Valley to the north. The same evil man had murdered her mother.

"I know of a place where we may hide for a day and a night, safe from discovery. It is not far from here."

This place was near the barranca's steep cliffs that looked down upon the Rio Papigochic, the abode of the silent ones, the ones who run through the rocks with bare feet, the Tarahumara.

Standing within a grove of oak trees, the sky had cleared. It became a sky nearly transparent and it was a blue neither had ever seen. He rode deeper into the bosque of oak trees and shrubs. They would rest.

As they rode, she behind him, the strength of her firm body pressed against his back. She had the soft smell of rosemary and laurel. The wind flung her long, black hair around his neck and her aroma clung to his body. They rode as one being.

When they stopped to rest, well hidden from the trail they had been following, they paused beside a trickle of clear water to refresh themselves and the horses. The man lay flat on his stomach, splashing water on his face and head, only to reinvigorate his weary body but not to remove the girl's fragrance.

The girl knelt, rinsing her face and arms, never taking her eyes that were as black and sharp as obsidian, from the man who had rescued her from the bestial demon who had abducted her.

The man rose from the meandering stream and once more held the reigns of his horse. The girl walked to him and placed her hand on his arm. He leaned toward her and kissed her forehead. Putting her arms around him, the man kissed her shining hair.

****

The Hacienda Dulce was in need of repair. The trees needed pruning, the fence was broken in places, and animals wandered aimlessly. The war had come and gone as it had all over Mexico. The owner, Don Eusebio Guadalupe Escobar, had been shot. The peons had left to join the insurgents. Don Eusebio Guadalupe Escobar's grave was in the patio beneath a large oak tree.

"I had to dig his grave myself," Doña Ursula Matilda Escobar said. "I had no coffin. He is there, simply under the earth itself. I dug one more for myself. Who will cover my bones, only God himself knows. May the angels assist. I will not leave this place of sorrows, dashed hopes, abandonment, and birds of ill omen."

The man stood silently, looking at the old woman in her worn dress that once may have been fashionable. She stood with a sense of authority that was now of value only to her.

"The gringo newspaper man you asked for – I will take you to his grave. But first..."

She walked to a trunk that was bound with silver and made of stretched pigskin. It sat in a far corner of the room. With a key that she took from a pocket of her dress, she unlocked the trunk. The lid opened with a creak and Doña Ursula Matilda Escobar removed a Colt .44, a belt with a buckle that had CS from the Confederate States stamped upon it and a diary filled with entries for stories that would never be written.

The girl stood silently watching, her hands clenched and held to her mouth, as if stifling a scream. Around her, the air reverberated with an anticipation of intense evil that seeped into the pores of her skin. She turned and fled.

The man and Doña Ursula Matilda Escobar walked to the patio where a mound of earth held a small, wooden cross. There was an empty hole a few feet away from it. The girl had disappeared and only her fragrance lingered in the still air.

Returning to the cool of the house, the man and Doña Ursula Matilda Escobar sat silently. Rifle shots sounded in the distance. The girl's voice came to him from far away, from the far mountains, from beyond the deep, mysterious barranca where the silent ones tended their goats. A caracara flew overhead, harried by two ravens.

An old, antique clock with a brass pendulum that had stood on its shelf since the beginning of time counted the minutes in the silence of the room and pounded them into the man's head. It sounded the hour that echoed into the immensity of the timeless universe.

He rose wearily with a calm acceptance, left the cool of the room and stood beneath the shadow of the portal. As he stepped out into the sun, a rifle shot spread a bloody rose across his chest.

The sky was now crystalline, serene, like a sky from some far off and beautiful place, a sky that had never seen death. Doña Ursula Matilda Escobar leaned against the doorframe, her fingers counting the beads of her rosary, and she looked out at the man lying in the dust before her.

"He only asked for the grave of the man Bierce," she said to herself. "I must dig one more grave."

A caracara sat with folded wings on a fence post, a raven clutched in one of its talons.

THE OUTCAST

He lived in a universe of his own invention where intuition and doubt never intruded with what went on around him. He was perpetually engrossed in fantasy and absorbed into oblivion. As he aged, like a cheese in a wine cellar, his passions often times came to him when they could no longer do him any benefit. Nothing, it seemed, could carry him into the mists of forgetfulness. He was proud, so he told anyone who would take the time to listen, that he recalled his own birth. But, within his mind, he questioned if whether he had given birth to himself. With such an iron-fisted hold on this idea, he knew that death had no power to ambush him. But there were times when old memories of other times would revive with no warning and, for no earthly reason that he could fathom, and they haunted his heart and soul with guilt and longing as sharp as a knife blade.

Sitting within his dank cell, pondering his possible reprieve, his cell mate, chained to an enormous block of granite, his bones nearly protruding through his skin, asked,

"What is the point of returning to your home, if all that you once knew has been replaced with things you can't relate to, or, if all of your friends have died or moved on to other more interesting places?"

But reality was different.

"I can't find my soul if it does not wish to be found."

And his hopes slowly rose from the ashes of his despair, only to be strangled by a fear that rose as well and stared with yellow eyes from somewhere deep within him. He then realized that his death would be but a birthing. The reprieve ceased to have any meaning. Serenity and acceptance closed his eyes and he sighed and left for another world, gathering with him his thoughts that carried the dusty, musty smells of a lifetime of wandering. He had fulfilled his mission in life. Or had he?

Each piece of the puzzle of his life had a reason for being where it was found, recognized or not. He gazed at the petroglyphs carved on the palms of his hands that only a gypsy could read, who wearing a red bandana with white polka dots tied to his head, with a black, drooping waxed mustache, and a gold ring in his left ear, said to him, in some mystical dialect,

"You will die an old man but you will live forever."

DREAM FROM THE SUNDANCE

Because they don't understand, they have chosen not to understand --where the desert and the mountains are, life and death sit silently waiting, smiling in the ever present now, the Sun. The night of the day becomes the day of the night and all becomes one in the Universal One where the desert is the sea and the sea a desert. A place where nothing is, is a place where all exists. The desert flows to the sea, the mountains rise and breathe, the earth shudders. Again, the night of the day has become the day of the night where all is at peace – and within the peace is the chaos of creation. All are flowing, all are becoming, peace is smiling as life and death are smiling still.

FINAL THOUGHTS

The desert conveys feelings of despair and euphoria.

Tucoy-hinantin-hucyuric-canchic, a Quechua phrase which means "We are all of one birth."

El grito del lobo – the howl of the wolf.

GLOSSARY

Abuelo: Spanish, grandfather

Achomawi: Indigenous people of Northern Califronia, also known as the Pitt River Indians

Aho: a positive affirmation used by most Native American people

Acequias: Spanish, irrigation ditches

Bisabuelo: Spanish, great grandfather

Bosque: Spanish, grove of trees

Brujo: Spanish, witch

Buharro: Spanish slang, buzzard

Cabron: Spanish slang, vulgar slang

Campo Santo: Spanish, Cemetery

Camposino: Spanish, worker

Capilla: Spanish, chapel

Caracara: a Mexican eagle

Carne asada: Spanish, a meat dish made with chilies and spices

Cenote: Spanish, a sink hole filled with water

Cerros: Spanish, hills

Chichen itza: a major Maya ruin in the Yucatan

Cui-ui, a fish found only in Pyramid Lake, Nevada

Diné: Navajo word for themselves, The People

Hogan: Navajo word for a home

Joven: Spanish, young person

Karnee: Paiute word for a home

Kuyuidikada: the Paiute people who live at Pyramid Lake, Nevada

Kola: Lakota, friend

Lengua: Spanish, language

Lianas: Spanish, vines

Matachines: Spanish, dancers in an ancient religious dance brought from Spain

Metakuye Oyasin: Lakota, all my relations

Mota: slang, Marijuana

N'de: the Apache word for themselves, The People

Nieto: Spanish, grandson

Padre: Spanish, father

Pesadilla: Spanish, nightmare

Ramada: Spanish, sunshade

Retablo: Spanish, religious icon

Sagrada tierra: Spanish, sacred earth

Selva: Spanish, forest

Tawa: Puebloan, the Creator

Tohono O'odham: Native American people of Arizona and Sonora, Mexico, once known as Papago

Vato: Mexican slang, an acquaintance

Viejo: Spanish, old man

Ya-eeh-te: Navajo, a greeting

Yamarika: a major division of the Comanche

Yoeme: Native American people of Arizona and Sonora, Mexico, also known as Yaqui

www.ingramcontent.com/pod-product-compliance
Lightning Source LLC
LaVergne TN
LVHW051452080426
835509LV00017B/1743